Telling Our Stories

Telling Our Stories

Personal Accounts of Engagement with Scripture

Edited by
Ray Gingerich
Earl Zimmerman
Foreword by Walter Wink

<u>Journeys with</u>
<u>Scripture Series</u>
<u>Volume 1</u>

Cascadia

Publishing House
Telford, Pennsylvania

copublished with
Herald Press
Scottdale, Pennsylvania

Cascadia Publishing House orders, information, reprint permissions:
contact@CascadiaPublishingHouse.com
1-215-723-9125
126 Klingerman Road, Telford PA 18969
www.CascadiaPublishingHouse.com

Telling Our Stories
Library of Congress Catalog Number:
ISBN: 1-931038-36-8
Book design by Cascadia Publishing House
Cover design by Merrill R. Miller

Library of Congress Cataloguing-in-Publication Data
Telling our stories : personal accounts of engagements with scripture / edited by
Ray Gingerich and Earl Zimmerman ; foreword by Walter Wink.
    p. cm. -- (Journeys with scripture series ; v. 1)
Includes index.
ISBN-13: 978-1-931038-36-2 (6 x 9' trade pbk. : alk. paper)
ISBN-10: 1-931038-36-8 (6 x 9' trade pbk. : alk. paper)
1. Bible--Criticism, interpretation, etc. 2. Spiritual life--Mennonite Church. I.
Gingerich, Ray C. II. Zimmerman, Earl S. III. Title. IV. Series.

BS511.3.T45 2006
220.088'2897--dc22

                                                              2006015075

12 11 10 09 08 07 06   10 9 8 7 6 5 4 3 2 1

To our treasured communities of faith,
through whom we have inherited
both the vision and the burden of
wrestling with Scripture.

Contents

Foreword

Walter Wink

When reading a serious theological book, I look for relief from the heavy sledding in the form of personal anecdotes, vignettes, sketches, parables, stories, jokes, puns, and other forms of "right brain" activity. Apparently others have made the same observation, so that an emphasis has emerged among scholars bearing the paradoxical moniker, "anthropological theology." Here is a tendency congruent with Mennonites (though I know too little of them), with their emphasis on experiencing God by truly living the teachings of Jesus. Anthropological theology simply goes one step or meta-level farther by telling us what such experience is all about.

This book grew out of a conference that sought to find some kind of unanimity in Mennonite circles in the only place it was to be found: at the intersection of the participants' own stories with the biblical story. For, as editors and conference conveners Ray Gingerich and Earl Zimmerman note, each person's story was relatively non-threatening when told in personal descriptive terms and not imposed as a dogma all must believe in. In the context of storytelling, even the more controversial issues could be broached and shared without leading to conflict. Each story was a gift to all, not a doctrinal position paper for others to approve or critique. And the teller of each tale had authority over it; no one else could controvert it so long as it remained in the story genre. The sharing in an Alcoholics Anonymous meeting is sometimes analogous.

But the biblical heritage carries our stories far beyond our own autobiographical storytelling, into a universal ambiance where the meaning of the text and its meanings for our lives are one. Autobiographical recitations can be flat-out boring. What makes them more than just entertainment—or its absence!—is the intent to bring about transformation. "Our story is not normative and faithful just because it is our story or my story. What makes biblical storytelling normative is if, after testing in the community of faith, it corresponds with our Lord's story, the story of Jesus" (Gingerich, 257).

Unlike many multi-authored books, virtually all the contributions to this volume are remarkably well-written and profoundly reflective. I hope this volume engenders new forms of communal exegesis capable of bringing about the transformation we all seek.

—*Walter Wink*
  Sandisfield, Massachusetts
  Professor Emeritus, Auburn Theological Seminary
  New York, New York

Acknowledgments

This book was made possible by the contributions of many people. We are especially grateful to the various people who wrote their stories for this volume. We deeply appreciate their willingness to make themselves vulnerable as they tell us about their personal journeys with Scripture.

We thank the committee that helped us plan the event "Our Journey With Scripture: A Colloquy," held at the Laurelville Mennonite Church Center on June 7-9, 2002. This includes Jane Hoober Peifer, pastor of Blossom Hill Mennonite Church; Keith Graber Miller, professor of religion at Goshen College; Malinda Berry, graduate student at Union Theological Seminary in New York; and J. Denny Weaver, professor of religion and history at Bluffton College. Their enthusiasm and work helped make the Journeys with Scripture project a success. They gave us the initial encouragement to edit this volume as well as helpful advice along the way.

We thank Michael A. King, of Cascadia Publishing House, for his vision for the possibilities of a book like this as well as the able way he coached us through the publishing process.

Finally, we thank Lilly Endowment for the grant which contributed toward the expenses of this project.

—*Ray Gingerich*
Harrisonburg, Virginia

Earl Zimmerman
Harrisonburg, Virginia

Part One
How It All Came to Be

CHAPTER 1

Finding the Storytelling Model

*In what odd and intimate ways have we each been led to this endlessly
"strange and new" text?*
—Walter Brueggemann

How the Concept of Sharing
Our "Journeys with Scripture" Emerged

All Christians acknowledge the Bible as the authoritative source and
standard for faith and life in the world. We recognize it as the essential
book of the church; it shapes our worship and our life in community. In
traditional language we refer to it as the "Word of God." Yet where does
the authority of Scripture lie? How do we understand the Scriptures to
be "holy?" Can we live with words like *inerrancy* and *infallibility?* Are
such descriptors of Scripture necessary to the faith? What meaning do
they have in the twenty-first century? Each Sunday morning, in the
gathering of a typical congregation, there are many responses to such
questions. It is becoming increasingly difficult for us to know how our
common confession of the authority of Scripture is guiding us in finding common ground amid the divisive issues we face.

Two contemporary issues in relation to which we turn to the Bible
for answers are violence and sexual ethics. Yet rather than uniting us, our
common scriptural source appears to contribute to the divisiveness.
Every church body is struggling with these problems. The basic fault
lines, unlike in the past, run through rather than between our confessional communities. Beneath the moral issues of the day lies the deeper
problem of how we understand and interpret Scripture.

How then does the Bible shape our communities of faith? This question has both academic and doctrinal dimensions. However, the Journeys with Scripture project began with the realization that another academic conference on biblical interpretation striving for more doctrinal clarity would not in itself address the problem of divisiveness.

As people we are inherently social. Our most divisive issues are likewise inherently social. This suggests that in addressing divisive issue we need to pay more attention to the social processes at work. Focusing on our experiences in social relationships and institutional connectedness fits the believers church tradition out of which this book emerges and which identifies the local congregation as the place where our understandings and interpretations are to be tested.[1] We all have personal stories of our journeys with Scripture interwoven with the communities and significant persons that nurtured our faith. Surely one place to begin is with a thick description of these common experiences.

These are the issues a few of us often wrestled with in the Bible and Religion Department at Eastern Mennonite University. When we met in the foyer between our offices, the conversation would often turn to such troublesome matters. The conviction that the issues dividing us have deeper roots than the particulars reported in the church press strenthened and gained clarity. That our understandings and perceptions of Scripture served as a taproot was indisputable. We needed a way to address these underlying and basic, largely unexamined prior assumptions rooted in our interpretation of Scripture, our common sustenance.

We sketched a variety of scenarios for how to proceed. Would an extensive conference on Scripture interpretation lead us in the right direction? That our denomination had not sponsored an open dialogue within memory, but nevertheless continued to issue definitive doctrinal statements, pointed to how deeply the unresolved dimensions of the authority of Scripture have been submerged into the subconscious of denial. Might a debate between scholars representing differing theological stances within the denomination creatively expose these tap roots?

But the intuited response was instant, simple, and direct: Such arguments would not change minds or establish the necessary fellowship for continued dialogue. It would only exacerbate tensions. Still the idea of engaging each other and the broader church would not die. It kept coming back into our conversations. How could we honestly engage the broader community of believers on an issue of this magnitude?[2]

By coincidence (or should we say Providence?) Walter Brueggemann published an essay in the *Christian Century* called "Biblical Authority: A Personal Reflection" (reprinted as Appendix A). This essay is a personal account of Brueggemann's religious formation in relation to the Bible, which for him is endlessly "strange and new." He talks about his own journey that began with the Lutheran congregation that nurtured him as a child, his seminary and graduate studies, and his years as a biblical scholar, teacher, and writer. He insists that "how each of us reads the Bible is partly the result of family, neighbors and friends . . . and partly the God-given accident of long-term development."[3]

The essay reinforced our belief that an academic conference focused on cognitive and doctrinal arguments about biblical authority and interpretation would hardly be a fruitful way to address the concerns with which we were wrestling. Brueggemann notes, "These issues live in often unrecognized, uncriticized, and deeply powerful ways—especially if they are rooted (as they may be) in hurt, anger or anxiety." This is a reality that we were beginning to recognize and finally heard articulated by a respected biblical scholar. If this was true, then Brueggemann's further argument was also true, "Decisions about biblical meanings . . . result from the growth of habits and convictions. And if that is so, then the disputes over meaning require not frontal arguments but long-term pastoral attentiveness to one another in good faith."[4]

Then came the suggestion: "Let's simply get together and tell stories about our personal journeys with Scripture." This was one of those "aha" moments. Storytelling in our postmodern age is an expression of "essence." As an authentic expression of a community member's experience, a story needs no further legitimization. It lies beyond the critic's analysis. For the one telling the story, it calls for vulnerability, an inward search, a potential revelatory therapy. For the listeners (audience) it offers the invitation to participate in another's sacred encounters and life-shaping experiences. It is disarming and, without further response, *ipso facto* provides a catalyst for the bonding of both friends and "opponents." Storytelling is the creating of this social fabric that is imperative to "learning and discerning in community"—a central component of an Anabaptist hermeneutic.

The genius, therefore, of "sharing our journeys with Scripture," as we would come to see, is not simply that it prepares the way for future theological work. For biblical understanding and personal growth, of both the storyteller and the listeners, sharing our journeys with Scripture is of the essence—it needs no further legitimation or goals.

We began to test the concept of sharing our journeys with Scripture with colleagues and co-workers. Among these were Jane Hoober Peifer, a respected pastor, and Keith Graber Miller, a colleague from Goshen College. They were both enthusiastic. And Keith, through his institution's relationship to the Lilly Endowment, was able to get funds to help convene such a gathering. Thus began the gestation of a dream.

What the Reader May Anticipate

The colloquy took place at the Laurelville Mennonite Church Center in Pennsylvania. It was an intense weekend of telling our stories and listening as others told theirs. For everyone it became a powerful and moving experience. Participants' enthusiasm for what happened as we shared our stories exceeded all expectations. Numerous persons remarked about our capacity to hear each other with respect. Despite our significant diversity (or was it because of it?), the stories of our journeys with Scripture were not debated, much less denigrated; they were affirmed and given new soil for transformation.

A conference pastor from Virginia remarked, "The Bible survives! How refreshing to be among people who have journeyed with the text and continue to acknowledge its power." Others said it gave them renewed hope for the future of the church. Key to this was listening to the deep Christian commitments and passions of the participants—passions that focused not on disagreement but on a common source of power and authority.

But our reluctance to tackle our more controversial differences also reflected our anxiety over losing the sense of community that had developed during our brief time together. Some of us sensed that we had a new ability to work at differences in the climate of trust that surrounded us. This milieu of hope and trust contributed to all that followed.

Intrinsic differences that emerged in the telling of our stories—prior in time and more deeply rooted in our experience than any controversial issues of the day—were the presuppositions that we brought to our interpretation of Scripture. We worked at identifying and clarifying some of our presuppositions. Out of that exercise grew what now constitutes chapter 26 of this book.

Closely related to the "presuppositions," but located at an even more subconscious level, was the particular "grid" (the theological sieve or controlling set of beliefs) that for each of us controls our life's work and that each of us, consequently, brings to our interpretation of Scripture. What, we asked ourselves, are our individual theological grids? How do they highlight certain Scriptures while filtering out others? Reflections on this exercise, including several grid samples, are found in chapter 27.

It needs to be acknowledged that the distinction between "presuppositions" and "theological grids" is somewhat arbitrary. One might set this up in different ways. But that is how it was articulated at the Laurelville conference, and we found value in continuing to use these categories. Nevertheless, the perceptive reader will recognize that the categories tend to shade into each other, something that is true for all of theology.

Common Subthemes

As the weekend progressed, we began to see common sub-themes emerge from our life journeys and our wrestling with biblical texts. Some of these themes reflect our common denominational background. Persons from other denominations will have other common themes reflecting their denominational culture. Others reflect our broader identification as Christians in relation to North American society and our world. Here is a partial but representative listing of common themes we identified:

(1) We belong to an Anabaptist "hermeneutical community" in which biblical interpretation is done in congregational settings where there is mutual accountability.

(2) Our Anabaptist biblical tradition tends to be suspicious of theological and creedal formulations. One participant said that we have a "lived theology."

(3) Many of us talked about the failure of the naïve answer book approach to Scripture, reflective of the churches and Sunday schools that nurtured us, and the challenges to both our intellect and faith as we encountered these concerns:
- historical-critical studies of the Bible;
- the problem of hearing voices of both oppressors and of the oppressed, within the Bible itself, sanctioned by the same God;

- the need to relate the Bible to ways of knowing other than traditional revelation, including sociology of knowledge;
- the Methodist quadrilateral of Scripture, tradition, reason, and experience (or other poly-authority schema) as a way to relate biblical authority to other authoritative sources;
- the hermeneutical circle involving the relationship between the Bible and our human experience.

(4) The imaginative, literary, dramatic, narrative, devotional, and contemplative qualities of Scripture were often woven together as strands of a single cord.

(5) The ongoing struggle with following Jesus' way of active nonviolence and suffering love in a violent world in which our own lives are so inextricably entwined.

Differences

Just as we noted common sub-themes, so also a cacophony of disharmonious, even conflicting, themes could be heard. Some of our differences reflect the experience of belonging to different age cohorts. Others reflect our different occupations, educational backgrounds, and families of origin. Still others reflect the liberal/fundamentalist divide that shaped North American churches in the twentieth century. Among the differences articulated in our time together are the following:

(1) The ways we had encountered Scripture in our formative faith communities:

- Many of us talked about our alienation from fundamentalist and dogmatic approaches to Scripture that we encountered in our home churches. Others worried that the church was slipping into theological liberalism.
- Some of us talked about rediscovering the power of allowing our lives to be shaped by the biblical tradition. Others struggled to distinguish tradition from dead trappings.
- Those of us in our twenties said that we had other "canonical" texts alongside the Bible. Others wondered whether such parallel sacred texts and aesthetic rituals do not mark yet another stage of acculturation to popular Protestant religiosity.

(2) Many of us in our fifties spoke of how powerfully the Vietnam War shaped us and the way we wrestle with Scripture. Others saw America's and the church's involvement in Vietnam as an aberration and

found greater compatibility between Western cultural values and biblical faith.

(3) Some of us were powerfully shaped by relating to situations of poverty, oppression, and violence in poor communities around the world—especially in the global South. Others saw some potential for healing and wholeness in capitalism.

(4) Some of us saw gender, ethnicity, race, and social class normatively modeled by the New Testament church. Others believed that faithfulness to Jesus in our day calls us to go beyond the practices of the first-century church as regards gender and racism.

The Purpose of the Book

We hope this book can be a resource to small groups and churches as well as college and seminary classes committed to understanding and interpreting Scripture amid challenges of our changing world. The stories that follow allow reader sto enter the experiences of the different writers and learn from their personal journeys with Scripture. We think this book can help us to better understand the personal and pastoral dimensions of our relationship with Scripture. Hopefully, it will enable listening to each other in ways that help us negotiate the deep divides among us.

In "The Model," which follows this introduction, we have stressed that stories cannot be isolated from the process and context in which they are shared. In fact, the process and the model that emerged in this colloquy may be the most creative, significant, and long-lasting aspect of the event. Of greater value than merely reading another's journey with Scripture in isolation is to engage that journey in community. Hopefully this book will encourage readers to reflect on their personal journeys with Scripture, and then to share their story in a listening and discerning community. That is our burden. We want to bring the Scriptures more centrally into the life of the confessing community.

We struggled with how best to arrange the stories. Should we classify the participants by vocational roles (e.g., pastors, administrators, and academics)? But that would add little to our understanding of the stories. Should we group story's according to the storyteller's theology? But who would determine the theology? And would such categorization run counter to the very purpose of narrating our journeys? A more promising categorization would be according to the personal faith journeys reflected in the stories themselves. Some of us are more contemplative or pietist, emphasizing our personal encounter and relationship with God. (Readers interested in these stories might begin with numbers 5, 13, 17, and 21.) Others of us are more rational and analytic, focusing on the search for understanding. (Here one might include numbers 8, 12, 19, and 23.) Still others reflect a struggle for identity, often as the result of having crossed social or cultural boundaries. (Illustrating this phenomenon might be stories 4, 7, 11, and 16.) The reader will sense that many of our stories readily fall into more than one category.

In the end, we decided that it would be best to allow the reader to personally discern these differences. They are, after all, matters of degree and interpretation. Consequently, we decided to simply list the stories in alphabetical order without imposing any prior boundaries on the reader's discernment and imagination.

This book is written on a semi-popular level so that it can be a resource for a broad audience. Nothing would make us happier than knowing that many different kinds of groups are using and adapting the process described here. We are convinced this process will enable us to listen to each other's journey with Scripture and to discover how the biblical stories interact with our personal experiences. They will help us learn how to listen carefully to Scripture and speak back to it from our own lives. We are searching for models of biblical interpretation that move us beyond limitations of past hermeneutical models. This book's serious academic intent should not be overlooked due to its popular style. We are audacious enough to dream that the model offered here will enable us to make Scripture come alive again for our generation. As people of faith, we are presumptuous enough to believe that it will empower us to rediscover that common ground and authority in our biblical tradition. That, in turn, will enable us to listen deeply and faithfully to each other on even the most divisive issues of our day.

Notes

1. *Confession of Faith in a Mennonite Perspective* (Scottdale, Pa.: Herald Press, 1995), 21-24.

2. Even within our department there were members who, though holding the Scriptures to be central to our tradition and to their own work, would not be engaged in the risqué and "futile venture" of involving the larger church.

3. Walter Brueggemann, "Biblical Authority: A Personal Reflection," *Christian Century* (Jan. 3-10, 2001): 14-20.

4. Ibid., 15.

CHAPTER 2

Developing the Storytelling Model

The model presented here was used at Laurelville for "Our Journeys with Scripture" Colloquy and is drawn from materials used for that event, edited lightly to make them more useful if drawn on as a guide for other colloquies.

Introduction

We share this model of "Our Journeys with Scripture" and the account of the Laurelville event itself (see the preceding Introduction) not as a model that can or should be mimicked or replicated in its totality. Nevertheless, toward the end of the Laurelville weekend it became evident to many of the participants that we were experiencing the beginning of something, not the end. And what we were experiencing was more than a series of stories. It was also apparent that the model—the calling together, the structure, and sequence of activities developed for this occasion—would readily lend itself to adaptation for use in a variety of other Journeys with Scripture settings.

The purpose here, therefore, is to help the ongoing sharing of our journeys with Scripture by lessening the need to start from scratch, and not as something that is worth preserving for its own sake. We present this model in narrative form: It is a story of what one group experienced and how that group went about birthing a particular event; it is not a set of prescriptions.

Telling Our Stories

Storytelling calls on us to capture past events and developments at an experiential level. To tell my story is to relive it—but only partly, not in its totality. The situation calls on me to sort out what is significant and determinative and what is only peripheral. Telling my journey with Scripture requires focusing on a certain strand of past events "that like peaks of some sunk continent jut through oblivion's sea." By highlighting these events with a kind of singular focus, we the storytellers make new discoveries about ourselves in sacred places we had long ago let slip into the subconscious. For the individual, to construct his/her journey with Scripture can be a "tingling" experience of self-discovery and renewed purpose. For the participating group, it may be a time of group identity and solidarity. Thus, to construct the stories of our similar yet very diverse journeys with Scripture, and to arrange for a special space in which to share these with sympathetic listeners, can be an authentic form of spiritual renewal both individually and corporately.

The special value in sharing our personal journeys with Scripture rather than delivering position papers on Scripture becomes apparent when in listening we realize that our focus is not first on analysis but on understanding and identifying with the storyteller. Listening to someone's story, especially that of a friend, is like being invited into their home rather than hearing them in a public space. Reciprocally, storytelling is like inviting friends into our home; it lets them see our interior furniture. And, like most opportunities, it offers a challenge. Telling our journeys with Scripture exposes us; it makes us vulnerable. We the storytellers will need to decide just how vulnerable we wish to make ourselves.

But precisely in this vulnerability we at Laurelville discovered that sharing our journeys with Scripture was also a "safe" activity. If it's someone's *story* we have different emotional responses than if it's an analytical think-piece. Not only was it safe because we knew that our turn was coming and we too would become vulnerable, but also as listeners we were drawn into the storyteller's life as participants in sacred moments—sometimes joyous, at other times painful. This experience of openness, of vulnerability to each other, of shared honesty with our own experiences in the fellowship of sisters and brothers with similar yet contrasting experiences stands on its own; it has no need to be further defended or legitimated. It has its own integrity simply as a personal story.

In addition to the value for individuals and the participating group to share their journeys with Scripture, each occasion will have a particular larger context offering a particular rationale for sharing our journeys with Scripture. For a larger more formal and more diverse group such as the one at Laurelville, this rationale needed to be written out (see Appendix B "Conceptual Background to Our Journeys with Scripture"). For a smaller group—assume a group from the congregation that meets regularly and finds that sharing its journeys with Scripture can be a fitting next step in getting to know and empower each other for the work of the church—some simple verbal statement of purpose may be all that is needed. Yet even here, identifying the purpose and formulating a few simple outcome statements will help maintain group cohesiveness and keep the process from spinning out into fragmented personalistic forays.

The Group Composition: Whose Stories Should We Be Hearing?

The attempt at Laurelville was to gather a cross-section of leaders of the Mennonite Church USA. We divided "leaders" into three categories: pastors, academics, and administrators. Since no funding to subsidize our transportation costs was available, we decided to invite only persons living east of the Mississippi. As a group that wanted to reclaim its biblical-Anabaptist heritage, it seemed important to be reminded that church gatherings and happenings don't have to be backed by wealthy donors to be "important." (In the end we did in fact have some support from the Lilly Foundation.)

The fact that we wanted a representative cross-section of a larger constituency within a fairly small group meant that the gathering at Laurelville needed to be by invitation only. Under other circumstances, for example in a Sunday school class, or the faith and life commission of a regional church district, or a small house church group, *all* members of the particular group would of necessity be included. That would be much simpler because it would eliminate the entire process of selecting and inviting certain individuals somewhat to the exclusion of others. Under certain circumstances, for example a Sunday school class, the disadvantage might be less inclusive representation of a larger body, such as the entire congregation.

Categories taken under consideration to compose a cross-section at Laurelville included the following:

- gender;
- race/ethnicity;
- sexual orientation;
- theological position/orientation;
- a mixture of leadership roles.

The first three categories listed above are the ones that have received the most attention in many Mennonite-related congregations over the past decade. Yet in the process of organizing the Laurelville Colloquy and observing, as best we can, what is happening in Mennonite Church USA, our conclusion is that the latter two categories are ones that need far more emphasis than they are currently receiving. Sharing our journeys with Scripture is "doing theology"—community theology. Creatively listening to each other's journeys is the constructive core of that corporate theology. This corporate exercise should also bring to our awareness that, for the Christian church, all theology is in the end corporate, that is community theology.

Because of the theological and ethical (lifestyle) tensions within the larger Mennonite Church USA (and we dare say, within every denomination today), it was especially important that the participants at Laurelville be representative of the theological spectrum of the larger church body. For the sociologist—and therefore for the theologian who seeks to do congregational theology—it seems superfluous to say that corporate theology calls for more than committee work and an electronic exchange of ideas. It calls for corporate gatherings where the means of communication is much "thicker," hardier, and stronger than when body-presence cannot be experienced.

Along a similar line of reasoning, we worked hard to make sure that the Laurelville gathering would not be dominated by academics but would also include pastors and administrators. The Mennonite church, like other denominations and church bodies, has invested significant resources over the past fifty years in institution building. Yet we are only in the beginning stages of developing a theology of how institutions should be structured and operated, and precious little in ethical structures has not been borrowed from General Motors or comparable secular organizations. The alienation between pastors, academics, and institution-managers is, we believe, deeper than generally recognized.

We further believe that a theology for the church needs to address structural issues beyond the traditional categories of church-state. There should be no illusions: Sharing our journeys with Scripture does not in itself make a theology. But for a tradition in which Scripture has been a significant formative component, the Laurelville Colloquy was, we believe, a critically significant step toward a new appreciation of our scriptural foundation and laying planks for the bridge needed to overcome the alienation and intra-institutional factions within the church.

The Process of Preparing Before Sharing: How Should the Story be Written?

No sooner had the invitations gone out than questions came back: Must my story be in writing? Exactly what should be shared? In response to these questions we drafted a short statement (see Appendix B "Guidelines for Writing about Our Journeys with Scripture"). Some persons, as would be expected, felt much more comfortable writing their stories than others did. Regardless of how widely one anticipates the stories to be made available and shared, we believe it imperative that the gist of the story be written in advance. Writing is an immense help in conceptualizing the key themes and sorting out the chaff from the grain.

The written story may vary in significant ways from those narrated at Laurelville. What is told in a given format of the story is determined in part by the purpose at hand, since not everything can be told. We tried to give the gathering a bit of a focus beyond the general and personal by mentioning two of the most controversial issues currently in the church—militarization and homosexuality. These issues were mentioned because they are in fact cutting-edge issues for which all sides of the church use Scripture as legitimation for their particular position. The issues were also mentioned to dispel the illusion that participants might come to Laurelville with no agenda, thinking "Our Journeys with Scripture" could be a wholly non-political event.

Structuring Our Storytelling Time: What Creates an Eliciting Ethos for Sharing?

There are no "correct" guidelines for creating an atmosphere that elicits sharing. Nevertheless we offer a few suggestions we attempted to incorporate into the structure of the weekend. For this type of participatory sharing, we decided that groups need to be small enough to encourage interpersonal bonding to develop quickly—ideally even before the first person begins to share. But it should also be large enough so that less secure individuals will not feel isolated and alone. The ethos should encourage vulnerability that, nevertheless, remains voluntary; it should elicit exposure without creating undue embarrassment, a sense of nakedness without the shame of nudity.

The physical space should be sufficiently large so that individuals can shift positions and places, but not large enough to allow participants, even subconsciously, to place themselves outside the arena of sharing even while they are listening.

We divided our group of twenty-three into two groups of eleven and twelve. This, over a six-hour period of sharing time, allowed each person to share about twenty minutes of narrative, with another five-ten minutes for immediate questions and comments. Twenty minutes for sharing, particularly at first, seemed on the short side of what was most desirable. Yet we discovered that twenty minutes of well-organized input was quite sufficient for sharing an abbreviated version of the longer journey and allowed for some underscoring of key themes and experiences. Persons over forty years old or those with a biblical-theological background could well have benefited by having another ten minutes. But in a group with some younger persons whose journey with Scriptures was by definition shorter, and with persons whose vocation was not centered in the Scriptures, the thirty-minute block seemed almost ideal and we suspect would be a good length in almost any similar group.

At Laurelville we had the benefit of having an outside trained facilitator for each of the two groups. We did not see this as a situation entailing conflict for which we would need mediators. But to know in advance that facilitators would be present offered a built-in safety factor that made it more attractive for persons who saw themselves at the fringe of the church's theological spectrum and in several cases may have been the determining factor in persuading such persons to participate in the venture. Nonetheless, we knew many of us would be quite far apart ideologically, and we found it helpful to have "non-vested" persons guide us through the dynamic process in an anxiety-allaying manner. Such presence of mediators might be less necessary in many cases, particularly in smaller groups.

Our facilitators also established rules of confidentiality that helped to provide an ethos of safety. On the first evening of our gathering all participants agreed that sharing outside of the "Laurelville Circle" would need to be in generalities (as opposed to specific details) and without attaching names.

Beyond the Initial Storytelling: Can Many Stories Become a Meta-Story?

How do we make sense out of the many stories? Or is there no further meaning to be gained? Every step in our planning up through the storytelling seemed to be a logically necessary next step to what had preceded. But as a planning team, which at this point in the process included the facilitators, we were unable to sense the "logically necessary" next step beyond the storytelling. Our objectives, which were relatively clear, included these:

(1) to have the two sub-groups interact so that each group would significantly share in the experience of the other group;

(2) to gain a deeper appreciation of the individual stories by stressing the key components, without however, repeating the stories;

(3) to create a process whereby we would discover a composite story—a meta-story, a narrative that captured the essential common experiences and transposed them into a nascent "communal theology."

The stories were shared during the first half of the Laurelville weekend (which began Friday evening and ended Sunday noon). Whatever happened after the storytelling by mid-Saturday afternoon could not be highly repetitious lest it be anti-climactic; it could not be focused primarily on individuals' inner experiences, lest we fail to create and discern a corporate ethos.

What emerged out of a process of ongoing planning through the weekend (sometimes jettisoning pre-conference plans) resulted in three critical developments, each of them going *beyond* the telling of our stories, yet each of them dependent on the storytelling-and-listening that had preceded:

(1) We experimented in "*putting it together*" to see whether in the many stories there was a larger story. The larger groups of eleven and twelve reported to each other on a few key insights that emerged from specific stories; on general themes that seemed to be repeated; and on in-

terpersonal relationships that developed in the sharing process (i.e., on the milieu or *ethos* that was experienced). This kind of reporting presented a new challenge to the groups internally, but it also tended to bond the entire body. The "analyzing" and packaging was of a type that did not cause the original experiences to dissipate; to the contrary, bringing together the experiences seemed to solidify the "reality" of what had already happened—so much so that there were a few new "aha" moments.

(2) We began to ferret out our *presuppositions*. Here again, we went beyond the sharing of stories but also beyond just putting it together. What were the values and concepts we bought to the reading of Scripture which informed both what we saw and how we understood? We were now asking these questions in a relatively non-threatening atmosphere. Having had the experience of having our stories accepted by our peers, we were able to risk exposing why we told the particular story in the way we did. (Part III, chapter 25 offers four sets of "hermeneutical presuppositions," with additional comments on the role they play in understanding each other's stories.) Such hermeneutical presuppositions involve the "almost before we begin to think" fore-meanings and prejudices shaped in us by our communities and effective histories.[5] While the four sets are written as each author's explicit, guiding principles for the interpretation of Scripture, it is helpful to keep in mind that each is imbedded in a given community and history.

To help make the connection between each set of hermeneutical presuppositions and the author's fore-meanings and prejudices, we provided a brief paragraph giving the background of each author (Part III, ch. 25). We did the same thing for each author of a "theological grid" (Part III, ch. 26). The reader can make further connections by relating them to each author's story of her or his journey with Scripture.

We began to share our "theological grids." This happened near the end of our time in an almost spontaneous way. What is the overreaching paradigm, or grid, through which I read Scripture? What is the controlling set of values that predisposes me to pursue the job/vocation that I have? And how does that same set of values function as a "grid," a theological sieve, determining both *which* Scriptures are most central to me and *what* it is that these Scriptures say? For some it was mission. For others it was peace and justice, evangelism, or liberation. (See Part V, "Theological Grids.")

This rather high level of abstraction moved us away from the immediacy of Scripture, but it exposed our life-orientations and it began to complete the interpretative circle of what we, individually and collectively, incorporate into our journeys with Scripture. Not every "journeys" event needs to be followed by a "grid' discussion. But writing up our stories and sharing them enables us to make new discoveries about ourselves. Only after we are aware of the grid we use—and we all *do* use one—can we allow Scripture to modify it or to reinforce it.

The Culmination:
Worshiping With the Scriptures in Our Midst

Whether our journeys with Scripture are shared over a series of weeks, as in a small group, or over an entire weekend, as in the Laurelville Colloquy, finding a fitting conclusion is important—and, perhaps one of the most difficult pieces to plan. Not to be ignored is an assessment of what has happened, and some reflection on where we go from here. Sunday morning at Laurelville included both of these, placed in the context of corporate worship—not, as is too often the case, a set of forms to check off or to fill out. In lieu of a sermon were Paul Keim's pensive, integrating and witty reflections on the film "Babette's Feast."

Critical to the model and critical to every journeying with Scripture, however, is the role of Scriptures itself. With the Scriptures in our midst we were given the opportunity first to talk back to Scripture, then to listen to Scripture as it talked to us. Allowing ourselves to "talk back" to Scripture—to point out the cacophony of voices we hear within Scripture, to vent our frustrations and anger at the discrepancies we find between God's promises and our reality, and to do this amid corporate worship with those with whom we had spent an entire weekend of struggling with the Scriptures—was immensely cathartic. And then to open our hearts and listen to Scripture as participants, spontaneously and unrehearsed, read passages from the Scriptures that emerged not simply out of a book but out of lives that had struggled with God and found some bit of refuge in the Scriptures! Such was the unforgettable culmination of the Laurelville Colloquy.

We present this as a model for sharing our journeys with Scripture. But in writing up the model we have shared a story. Stories are not presented to be replicated. They stand as guides and encouragement, as signs of empowerment to fellow travelers seeking the Way amid difficult and diverse issues.

We now invite you to listen to the stories as you read them in this next section. Read them straight through, or read them selectively. Read them as devotional pieces and as theology in the making. Read them as a way of listening to a small group of fellow journeyers, and read them as an instrument to discern more clearly God's voice to you and to the church.

Note

1. For a discussion of the interpreter's need to appropriate her or his personal fore-meanings and prejudices in the task of interpretation, see Hans-Georg Gadamer, *Truth and Method*, 2nd. Rev. ed. (New York: Continuum, 1994), 265-271. It is a fallacy to work from the premise that one is a neutral reader, objectively interpreting a text. There is no such thing as reading the text or doing the history straightforward. According to Gadamer, our fore-meanings and prejudices positively inform the hermeneutical task.

Part Two

Telling Our Stories

CHAPTER 3

Scripture is a Snake

Malinda Elizabeth Berry and Liz Landis

Prelude

The Prelude is a version of the stories Malinda and Liz wove together for their presentation to their small group during the colloquium at Laurelville. What follows the opening section of this document is a fuller version of Malinda's story followed by Liz's story.

LIZ: We're here because we didn't feel like we had a choice not to be. As it stands, we're the only "under thirty" types here—this is of course to not offend those of you who like to think of yourselves as hip, happening, and cool—because we of course appreciate that and why else would we have accepted this invitation if you weren't?

MALINDA: This kind of conversation is important to both of us because we are women who belong to the church, who care deeply about the faithfulness of its members, and want to share with those who will listen about what our vision is for the particular body of believers who call themselves Mennonites.

LIZ: These reasons for coming do not negate the very real fact that I stand here before you feeling like a misfit. I do not teach in a related department at a well-known college or seminary, nor am I a Ph.D. candidate anywhere at this time. My only claim to fame is that I have recently graduated from a Mennonite seminary with more questions than when I began two years ago, and for some reason I've been told this is good.

MALINDA: I'm here because I love this kind of thing and value the relationships I have with many of you gathered here this weekend. I've recently decided to make my dissertation mantra the following: "It's time to end male supremacy" (biblically based or otherwise). And for me this means calling out the boogie man of sexism and speaking truth to the power of male domination, often referred to as patriarchy that acts as a serpent whispering lies in our ears. Lulling us into complacency and acceptance of the way things are.

LIZ: *Ssscripture.* The word itself seems to have a serpent-like quality and like a snake Scripture waits for the right moment . . . wham: it strikes and I feel the searing pain of is fangs piercing my flesh as the venom begins coursing through my veins. I fear contorted muscles, the onset of paralysis.

MALINDA: "From whence cometh my help?" Is there an antidote? Something that will stop the flow of poison polluting my body, seizing my mind?

LIZ: "Trust in the Lord with all your heart, lean not on your own understanding. . . . "

TOGETHER: Stop! It's Bible Memory: content devoid of context!

MALINDA: So this is where we find ourselves. In a place where the Bible is something we "study" and "memorize" and turn ourselves over to, letting the "Word of the Lord" speak to us today. Scripture is not a serpent, it is our solace. "A very present help in times of trouble." But there is no room made for context, social location, all the things that make me, me because the Bible *tells* me who God is and must be. And we don't get to answer back.

But our stories demonstrate the fact that we have received the Bible as a series of encoded messages, and we are weary of being told we haven't used the right decoder ring because the meaning we have made doesn't make sense to others.

Maybe the real reason we are here is that we want to be snake-handlers, and that means getting a good grip on this snake that's called Scripture, to engage despite the risks, milking this reptile to secure antidote for others.

Malinda's Story

The story of my relationship with the Bible, the Christian Scriptures, is a story of personal development.

I am part of a generation of biblically illiterate Mennonites. Oh sure, I learned to recite the books of the Bible and describe the continuity between the two testaments. I could even tell you about the Apocrypha. But there is a great deal to the Bible about which I have been willfully ignorant.

The fact that I grew up in a heavily populated Mennonite area of the United States, in the light and shadows of well-known church institutions, may make my disclosure a bit shocking. Even worse, though, is the fact that I was very attentive in my Mennonite Sunday school classes and quite a good student at the Mennonite high school and college I attended.

As I think back on those experiences, I must confess that I got away with being biblically illiterate not because the Bible was ignored in my setting but because I thought I was past the Bible, and memorizing Scripture was not my idea of time well spent. Moreover, by the time I got to junior high, I didn't want to hear any more Bible stories because my valiant Sunday school teachers—armed with Herald Press's Foundation Series (our denominational materials)—just kept telling us the same old stories over and over. I knew all those stories already, my reasoning went, so I stopped paying attention to the Bible.

I also remember one occasion when I was in high school, and for some reason I no longer remember, I was trying to find the "Christmas Story" in the synoptic gospels. I of course did not find a neat and tidy version of "The Nativity" as I had expected. That made me mad. I felt I had been lied to; here I thought the version of "Christmas" I had heard about every December was in the Bible in one complete narrative. As I reflect on this, I think that based on my adolescent logic I felt I had been lied to because what I thought was real was actually someone's imagining. That could and should have been a good thing.

Instead I wanted to know why St. Francis could imagine the crèche but I was not allowed to imagine Paul as a crusty old man who I didn't need to listen to or God as a female-ish entity or Jesus as a jolly, short, chubby Palestinian guy instead of that emaciated weakling dressed in white on Grandma and Grandpa Hostetler's wall. Why was someone else's imagining of what the text means more credible than mine? Once I got to college this struggle continued but with clearer political overtones. For example, *Why does everybody think Mary Magdalene was a prostitute who had unrequited hots for Jesus"* I wondered. Not to be outdone by the light-bulb flash that the psalmist describing the Good Shepherd was not talking about Jesus!

About my second year of high school, our Sunday school teacher tried his best to get us excited about studying the Old Testament. (This was the summer after our previous teacher tried to get us to read John's Revelation.) We needed to understand Israel's history, he declared. Cynical youth that I was, I blew off this admonition with a, "Well, I'm not Jewish, and besides all we Mennonites care about is the New Testament." With that, I turned my back on the Bible again.

By the time I had graduated from high school, I was sure of one thing about the Bible: I'd had it with patriarchy, which seemed most insidious in the church and its interpretation of the Word of God. I was appalled that Lot was going to "feed" his daughters to the ruffians pounding at his door, troubled that David got away with a major plot against Bathsheba and Uriah, and scandalized by the sad story of Tamar's rape. There were a few things about the Bible my Sunday school teachers forgot to tell me—especially about what I perceived as the Bible's dark side.

Despite my resistance to the biblical text's bad parts, I found myself trying to commit to reading the Good Book. These off-on commitments took the form of New Years' resolutions. I figured that as the owner of four Bibles, I ought to at least read one version of the text. Moreover, in all my raging against the patriarchal biblical machine, I had to admit that I really did not know the Bible. My one-year Bible had a daily reading plan that consisted of a reading from the Old Testament, Psalms, the New Testament, and the Epistles. I struggled to make sense of what I was reading not only theologically but literally as well. All those hard-to-pronounce names and places, slain lambs, floods. What was it all about? After about a month or so, I would give up. Looking back, I think I feared that if I really read and studied this set of texts, I might decode the gospel message as dramatically as Paul, and I was not ready for that much transformation.

In college, I loved my religion and ethics courses. Delving into issues and ethics that allowed me to pontificate and posture was an important stage of development for me. My introduction to feminist and womanist theology was instrumental in focusing my moral vision. In these contexts, I found I enjoyed working with the biblical text because the Bible became a tool for me as I patterned my thoughts according to an ethical and theological framework. However, I neglected to develop a reverence for the sacred nature of the texts I studied. The Bible functioned as tool—nothing less, nothing more.

Being at Associate Mennonite Biblical Seminary was a watershed experience for me. I found a place where I could ask tough questions of the biblical text and also—through worship and study—experience the Bible as the sacred Words of God. I went down into the book stacks in the library and pored over volumes that helped me voice my questions. For me, the power of the Bible has come from finally paying attention after all these years.

When I chose to begin paying attention, I learned about the story of Vashti. We find Vashti's story in the book of Esther 1:9-22. In fourteen verses, this woman makes quite an impression on readers. She is married to Xerxes, king of the Persian empire, and one evening he sends some eunuchs to bring Vashti into his presence. The queen refuses to go because she knows he's been eating and drinking to the point of overindulgence. His summons is merely a way for him to show her off in front of his male guests, and the narrative suggests that she will not be handled in such a vulgar manner. Because of her choice to disobey Xerxes, she is no longer a queen. In her reflections on this part of Esther, Sidnie White Crawford writes,

> "The character of Vashti the Queen serves as a foil to Esther the Queen, and very different fates await each. . . . The minute she opposes her husband the king, the entire machinery of the state descends on her head. and she loses all status and power. To many modern commentators, Vashti is a feminist hero, opposing the male power structure with what little independence she has. . . . However, in the story, Vashti fails, and Esther succeeds. What message is the author trying to convey? Can we reconcile that message to our differing ideas about the status and role of women in society?"[1]

In my own life, Vashti has become an increasingly important figure for three reasons. First, she is a feminist hero for me. She urges me to remain steadfast in my commitments to working for "gender justice." Secondly, Vashti reminds me that this work is not without sacrifice. Through the example of this Persian queen I must ask, "Am I ready to pay the price for being faithful to God's *shalom* when it comes to integrity and building right-relationships?" Finally, Vashti is a woman of action. Esther is certainly bold in her willingness to risk so much for others, but unlike her predecessor, her methods are not those of the activist.

As a woman of color, Vashti's story not only challenges me to know and remember my own worth but to have the courage to tell others who I am.

I come from a privileged class and a privileged family, so I have never looked to the Bible as a source of liberation from socioeconomic troubles. But I also have stories from my family which have stirred in me a deep commitment to women's liberation from sexism and patriarchy. My commitment to this vision and the work it involves comes from experiences of anger and pain. As I study the stories of biblical women like Vashti and Bathsheba, I have come to look to the Bible as a place where I can find, and thus more fully trust, a God of women's work. My work is to study the Bible, my sacred text, full of stories about women who have survived and suffered and extended hospitality and hope.

There are many writers, poets, and songwriters whose verses and lyrics capture the deep sense of what I mean by the phrase *women's work*: Toni Morrison, bell hooks, Elizabeth Johnson, Jan Richardson, Maya Angelou, Tori Amos, Tracy Chapman, Indigo Girls, and the women of Sweet Honey in the Rock. Their words, vision for life on Earth, music, embrace of womanhood—this is also their work in the world. Their work has become an interpretive foundation for me, calling me to a place mindful of the past yet insistent that it must be kept in perspective. For women of all colors everywhere, the past cannot be allowed to be the sole architect of the future insofar as that past is steeped in death-dealing silences, fear, and bondage. Both my self's and my community's text can sit together in the shade of the Tree of Life, at peace and unafraid.

What does all of this mean for me? It means I prize a hermeneutic of freedom and safe passage. It means the trail to a radical freedom in Christ has been blazed. In my generality, I am a Christian, and we Christians are people of the book. In one facet of my particularity, I am a woman—a woman of books. God speaks to us and dares to hope that we will hear the stories God is telling.

In this place of questions and struggle, I have learned to see the Bible in narrative terms. Whether my parents and home congregation intended that to become my hermeneutic, I cannot say for certain. Regardless, I feel my greatest connection to the Bible when I approach it as an anthology, an edited collection of all kinds of writing by all kinds of authors. Yet I have no doubt that I have a "biblical faith." Thanks to my goodly heritage, I am not about to give up on the Bible; rather, I must confess to my strong desire to convert others to my way of reading and living with this book. I want us all to be allowed to imagine and read out in the open and not be accused of heresy, apostasy, being New Age, or being just generally un-Christian. I find myself reacting to the rigidity of Christians who equate the Bible with faith and believe that slapping a Bible verse on something makes it Christian and that whatever is not biblically stamped is secular and problematic. On the other hand, I have concerns about the outright rejection of the Bible and biblical religion, a reality in some circles. I find Elisabeth Schüssler Fiorenza's articulation of this dynamic helpful. She writes,

> A postbiblical feminist stance is in danger of becoming ahistorical and apolitical. It too quickly concedes that women have no authentic history within biblical religion and too easily relinquishes women's feminist biblical heritage. Nor can such a stance do justice to the positive experiences of contemporary women within biblical religion. It must either neglect the influence of biblical religion on women today or declare women's' adherence to biblical religion as "false consciousness.". . . Feminists cannot afford such an ahistorical or antihistorical stance because it is precisely the power of oppression that deprives people of their history.[2]

Now as I read the Bible, feminist and womanist[3] perspectives often function as my primary interpretive lenses. The gift of these perspectives to me is courage. My passage has been paid; I have little to fear; I have the power to be a visionary. I can demand that we, the church, look for the sacred in both the light and the shadows, requiring that our moral vision goes beyond what is right or wrong. If we do this, then we will see each other so closely, listen to each other so intently that we can taste one another's tears of joy *and* sorrow. I feel my bright day dawning and courage bubbling in my veins. As I study, more important to me than satisfying my christological questions has been the cultivation of women role models from the stories of Scripture—women like Vashti and Martha who know their worth. When it comes to the Bible, then, these women become us and we become them.

We are Vashti. With our heads held high, we will not be party to men's manipulations.

We are Bathsheba. We are angry because the powerful stole from us what they had no right to touch.

We are the Cannanite woman. We seek justice for those close to us, knowing that even men are not above reproach.

We are Martha. We fuss over details *and* we are committed to Jesus' moral vision.

We are these women.

And we have survived.

And we will continue to live on into the future because our stories and our lives are sacred.

Liz's Story

My earliest memory of Scripture, though not the most formative, is by far the most pleasant. Thus, here is where the journey begins, winding around twists and turns, climbing, descending, and circling back, as all the time I gasp for breath.

As a child my experience with the biblical text rested within my immediate family and within the wider community of Salford Mennonite Church, a congregation in the Franconia Conference. It was here that I heard the stories of people from far-off lands who lived long ago but whose memory was kept alive through our recitations, our reenactments, and our own life's parallels. I did not doubt that Jonah, ingested by a whale, survived in its belly via a miracle and after being spewed forth quickly changed his ways and turned to serving God, as was God's desire. Similarly the battle of Jericho sprang to life in my mind, complete with the sound of trumpets and toppling stone. And like David, I too could challenge an ornery giant, despite my age or size. (Never mind the implications of this story for Mennonite peace theology. For a church trying ever harder to compete with the whistles and bells society had to offer, this story has surfaced as the church's best bet.)

All this is to say that for me Scripture functioned primarily as story amid community. The stories unfolded their magic and mystery as I sat around a table with others my age during Sunday school or as I listened to pastor John Sharp embody Pilate, complete with what may have been his accompanying fears and emotions, at the time of Christ's crucifixion. In many ways, these were stories fashioned after our own experience and in turn, they shaped who we were and would become.

A life fashioned after the Scriptures was expected. Within these stories, leaping from the tattered pages of John Ruth's Bible or the nearly perfect pages of my younger collection of stories, complete with colored pictures (more whistles and bells), God's followers resided. From such stories, attributes could be gleaned, lessons in morality explored, hope for the future found. With the Ten Commandments memorized, the books of the Bible flowing from my lips in singsong fashion, I had nothing to fear and felt fully accepted as a participant in the faith community.

Snake in the Parsonage

I found it in the cellar,
sleek and curled around
empty Mason jars when I went down
for pickled beets, cried for my father
to come with a shovel.
This parsonage an ongoing irritation
for my mother, a square white house
in the middle of a barren plain.
All year, a strong wind
driving grit through every crack,
the steep, narrow stairs,
the laundry lines strung
beside the gravel road.
All of it planned wrong, she said,
rinsing the sheets once more.
As if we were reading the Bible
backwards, this four-square manse
set down like the holy city
of Revelation an eternity ago,
reversing its stories of miracles
and its weeping prophets.
And now we were back to the beginning,
one family in a desert
with a serpent, even before
the Garden, when creation
had barely begun. Nothing
on the horizon of this flat land
except the setting sun, evening
after evening, so brilliant
in its fuchsias and golds,
everything waiting to begin.[4]

On more than one occasion, my experience as a woman has left me feeling as if I have experienced the Bible backwards—similar to Janzen's notion, but having yet to arrive in the garden, blossoming with color, basking in the glow of the setting sun, "everything waiting to begin."

Before I can reach the warmth and safety of the garden, the snake, awakened by the voices of those who are recently new to the garden, or merely hoping to catch a glimpse of what lies beyond its gates, strikes.

This "snake" is Scripture, not dangerous as a canon itself, but in the way I have experienced its use by those seeking to win their argument, demanding that their way be hailed as the "right way."

Following a move to Lancaster County, Pennsylvania, on the brink of junior high school, my family began attending a Mennonite church sitting high atop a hill just outside a well-know tourist community. Initially this place seemed almost perfect. The people were friendly, there were children my age, and after all, it was "Mennonite." However, beneath the warm, welcoming smiles of the congregants a storm was brewing.

The storm rose as a fierce tornado, leaving nothing in its path untouched, tossing bodies about as if they were nothing but limp rag dolls devoid of spirits, and spewing others so far that they were never to be seen again. Screaming over the storm was the phrase, "He's not biblical enough." This phrase became the mantra of a band of congregants seeking to oust the pastor via a petition only a few were invited to sign. Perhaps there were numerous reasons they felt this way, yet the one that always surfaced was his affirmation of women's leadership abilities.

One example of the enormity and divisiveness of this issue stands at the forefront of my mind. A very capable, energetic, and gifted woman taught my senior high Sunday school class. She was able to engage everyone, eliciting questions and joining us on the quest for insight and answers. Naturally, or so I thought, I revered her as a woman leader and regarded her as one of the many women my pastor was seeking to empower. So, at a congregational meeting held at the conflict's peak, and in response to an exploratory committee's proclamation that women could not hold positions of spiritual leadership within the congregation, I stood up and said, "But what about Marion? She's already doing it. Aren't the youth considered part of the congregation?"

As I now reflect on my outburst, which was probably not an outburst, but a question voiced only after being called upon, I don't recall a memorable response at the moment of my inquiry. However, a few short weeks later our Sunday school teacher resigned, and I learned that she was opposed to leadership roles for women. When she became aware of the message she was sending, she quickly stepped down.

With no end to the conflict in sight and droves of people seeking refuge elsewhere, my pastor handed in his resignation. Shortly thereafter Mennonite Board of Congregational Ministries stepped in to journey with us through the healing process and the search for a new pastoral leader. Though I participated in many meetings to follow, even traveling back from college, as well as the concluding "healing" service, healing and wholeness have seemed nearly unattainable.

I have little doubt that the last six years of my life have been reactionary. However, I am keenly aware of the need to move beyond such a place—to reclaim the sacredness of the garden and the snake. My recent studies at Associated Mennonite Biblical Seminary have equipped me with tools necessary to reflect on the biblical text and make sense of my experience personally, in relation to the text and within community, all the while incorporating this experience into a larger journey. For the journey to continue, I needed to remind myself that such an experience must exist as only one of the many winding twists and turns in the road. The pain of the circumstance, no matter how great, cannot cause the journey to end, though it may come for a time to a crashing halt.

Within my crashing halt and the ensuing doubt and confusion, I encountered the breath of God through the people of God. Although this may sound a bit removed from a literal journey with Scripture, the people of God provided me with a secure, welcoming space in which I could cry, question and, in doing so, begin to experience Scripture in a way similar to my encounters as a child. The Book as narrative, as collected stories of the people of God, again came to life, only this time nuanced by time, experience, and the meaning of the text itself. It was in these nuances that I began to see hope, hope in a God who, through the person of Jesus and others (women included!) was interested in proceeding backward, if "frontward" was defined by the norm, the status quo.

So I venture forward, albeit backward. Surely there will be many more twists and turns, some equally as sharp as those I have previously encountered, others a bit more dulled. At twenty-five years of age, I am striving to act less like a victim and more as someone empowered to seek out and embody, though the task appears arduous within the context of

Lancaster County, a county which houses a branch of the Mennonite church that continues to discourage and forbid women from pursuing pastoral leadership. This practice oppresses all who are involved. It oppresses women and families. It oppresses children who, if they are female, experience life as less than, even though they many not be sure why, and if male, perceive themselves as overly capable. Again the question must be asked: *From whence cometh our help? Is there an antidote? Something that will stop the flow of poison from polluting the bodies of all who are to come?*

The antidote, perhaps, lies in the journey itself. In a willingness to engage the Scriptures, the community, and all they have to offer "despite." For it is on this journey that I have and continue to encounter the breath of God through the stories, voices, and encouragement of the people I bump into—the people who offer me a garden rooted in Scripture explored backward, with "Nothing on the horizon . . . except the setting sun, evening after evening, so brilliant in its fuchsias and golds, everything waiting to begin."

Notes

1. Sidnie White Crawford, "Esther," *The New Interpreter's Bible,* vol. 3 (Nashville: Abingdon Press, 1999), 883.

2. Elisabeth Schüssler Fiorenza, *In Memory of Her: A Feminist Theological Reconstruction of Christian Origins* (New York: Crossroad, 1998), xlviii-xlix.

3. For a treatment of how womanism interacts with the biblical text, see Delores Williams, *Sisters in the Wilderness: The Challenge of Womanist God-Talk* (Maryknoll, N.Y.: Orbis Books, 1993).

4. Jean Janzen, from her collected works, *Snake in the Parsonage* (Intercourse, Pa.: Good Books, 1995).

2. Maya Angelou, "On the Pulse of Morning" (New York: Random House, 1993).

CHAPTER 4

Confessions of the Laborer Who Arrived Late in the Day

Jo-Ann Brant

When I told my mother I was going to an event at which we would share about our personal journey with Scripture, she responded, "Oh dear, Jo-Ann, you had better take the fifth." I began my journey with Scripture at age twenty, as a biblical near-illiterate who had never put the words *authority* and *Bible* into the same sentence. I was raised in the United Church of Canada, and although I had attended Sunday school regularly until the age of thirteen, had been active in church youth groups, and had even served on congregational and national church committees, I had only the most general notion of what the Bible contained.

To this day, I have to stop myself from adding to Pilate's question "What is truth?" the question "Is it not changing law?"—Tim Rice's expansion of Pilate's line in Jesus Christ Superstar. The source of most of my knowledge of the Bible came from the movies "The Ten Commandments," "Godspell," "Jesus Christ Superstar," "Joseph and His Amazing Technicolor Dream Coat," the Byrds' lyrics, and novels like *The Big Fisherman* and *The Silver Chalice*.

I began to read the Bible only after being introduced to the conclusions of nineteenth- and twentieth-century higher criticism. I had entered university with the intention of heading to seminary once I had a B.A. in history in hand. In my second year, I decided some remedial reading in Bible would be a good idea, so I enrolled in a course on the

Hebrew Bible. The Bible became a historical artifact, the product of the communities that transmitted it first in oral and then written form to subsequent generations. When I began to study the Christian Scriptures, I followed in the footsteps of liberal theology and Rudolf Bultmann looking for the *kerygma* of the text and discarding those things that seemed alien or irrelevant to me, such as purity laws or limitations on women, as husk or something to be demythologized. I did make up for lost time by reading the Bible cover to cover in the summer between my second and third year of university. In the context of a large secular university, where saying "I am a Christian" was tantamount to confessing, "I am brain dead," I did gain a special reputation among serious students for having a relationship with Scripture. For example, English majors working on their senior theses on Donne and Milton had me read over pieces of poetry and pick out the biblical allusions. I contemplated having cards printed out:

Jo-Ann Brant
Hermeneutical Consultant
Texts Interpreted

Looking for a more personal relationship with Scripture during my developmental years strains my memory, which is otherwise full of recollections of crises, frightening moments, and surprises. The guidelines for writing this document led me to focus upon the following two church discussions, but they are not so much encounters with Scripture as moments when I asked for the first time what role Scripture ought to be playing in the life of the church. As I considered the possibility of a future in pastoral ministry centered on ordination, I followed two debates of the United Church with some interest.

The first debate on lay ministry occurred at the General Council meeting in 1977, which I attended as a youth delegate. I recall three observations I made at the time that affected the path I would then follow. The notion of ordination was founded upon ecclesiological tradition rather than a New Testament paradigm. The ordinations I witnessed were powerful moments of consecration in which I could see the power of the Holy Spirit descend upon the candidates as clearly as if it were a dove. Scripture played little role in the discussion that to the best of my memory ended with the resolution that the church would continue to require an ordained clergy. These observations led me to question whether I, such a flawed human being, was suited for ordination. I began to back away from the idea of pastoral ministry and focused on study of religion and the Bible with a fuzzy notion that maybe the church needed more Bible scholars.

When the second debate came around, I was drifting about and finding it difficult to be engaged in the church and to commit to a future course of studies, driven by fear into what seemed like security in teacher training. The second issue, whether to ordain practicing homosexual candidates for the ministry, came to the floor at the 1984 General Council meetings. The Wesleyan tradition still informs the United Church's decisions. The Wesleyan distinction between justification (an act of grace that gets the sinner through the door of the church) and sanctification (a process that happens once one is in the church) meant that we did not feel compelled to worry about who we let into the church, but ordination made the purity question relevant for its clergy.

I sat, looking in like an anthropologist, watching what effect the decision of the General Council had on individual congregations. I watched the political maneuvers of leaders orchestrate the decision that "all persons, regardless of their sexual orientation, who profess Jesus Christ and obedience to Him, are welcome to be or become full members of the Church," that "all members of the Church are eligible to be considered for the Ordered Ministry" and "that all Christian people are called to a lifestyle patterned on obedience to Jesus Christ." From where I sat, I could see the decision descend on most of the delegates and then subsequently on members of the church-at-large like lightening from on high or a sort of surprise surgical strike. Given the number of homosexual ministers already leading congregations, the decision about who churches would call to ordained ministry was left up to a congregation. The United Church would go on ordaining candidates with the appropriate education.

My detachment ended as I began to watch individual people, in particular a couple who belonged to my mother's congregation and with whom we shared Christmas dinner every year. He was uncomfortable with the church's decision. He sought out and then engaged in a form of Bible study that supported his negative reaction and soon decided that he and his wife had to leave my mother's congregation along with a group of about twenty other people. As I watched the congregation rip apart, I felt personally torn. I especially grieved for her; she had lost her voice when her sixteen-year-old daughter died of meningitis, and their congregation was a home amid the world's pain.

By this time, I had read Paul's letters well enough to suspect that both sides missed the mark at which Paul was aiming. The leaders had failed to bring the people along. And the Bible was not a handy reference book to find material to crank up one's rhetoric. Moreover, even if you thought your church was wrong, you did not walk out and say who is with me and start another one so precipitously. (Incidentally, the group that left my mother's congregation has split two more times. The most recent issue has been whether the Bible sanctions the existence of a woman's sewing circle.)

This experience has informed my reaction to the disagreements and decisions of Mennonite Church USA. It grieves me now to watch congregations ripped from their denominational home, and I do not know what to say to those who want me to engage in a debate using the Bible in a way in which it was not designed to be used. I find no resemblance to Jesus' jurisprudence modeled in the Sermon on the Mount. Unlike the acquaintances in my mother's congregation, when I have found myself to be a dissenting voice, I have decided that I will follow in the apostle Paul's footsteps and submit to the authority of the church while disagreeing with it.

A variety of forces in my life put me back on a trajectory to graduate school and the study of religion at McMaster University in Hamilton, Ontario, where I hooked up with the Mennonites. I married a man who had been raised in the Mennonite Brethren Church. I had been attending a Presbyterian church with a number of other grad students because of the erudite preaching of its minister. When we married, we decided it was time to get serious about church membership and try the one Mennonite congregation one weekend and a neighborhood United Church the next, then choose. I walked into the Mennonite church, they put me on a committee, and that was the end of that.

I wish I could say that I had come to a more Anabaptist understanding of Scripture before joining the Mennonite church or beginning my teaching career in a Mennonite institution. My conversion to the Anabaptist tradition had been to a way of being church rather than to a particular view of Scripture. Not yet having read John Howard Yoder, I initially feared that I would be found out in my first year of teaching.

In retrospect, I realized that the intimacy that I quickly experienced in attending Hamilton Mennonite Church had much to do with the way that I had begun to read Scripture during the course of my graduate work. My master's thesis, "Pauline Mimesis: An Ethic of Self-Renunciation," and my doctoral dissertation, "A Second-Best Voyage: Jesus and Judaism on Oaths and Vows," both read as though I were raised in the bosom of a Mennonite congregation. My experience in the classroom led me to the awareness that I treated Scripture more seriously and often gave it more substantial authority than my students who claimed to believe in its infallible inerrancy.

In my second year of teaching at Canadian Mennonite Bible College, I engaged in an open debate in chapel about the authority of Scripture. One student, who was in my course on the book of Hebrews, had begun to lead a number of bright students toward the positions that one ought not engage one's imagination while reading Scripture and that the Bible did not employ metaphoric truth, which he equated with fiction, but was literally true. I recall quite vividly how he accused me of treating the Bible as though it were Shakespeare, to which I retorted, "Better that than an Archie comic." (I'm afraid that my impulsiveness gets the better of me sometimes.) His influence over other students ended rather abruptly when he stated, "There is no metaphor in the Bible. Every word is true. We are sheep." I looked about the chapel and could see the whirling gears of over one hundred imaginations conjuring up a picture of us as sheep.

The people who look over my shoulder as I read the Bible and interpret it in a way that gives it authority in my life are not people I encountered in my family or in church but rather the scholars whose work I have read. I have been influenced by Eric Auerbach, who has taught me to read the Bible as a representation of reality and to understand its authority in a particular way. One line from Auerbach's book, *Mimesis*, struck me immediately as true and continues to echo about in the hollows of my cranium: "Far from seeking like Homer, merely to make us forget our own reality for a few hours, it seeks to overcome our reality: we are to fit our own life into its world, feel ourselves to be elements in its structure of universal history."[1]

Rather than reading the beginning of Genesis as an account of how the world came into being, I read it as *mimesis*, an account of the nature of the world and the relationship between God and that created order. I read it against the backdrop of Ancient Near Eastern myths in which the earth is created from the carcass of the mother goddess, the beast of chaos, and humans are created as slaves to the gods. I then ask what demands the text makes on God's people if we are to live in this reality.

I have found the language of Paul Ricoeur most helpful. What I know of the origins of the universe, the geology of our planet, and the evolution of our species does not allow me to naively believe that this text is the history of our world. Similarly modern knowledge about anatomy and mental illness requires that I not treat the Bible's conception of these things as "authoritative." I cannot selectively shut off aspects of my consciousness and say, for example, I will depend on the findings of modern biology and physics for the technologies I will employ but I will pretend that their findings are not true. Instead, I choose to live my life "as if" God pronounced the world good at its creation and "as if" he fashioned human beings in his own image from the stuff of that world.[2]

Meanwhile the resurrection defies medical science. Rather than trying to accommodate science to a belief in resurrection or even to get my head around what resurrection is, I try to live my life "as if" death has no dominion. While this faith has not been put to the test, I try to avoid assenting to political propositions that have as their basis the notion that might makes right, a notion that belongs to a mytho-poetic order other than that of the Bible.

While much of my doctoral work required that I treat the Bible like Josephus or the Qumran material as a source for historical reconstruction, in my more personal engagement with Scripture I was influenced by Martin Buber. I sought to be addressed by the authors of the Bible and the characters represented in its stories as if they spoke directly to me and then to respond honestly to what I heard. Jesus calls me to look for God in the face of the other, to see the kingdom of heaven around me in the mundane, and to look to change my world not by defeating my enemies but by being more circumspect about my own actions. More recently I have found the writings of Emmanuel Levinas challenge me to another perspective on my relationship to the other. I am more cautious about the characterizations I impute upon figures in the Bible, in awareness of the harm I risk doing to them and myself. Jezebel is no Jezebel and Jesus is not "the Christ"—not someone reducible to a confessional statement.

I cannot gloss over the violence in the Bible and say, "Yes, every one of those Canaanites was wicked; every infant and beast in Sodom deserved death." If I take the authority of the Law and the Prophets seriously, if I speak the Shema, "Hear O Israel, the Lord your God, the Lord is one, Love the Lord with all your heart, soul and might" when I arise in the morning and when I lay down at night, if I do what the Lord requires, "to love justice and walk humbly with my God," if I do all that—then I must ask the question whether such violence and conquest is even of God. If I do not lament the suffering of those who make possible the story of Israel, will I lament the suffering of those upon whom the affluence of my life depends?

The conquest story is a stumbling block for many of my most thoughtful and dedicated students because they have gotten the idea that to question its justice is to question the authority of the Bible, and once you question one passage, the Bible falls apart like a house of cards. My question for them is then, "By what authority do you ask the questions of right and wrong?" They generally come back with an ethic that is thoroughly informed by the Bible. We ask these questions because we believe that the Bible is true: God exists and he cares about what we do and that people suffer.

One great regret about my upbringing is that I did not commit verses of the Bible to memory. While Scripture does not find its way to my lips, it has found its way to my heart. As I have pondered the patterns of repetition and the reception of stories and divine proclamations in their original milieu and asked myself what reading habits I want to instill in my students, I have became the beneficiary of my own lessons. When I began to read the text for and with my students, my preoccupation with the questions of historical criticism gave way to a growing awareness of the habits of the heart that the stories instilled in me. I began to replace notions of faith as an epistemological disposition with faith as trust, and I began to find affirmation of core Anabaptist convictions about nonviolence, justice, simplicity, mutual aid, and communal accountability.

I thank Stanley Hauerwas and other narrative theologians for making me conscious of how I make sense of my life by narrating its episodes as though I stand in the biblical narrative and encouraging me to be more consistent in my story telling. The conflicts I have had with individuals move toward reconciliation and forgiveness. I try to make the story of my life a confession rather than a rationalization. I count myself blessed rather than a victim. As the years have gone by, I have become thoroughly Anabaptist. The Bible informs my patterns of thought and provides reference to make meaning out of the dizzying mess that I experience in my daily life. I am the laborer who arrived late in the day and received a full day's wages.

Notes

1. Eric Auerbach, *Mimesis: The Representation of Reality in Western Literature,* trans. Willard R. Trask (Princeton: Princeton University Press, 1968), 15.

2. Paul Ricoeur, *The Symbolism of Evil* (Boston: Beacon Press, 1967), 355-357, uses the language of wager and second naïveté.

CHAPTER 5

Encountering the One Behind the Bible

Owen E. Burkholder

I was born the second of what would be seven children to church plant-ing parents in northern Alberta, Canada. A year before my birth, Paul and Doris Burkholder arrived in Bluesky with their son Tim. They were the first couple to leave the mother church at Tofield to establish mission stations in the north.

It became clear to me that my parents' lives were shaped by the God of the Bible. How could we explain the obvious differences between our expected lifestyles and those of our school friends? Tim and I asked that question many times! Our parents almost always answered that with ref-erence to the Bible. Very early, I took notes of sermons I sat through. There was always a reference written at the top of those notes.

The vacation Bible schools that were a primary means of outreach to the community used the Mennonite Publishing House materials— stories of the Bible. There were Bible memory and Bible reading incen-tive programs in our little church in Bluesky. Students' names, written on paper apples, were pasted on a paper apple tree in front of the church for each of the books of the New Testament that was read. I remember lying about how many chapters I read just to see my name on that paper tree.

In our public school, we received New Testaments from the Gideons in sixth grade. I faithfully read that little book until the cover fell off. Then I sewed on a cloth cover and continued my reading. One classic story comes from an Easter holiday campout one spring when we had an extraordinarily fast thaw. The snow melted so fast that the Snow-shoe rabbits were dreadfully exposed in their white coats against the dark earth. What fun we boys had trying to corner and catch rabbits on that camping trip. (They always eluded us!) But one morning while the rest of the gang was out chasing rabbits, Owen was in the tent reading his New Testament!

The more meaningful encounters with Scripture took place in my bedroom during junior high and high school. There I began to en-counter the One behind the Scriptures; I began to know and interact with this God. I learned to argue with the texts I couldn't understand: I remember my fury on reading that a priest who had a crushed testicle couldn't approach the altar in the tabernacle. I stood in my room and yelled out loud, "Why not?!" As I reflected, I asked myself if the New Testament made any difference. I was drawn to the story of Philip and the Ethiopian eunuch. Here was some vindication: In the early church, one of the first witnesses was a eunuch. I had learned a key hermeneuti-cal principle: the New Testament takes precedence over the Old.

It is clear to me that it was my father who gave me the basic appreci-ation for the Scriptures. This was then reinforced by Bible school teach-ers, boys club leaders, visiting speakers, and our active participation in conference activities.

Following high school, I studied at Ontario Mennonite Bible Insti-tute in Kitchener, Ontario, for a year. There I experienced my first crisis in relation to the Scriptures. I had grown up with a fairly literal and di-rect approach to the Bible. Now I encountered the first inklings of some more critical questions. What of the creation accounts? We were shown a more theological approach that downplayed some of the literal pieces that somehow had become part of my being. A valuable service of this Bible school experience was the gentle introduction to broader views of the text. It was also here that I experienced an epiphany, where God met me in a forgiveness experience that has transformed my life. So the real-ity of God's presence was mediated to me beyond the critical questions about the Scriptures.

My years as a student at the University of Alberta in Edmonton from 1967 to1970 were a huge challenge. The sexual revolution, the hippie movement, and the Vietnam War were major influences, even up north. When our tuition was raised from $300 to $400 annually, I remember marching in protest with about 3,000 across the High Level Bridge to the Alberta Provincial Capital buildings. There I became disillusioned with my fellow protestors who wouldn't even listen when the Minister of Education tried to speak. I remember the tension I felt as I moved between the wide open atmosphere of the university and the more confined atmosphere of the Mennonite congregations outside of the city. Intriguingly, as I reflect on it now, the affirmation I received from those traditional communities assured me that here was a lifestyle of integrity—even if it wasn't up-to-date.

The deaths of Martin Luther King Jr. and Robert Kennedy in 1968 were very difficult. We were in an anti-authoritarian atmosphere to begin with, and the killing of these hopeful leaders fueled the cynicism.

This was the challenging context for my journey with Scripture. I continued to read, but with different eyes. I needed to test the assumptions I had made about Jesus. I asked a lot of questions about things like miracles. I was particularly concerned about the basic claim that Jesus was the only way to salvation. Amid these questions, I was asked to teach the junior high Sunday school class in Edmonton and occasionally to preach. Those tasks kept me close to my community of faith. I remember working through the "I am" texts of the gospel of John and knowing that it was an "either-or" situation: either writers of the text were speaking the truth or the whole deal was a hoax.

In autumn 1968 I was asked to participate in the U.S. Congress on Evangelism in Minneapolis convened by Billy Graham and other evangelical leaders. There, amid the Vietnam War, I heard Myron Augsburger tell that assembly of evangelicals that "We don't kill those we are trying to redeem." As he completed his address, I was in tears as I felt integration with and vindication for the positions of my community of faith.

After receiving my B.A. in English, I did a private voluntary service assignment in Youngstown, Ohio, where Fred and Carolyn Augsburger had planted two churches. They were looking for help with a youth program in this racially mixed city. I had met their daughter Ruth Ann at the Ontario Mennonite Bible Institute three years earlier. We had corresponded, and she had told her folks about my interest in a Voluntary Service assignment. Three significant things happened in those two years: I was exposed to black culture, I was exposed to the charismatic movement by Fred and Carolyn, and I married Ruth Ann.

In that setting, the more direct, literal approach to Scripture was re-inforced. The Augsburgers were trying to do mission work out of their traditional understandings that at first included many of the "plain clothing and covering" expectations of their sending communities. Their city experiences and their family needs made them receptive to the more immediate presence of Jesus through the Holy Spirit. As Fred's ministry in renewal meetings expanded, he was used in some remarkable ways to bring healing to many. As I assisted with the work in Youngstown during his many absences, the Scriptures that explored the gifts of the Holy Spirit became more important in my thinking.

Ruth Ann and I returned to Alberta for summer 1972, so I could work in construction to make some money for attending seminary in the fall. There at Bluesky I was ordained to the ministry to serve as the associate pastor of the congregation so my father could attend the Men-nonite World Conference in Brazil that summer. It occurred to me then, and I'm still convinced, that the leaders of the Northwest Conference wanted to give me the signal that I should return to Alberta following my seminary work. In any case, my ordination was further affirmation from my community of faith.

In the years 1972 to 1975, Eastern Mennonite Seminary in Har-risonburg, Virginia, was still largely in "pre-critical" days in terms of ap-proach to the Scriptures. David Ewert from Manitoba, Canada, was a guest lecturer for those three years. His scholarly narrative approach to the Scriptures was crucial to me. Exposure to the biblical languages and the theological journals was also significant. Seminary gave me the tools to study on my own.

During seminary, Ruth Ann and I participated in the beginning of Community Mennonite Church in the former Chicago Avenue Men-nonite Church building. I was called to serve as its half-time pastor from 1975 through 1980. The other half-time assignment was with Shenan-doah Valley Youth for Christ, which gave me continued exposure to one portion of the evangelical world.

The young crowd at Community Mennonite Church was at least as affected by the autonomous and restless nature of the late 1960s as I was. I suddenly felt compelled to make a case for the importance of leader-ship. It remains a mystery to me why people responded so positively to my leadership. I was candid about my questions and about my life's journey. People found it helpful when I interacted with the text of Scripture and then shared what I discovered. My preaching seemed to provide a gathering point for this young group. This, of course, was only a part of the genius of Community Mennonite Church. The congregation was organized around an intentional small group model. This meant that deep relationships were being formed and were shaping the life of the group.

It was during these years that the Mennonite church did a study on "Biblical Interpretation in the Life of the Church." Engaging that process alongside my seminary studies was very helpful.

The transition to a full time pastoral assignment at Park View Mennonite Church, a mile and a half from Community Mennonite, again shifted the terrain for me. Here was a more academically and professionally inclined congregation. I soon learned that my only hope in preaching was to stay with the biblical text. If I ventured very far into any field, I would bump into someone's Ph.D. So my approach was to study the text and try to shed some light on it for our situation, usually including a sizable dose of storytelling. In that way people were invited to deal first with the text and secondarily with my approach to it.

Meanwhile I was accumulating years of pastoral and family experience. I was invited to preach in renewal meetings here and there. I developed a series of sermons on Isaiah's call based on Isaiah 6. I found a theological anchor in balancing God's holiness and God's love through the amazing concept of "God with us."

As pastor, my quest was now "how" rather than "if." I was convinced that God was in Christ and that this reality was somehow available to us through a Holy Spirit. My experience did not negate the witness of Scripture. Then how was God working in the world? What was the way of Jesus in some of the pastoral situations that presented themselves?

Beyond the textual studies for sermon preparation, I continued to read the Bible devotionally. My pattern was to place markers in the Old Testament law/history, writings, and prophets as well as in the New Testament gospels and epistles. As I read through the Bible and mixed these texts together, the breadth of God's work and the reality of human responses in salvation history began to shape my worldview.

When I was assigned conference and then denominational leadership tasks, I became better acquainted with the range of interpretations that exist across the Mennonite church. I have found myself functioning as a bridgebuilder, trying to make sure people understand each other. I discovered the value of waiting for consensus as the variety of approaches are worked out in the church. This stance has been challenged many times by folks who are sure I need to champion one approach or another.

Our family experiences have deepened both my faith and my puzzlement. My father survived a cardiac arrest at the age of fifty-eight and lived until he was eighty. But my wife Ruth Ann's mother lived for seven long years with the results of a stroke that took her speech and mobility before she finally died. We have experienced mental health challenges in our family system as well as questions about sexual orientation and its expression.

I now come to the text with a new level of neediness. I find myself in dialogue again with the One. Just what were the contexts of some of those promises? Most often I receive hope from the scope of God's grace made known to us through the Scriptures.

CHAPTER 6

Scripture in Congregational Life

J. Ron Byler

Teach us your word, reveal its truth divine;
on our path, let it shine.
Tell of your works, your mighty acts of grace;
from each page, show your face.
As you have loved us, sent your Son,
And our salvation now is won,
O let our hearts with love be stirred.
Help us, God, know your word![1]

"Then Jesus said to him, 'What do you want me to do for you?' The blind man said to him, 'My teacher, let me see again.' Jesus said to him, 'Go, your faith has made you well.' Immediately he regained his sight and followed him on the way."
—Mark 10:51-52

The Gospel writer gives us quite a contrast! First, a rich man comes to Jesus asking how to inherit eternal life (Mark 10:17), then the disciples want to sit at Jesus' right and left hand (Mark 10:37). Now, on the road out of Jericho, the blind man, Bartimaeus, can't even voice his request. "Son of David, have mercy on me!" he shouts. "What do you want me to do for you?" asks Jesus. Bartimaeus asks Jesus to be able to see again and Jesus can grant the blind man's request because, unlike the rich man and the disciples who do not seem to understand that they do not measure up on their own, Bartimaeus knows he needs Jesus' help.[2]

As followers of Jesus two millennia later who study Scripture and seek its meaning, do we understand that we need Jesus' help? Or do we depend solely on our own knowledge and study to discern what these ancient texts mean for us today? Do we cry out, "Jesus, help us to see?" Do we recognize that we are dependent on the Spirit to show us the way? Do we look for God's acts of grace on each page? Are we aware when God's Word does shine on our path?

In his article, "Bible Boy: My Quest to Understand Scripture," Norman Kraus speaks of the Bible as "the church's record of the Word of God that finds its climax in Jesus, the embodied Word." The Bible, Kraus says, is inspired by the same Spirit which is now in us, the body of Christ, the church.[3] How is that Spirit "in us" today? How has that Spirit spoken through this book to give shape to our lives? I find I can speak best of my personal journey with Scripture by talking about my journey with the church.

Congregational Roots

The year I was born, 1952, was also the birth year of Neffsville Mennonite Church, my home congregation in Lancaster County, Pennsylvania. At the mid-point of the twentieth century, writes Roy Burkholder, congregational historian, many Mennonites were attracted to *fundamentalism* through radio preachers, Bible conferences, and the Scofield Bible courses in contrast to the *legalism* they perceived in too many Lancaster Conference churches.[4] At the East Chestnut Street congregation, dissatisfaction over the "outward" expressions of faith as spelled out in the *Rules and Discipline* of Lancaster Mennonite Conference (no radio, frock tail plain coats for men, black stockings and strings on their devotional coverings for women), plus a dispute over a deacon ordination, gave birth to the Neffsville congregation.

Many of the young leaders at Neffsville received their biblical training through the Scofield dispensationalism courses which taught that God dealt with humans differently in different eras, or dispensations, throughout the Bible. From a Scofield perspective, Jesus' teachings in the Sermon on the Mount, for example, are not meant for us today but for an age after the rapture of believers.

While I had little understanding of Neffsville's moorings during my growing-up years in this congregation, these moorings influenced how I learned to view Scripture. My perspective might have been more whole had I understood H. S. Bender's critique of fundamentalism as a danger to Mennonites "because it pushes Mennonites from obedience and discipleship to the inner experience of justification and sanctification, thus becoming subjective, emotional and introspective."[5]

The Neffsville congregation nurtured my call to ministry and it taught me to love God. But it also taught me an understanding of Scripture that turned my focus inward on personal piety, making me less able to see the outward applications of the Christian way in the broader community around me.

Incidentally, for a fuller perspective of the Neffsville congregation, I should add Burkholder's observation that, while few members may have heard of or read John Howard Yoder's *The Politics of Jesus*, the congregation repeatedly called pastors who had received training at Mennonite colleges and seminaries.[6] Anabaptist history and theology, the works of Yoder and others, "provided the intellectual and theological framework for their teaching, preaching and pastoral leadership."

Like the beggar on the road to Jericho, we cry out, "Jesus, help us to see."

High School Years

During high school, I became involved with Youth for Christ (YFC). I still own my red YFC Bible with an inscription by Billy Graham inside: "The Bible is the most important Book the world has ever known. Every young person should have a good, readable copy for his very own. It should be carried to school as well as to church, for it is the greatest of all textbooks. 'Let the high praises of God be in their mouth, and a two-edged sword in their hand'" (Ps. 149:6).

As YFCers, we learned to speak of the Bible as our sword. One of my fondest memories from those years was Bible quizzing. We would study several chapters, practically memorizing them, then would compete to answer questions from these passages. These were wonderfully enriching experiences led by people who loved God's word.

While we regularly asked what the Bible *says*, we rarely thought about what the Bible *means*. The late 1960s were turbulent years in the United States—troubled race relations, the Vietnam War, and more were part of the context of my high school years but not part of my memory. I can remember being vaguely aware of Martin Luther King Jr.'s death and knowing that killing was wrong but also feeling that King was a troublemaker and probably had it coming to him.

Like the beggar on the road to Jericho, we cry out, "Jesus, help us to see."

Social Awakening

I drifted away from the church during my early college years but still ended up on Messiah College's urban center in North Philadelphia. The director of the center, Ron Sider, introduced me to his book, *Rich Christians in an Age of Hunger.*[7] Ron made a strong case for radical Christianity, a faith based on a belief that God's Word has something to say about how we live our daily lives. "If the Christ of Scripture is our Lord," said Ron, "then we will refuse to be squeezed into the mold of our affluent, sinful culture. . . . Only if we are thoroughly grounded in the scriptural view of possessions, wealth and poverty will we be capable of living an obedient lifestyle" (26-27).

Here was someone who took the *meaning* of Scripture seriously! I can remember Ron telling us that the Bible has more to say about wealth and being rich than about almost any other topic. Why didn't Christians take these words seriously? Ron taught us about the jubilee principle, the sabbatical year, laws on tithing and gleaning, Jesus' new community, the Jerusalem model, economic koinonia and more. North American Christians, taught Ron, were much like the rich Corinthian Christians who feasted without sharing their food with the poor members of the church (1 Cor. 11:20-29). "The Bible clearly teaches that God wills fundamentally transformed economic relationships among his people."

Sider wondered, "Do we have the faith and obedience to start living the biblical vision?" I responded with a resounding "yes" and worked with Ron as he formed Evangelicals for McGovern and later Evangelicals for Social Action.

Several years after college, I moved back into the northwest part of Philadelphia in the Germantown section of the city, a largely African-American community. My work with *The Other Side* magazine and with the worshiping community, Jubilee Fellowship, a congregation with informal ties to the Mennonite church, encouraged my interest in biblical studies. Eventually I attended and graduated from Eastern Baptist Theological Seminary, not because I wanted to be a pastor but because I had a deep hunger to understand Scripture. What relevance did these books we call Scripture have for my life?

What I remember most about Eastern Baptist Seminary is Dr. Tom McDaniel, professor of Old Testament studies. Gerhard von Rad, Otto Eissfeldt, and methods of biblical criticism shook the foundation of my assumptions about the Bible. Dr. McDaniel rebuilt that foundation with a love for Scripture and a love for the God revealed in it. It was McDaniel who first helped me ask the question when I read Scripture, "What did these words mean for those who wrote them and for those who first received them? And then (and only then), how can we apply this text to our situation today?"

The words of the Psalmist (9:1, 2) took on new meaning: "I will give thanks to you, O Lord, with all my heart; I will declare all your wondrous deeds. I will be glad and exult in you; I will sing praise to your name, most High."

It was also in Philadelphia, a number of years later, that I participated in an alternative seminary, a movement that professed the church to be a body "called out," a body distinct from culture and called to a mission of reconciliation; concern for the poor; and new understandings of power, justice, and community. It assumed the institutional church had been largely co-opted by the values of the culture and needed to be revitalized.

The word of God, we stated, should not be studied in ivory tower abstract detachment, but in real dialogue with the struggles of the world and our own place in it. Our goal was to develop skills of biblical and theological reflection as tools for ministry and witness in society.

Like the beggar on the road to Jericho, we cry out, "Jesus, help us to see."

Scripture in Congregational Discernment

In the late 1970s, I moved to Harrisonburg, Virginia, where I attended the Broad Street Mennonite Church, a congregation originally founded in the 1940s as a mission to the African-American community. While the motives of the founders of this mission to share the gospel with the African-American community were genuine, their actions, which they believed were based on Scripture, demonstrate how far off the mark our understanding of Scripture can sometimes be.

Harold Huber, Eastern Mennonite University archivist, reports that in November 1940, the executive committees of Virginia Mennonite Conference and the Virginia Mennonite Mission Board met together to formulate policy "to govern relationships between the colored and white in [Virginia Conference] Mennonite church fellowship." Their recommendations read as follows:

> In view of the general attitude of society in the South toward the intermingling of the two races and inasmuch as we desire to adopt a practical working policy with the view of promoting the best interests of both colored and white, and since as a matter of expediency we must make some distinction to meet existing conditions, we propose the following course of procedure in establishing a Mennonite colored congregation [the fledgling Gay Street Mission, later Broad Street Mennonite Church]:
>
> Aim: To build up a colored congregation under a separate but auxiliary organization of the Virginia Mennonite Conference.
>
> Baptism: . . . the applicant should be greeted by a colored brother or colored sister.
>
> Salutation and feet washing: . . . we do not recommend the practice of these two ordinances between white and colored.
>
> Communion: . . . provision be made for the use of individual cups at the communion table and that participation in the communion be restricted to the colored and those who are regular workers among them.

Some leaders immediately challenged these policies and a resolution was passed in 1955 that these practices "no longer express the thought or practice of this conference . . . and that we confess our former spiritual immaturity."

By the time I attended the Broad Street congregation, its members were primarily white. We struggled to understand our identity within an African-American community. We too had a respect for Scripture and its meaning for us, but our focus was less on the Great Commission and more on God's desire for justice for all people.

Like the beggar on the road to Jericho, we cry out, "Jesus, help us to see."

Germantown Mennonite Church

In 1989, when my family moved back to northwest Philadelphia, we began to attend the Mennonite congregation nearest to our home—Germantown Mennonite Church. The historic Germantown meeting-house, the first Mennonite congregation in North America, was the site of the first anti-slavery protest in the New World. This Quaker and Mennonite anti-slavery declaration, says Elaine Sommers Rich, was simply an application of Jesus' counsel, "Do unto others as you would have them do to you." Can you imagine the prayer and study of Scripture, the agonizing over consistency of word and deed that must have preceded this declaration?

When we first began to attend Germantown, the congregation was in a period of steady growth. We were attracted to the congregation's vibrant worship. The congregation included a number of young families and was also struggling with what it meant to be an urban congregation, a relatively rich congregation in a poor community.

We quickly became aware that the congregation included a significant number of gay and lesbian Christians, though this was before an eventual rift with Franconia Conference (a denominational cluster of churches which eventually excommunicated the congregation) was visible. While we heard quite different perspectives in the congregation about homosexuality, these varying viewpoints did not seem to impair the congregation's ability to be sisters and brothers with each other. I remember the words of the pastor when I asked him about the situation: "We have simply agreed that we are brothers and sisters in Christ and that we will all worship together."

The early 1990s brought much study of Scripture in the congregation. What do we believe the Bible teaches about homosexuality? How are our perspectives shaped by our relationships with each other, gay and straight together?

I remember a tract written by a member of the Germantown congregation who had been trained in a well-known evangelical seminary. The tract, "Why I Changed My Mind," detailed this member's struggle to reexamine biblical texts related to homosexuality that he thought he already understood so well. "Integrity and faithfulness to the biblical witness are core values for me," he stated.

In the end, this member chose to cite Ephesians 4 and Galatians 5 as evidence that had compelled him to change his mind about homosexual

Christians. "I see qualities of life—the fruit of the spirit—and gifts that have built up the body of Christ in gay and lesbian Christians who are in covenanted relationships with each other." Summing up the congregation's long discernment process, he concluded, "I cannot exclude from congregational membership persons who confess Christ as Lord and who exhibit fruits and gifts that I can attribute only to the Holy Spirit."

I observe that the broader Mennonite church has also undergone a community discernment process concerning homosexuality and faithfulness and has issued well-thought-through documents Mennonites have come to know as the Saskatoon 1986 and Purdue 1997 statements. These documents were written after serious research and listening, earnest biblical study, and prayer and deep discernment within the body of Christ.

These denominational statements on homosexuality, which limit full sexual expression to heterosexual marriage, represent our best corporate understanding as a Mennonite churchwide community about what God has revealed to us through Scripture and community discernment. Similarly, our brothers and sisters at Germantown have taken biblical study and community discernment seriously. This discernment process included extensive respectful discussion with Franconia Conference leaders, but, in the end, this congregation felt led by God to go in a different direction than the conference.

What are we to make of these different directions within our own body? How do we affirm serious community discernment of Scripture within the congregation as well as within the larger body of Mennonites? Perhaps the current debate within our body has as much to do with our views of community discernment of Scripture as it does with our views about homosexuality.

Like the beggar on the road to Jericho, we cry out, "Jesus, help us to see."

Summing it Up

"In the end," says David Ewert in his book, *How to Understand the Bible,* "we must confess with the sixteenth-century Reformers, both mainline and Anabaptist, that the Bible alone is our ultimate authority and guide in a world that is often confusing."[8]

The article on "Scripture" in the *Confession of Faith in a Mennonite Perspective* states, "We seek to understand and interpret Scripture in harmony with Jesus Christ as we are led by the Holy Spirit. . . . we participate in the church's task of interpreting the Bible and of discerning what God is saying in our time by examining all things in the light of Scripture."[9]

If God's Word was inspired by the same Spirit which is now in us, the church, what does that mean for our discernment of Scripture within the body of Christ in our congregations, our conferences and our denomination? When our discernment about what Scripture means differs, what becomes our recourse?

One response is that we will need more discernment. God has not finished speaking to us through God's Word and through the community. We must continue to pray, study, and discern together.

Another response is to actively observe the result of Scripture's influence on our lives. Does our discernment help us to follow Christ's example? Does it break down the walls that divide us? Does it help us to love one another? Does it help us see through Jesus' eyes of love so that we can follow him on the way?

Neffsville and Jubilee Fellowship, Broad Street and Germantown, and now Eighth Street, my congregational home in Goshen, Indiana— they all share a common desire to hear God's Word as mediated to us through Scripture. If we hope to understand Scripture's meaning for our lives, this shared reverence for Scripture must be accompanied by an equal respect for the tradition of the church, a commitment to ongoing community discernment, and an openness to the Holy Spirit to show us new meaning and application.

Like the hymn writer, we can affirm a basic truth of Scripture: "*As you have loved us, sent your Son, And our salvation now is won, O let our hearts with love be stirred. Help us, God, know your word!*"

May we continue to be like the beggar on the road to Jericho, crying out, "Jesus, help us to see."

Teach us to love with heart and mind and soul.
You, O Christ, be our goal.
Break down the walls of prejudice and hate.
Leave us not to our fate.
As you have loved and giv'n your life,
To end hostility and strife,
O share your grace from heav'n above.
Teach us, Christ, how to love![10]

Notes

1. K. L. Cober, "Renew Your Church," verse 2, in *Hymnal: A Worship Book* (Elgin, Ill.: Brethren Press, 1992), no. 363 (a hymn in public domain).

2. Ched Myers, *Say to This Mountain: Mark's Story of Discipleship* (Maryknoll, N.Y.: Orbis Books, 1996), 134.

3. Norman Kraus, "Bible Boy: My Quest to Understand Scripture," *Dreamseeker Magazine* (Spring 2002): 5-7.

4. Roy Brubaker, *Pathways to Renewal: A Narrative History of Neffsville Mennonite Church, 1952-2002* (Neffsville, Pa.: Neffsville Mennonite Church, 2002).

5. Harold Bender, "Outside Influences on Mennonite Thought," *Mennonite Life* (January 1955): 48.

6. John Howard Yoder, *The Politics of Jesus* (Grand Rapids: Eerdmans, 1972).

7. Ronald J. Sider, *Rich Christians in an Age of Hunger* (Downers Grove, Ill.: Intervarsity Press, 1977).

8. David Ewert, *How to Understand the Bible* (Scottdale, Pa.: Herald Press, 2000).

9. *Confession of Faith in a Mennonite Perspective* (Scottdale, Pa.: Herald Press, 1995), 21.

10. K. L. Cober, "Renew Your Church," verse 4.

CHAPTER 7

A Great Many-Winged Bird

Lin Garber

The topic assigned here is not one that I would have voluntarily rushed to focus on. But I do understand that the struggle with varying understandings of Scripture is at the very center of the disagreements that roil the Mennonite Church USA and many other denominations today. Although I will not be able to establish impeccable orthodox credentials nor do I have interest in doing so, I do hope to show myself a fellow believer with other Anabaptist seekers, one worthy to hear and be heard, to give and receive counsel.

Of the four major divisions suggested for our presentations, the second, "On the Way," asks what crises I encountered and what issues the community struggled with that shaped my journey. (For the various segments suggested, see Appendix 2: "Conceptual Background to Guidelines for Writing About Our Journeys with Scripture.") That second division may be the most crucial one for me to engage in this context. That is to say, I am conscious of being the only person publicly identified as gay who has accepted the invitation to participate in this discussion.

First, as to the community that introduced me to Scripture in the form of the Holy Bible: I grew up in a traditional Mennonite community. This meant that Scripture for us was centered on the story of Jesus and his ministry, on the Sermon on the Mount, and on instructions for how a Christian life should be lived in relation to the needs of the world around us.

But something occurred to me as I was contemplating this: The words of the King James Version were a constant background to our lives in those days. By osmosis as much as by intention, many passages were inscribed in my synapses in a way that still brings them forth at unexpected times. The very sound of the words helped frame my aural environment, and often it was as much the music of the sounds as the meaning they conveyed that stuck with me.

Walter Brueggemann, in his *Christian Century* article on "Biblical Authority" (see Appendix 1), refers to James Muhlenberg, who asked his students to "attend with educated alertness to the cadences and sounds of the text in all its detail." That request quite literally resonates with me.

Recently our congregation, along with many other folks, has been taking something of a crash course in Islam. I was interested to learn that the very music of the Arabic language of the Qur'an is considered to be inspired and inspiring and that its production by the prophet Muhammad is considered to be a foundation miracle of Islamic faith. Similarly, today, and for most of my life, I have found myself often reverting to the language of the King James in preference to the perhaps more intellectually respectable versions our scholars have been producing in such profusion in the last half-century.

Whether the intended original meaning is corrupted or not, very often the noble cadence of that text in itself provides for me a kind of anchor that I had not always realized was meaningful for me. Just as one example, the marvelous benediction from the epistle of Jude that our uneducated farmer ministers could intone so majestically still sings to me: "Now unto him who is able to keep you from falling, and to present you faultless before the presence of his glory with exceeding joy, to the only wise God our Savior, be glory and majesty, dominion and power, both now and ever. Amen." Today I have some gender-inclusion problems with these words, some theological qualms, and some questions about priorities. But their very sound still has the power to give me a calmness and an assurance when things threaten to go all out of control, as they do almost daily.

I think there is a downside to that phenomenon. To the extent that music can hypnotize us, can lull our critical faculties to sleep, it can obscure falsehoods and distortions that may inhere in a text and lend them a subliminal acceptability such that we often don't recognize that they are there. I wonder if that is part of the dynamic behind the new currents of belief that were entering the church of my childhood, currents which insisted that every single verse of the Holy Bible that we each carried with us to every service of worship was of equal value. That meant that the Old Testament was as inerrant as the New, that Jude had the same authority and value as Jeremiah, that every commandment, explicit or implied, was to be obeyed to the letter.

There was tension in my little community as a result. Some of us were secretly aware that some things in the Bible were in direct contradiction to other things in the Bible. But if anyone were so foolhardy as to point that out, we would immediately be countered with the ultimate proof text of 2 Timothy 3:16: "All Scripture is given by inspiration of God, and is profitable for doctrine, for reproof, for correction, for instruction in righteousness." I was already the skeptic at ten or so, and I would protest that more evidence than that was needed, preferably something from outside the Bible. I quickly learned, however, after the storm of indignation that would ensue, to keep my protests to myself.

On my own journey, I have become increasingly unwilling to place boundaries around inspiration, to put it into cages. The image used by animal rights activists to show the cruelty of egg factories, where hens are jammed into pens too small to move about in and their wings are clipped, is what comes to me when I think of the Spirit—the dove of inspiration—having boundaries set around it. That includes the cage of a printed text.

Some versions now render that verse as "all Scripture that is inspired," and in so doing put inspiration into one kind of cage. Some readers mentally insert a caret and say "all *canonical* Scripture is inspired." That is another kind of cage, and in both cases an occasion for dissent is being established. Instead of listening to the inspiration itself, we will quarrel over what is and what is not inspired, what is and what is not canonical.

Another approach to Scripture has been that taken by a tradition rooted in England, first in the Church of England, then by Methodism. There we were introduced to the "three-legged stool" upon which theology rests: Scripture, reason, and tradition (usually embodied in "the Church"). Wesley and the Pietists added "experience" to make a four-legged, quadrilateral stool. Whenever I hear a Methodist preacher expound on the four-legged stool, something in me keeps saying "Yes . . . and . . . and what else. . . . " waiting to hear some acknowledgment of the role of the Spirit in all of this! And it has struck me that the metaphor of the stool, however many legs it has, is a fitting one for the inevitable re-

sult of that omission: it produces a piece of furniture suitable for the accommodation of the human fundament, but it is necessarily earth-
bound. I want these folks to let the Spirit come down and pick up that
homely object and bear it, and its occupants, up to the skies!

I have learned from my Quaker sojourn, and in other contexts as
well, to sense a movement of something that originates from outside me
and to listen to what it is saying to me. That is what I understand to be
inspiration—literally, an intake of breath, the *sine qua non* of life, that
ultimate gift of God. Now it is from Scripture itself, reinforced by the
Quakers, that I learned what is to me the key truth that seems so often
overlooked or disregarded by today's literalists and by those folks who
are glued to their stools: *We have ready access to the same Spirit that inspired Scripture.* It is spelled out in the Gospel of John, in three chapters
in succession: "When I go away, I will leave you with a comforter, a *par-
aclete.*" Not a book, but a Spirit.

Recently I talked about the Apocrypha to our congregation, including the use made of it by Menno Simons, and about themes from the
Apocrypha that have been used in the arts. I noticed that works of art
based on Apocryphal themes often appeared, even from an art-critical
standpoint, to be less inspired as a rule than many based on themes from
the 66 books of the Puritan canon. I simply introduce that observation
here; I have not done any systematic investigation that would make it
definitive, but it does interest me in connection with how the canon was
formed. Is there in fact some intrinsic mode of inspiration that guided
the canonical process?

But allow me to address the issue my community struggled with
that made me grapple anew with Scripture. After a period when it
seemed of only slight relevance to my life and faith, there was indeed one
such major issue. I was amazed, when I was urgently sent to the texts
imagined to be relevant to same-sex orientation, to discover that this
project is actually exciting! But the standard selection of six or eight
"clobber texts"—from Leviticus, Romans, and 1 Corinthians—were
not talking about anything I recognized from my own experience. Certainly the society of Sodom bore no resemblance to the gay community
as I knew it!

It was in the love story of Jonathan and David that I found common
ground with my own experience. I knew exactly what Jonathan was feeling when he "made a covenant with David, because he loved him as his

own soul." I understood the tension between father and son when Saul accused Jonathan of bringing shame on his mother through his love of David. And I knew exactly what David was singing about, in his lament over the death of Jonathan: "Very pleasant have you been to me; your love to me was wonderful, surpassing the love of women."

In the Brueggemann article cited before, I appreciate his highlighting of the contrast between Deuteronomy 23:1-8 and Isaiah 56:3-8. Throughout the Bible there is a remarkable flow of references to eunuchs, reinforcing how these once-despised souls were assured by Isaiah of their high place in God's affections. Brueggemann stopped short of the New Testament: I was enormously excited, years ago, when I discovered how the apostle Philip, after sharing the reading of Isaiah with the Ethiopian eunuch en route to Gaza, couldn't sustain his prejudice and had to go ahead and baptize him. Then, lest he have second thoughts, he is whisked away by an angel of God!

I happen to believe, after further reflection on these stories, that it is wrong to say that the Bible has nothing to say about same-sex affectional relationships, and certainly that it is wrong to insist that whenever the Bible mentions "homosexuality" (which of course it never does), it does so only to condemn it. Even such tolerant scholars as Pim Pronk and Walter Wink have fallen into that trap. But they fail to see what has become clear to me: the eunuchs spoken of in the Bible were the gay men of their time! And aside from one verse in Deuteronomy, every mention of eunuchs is either neutral or positive.

This one topic illustrates magnificently something I have come to appreciate about these texts: They provide pointers to aspects of eastern-Mediterranean history and culture that were the context to some stark and bewildering passages. And suddenly the whole project became a richly textured experience indeed. Brueggemann again spells it out beautifully: "It becomes clear that the interpretive project that constitutes the final form of the text is itself profoundly polyvalent, yielding no single exegetical outcome, but allowing layers and layers of fresh reading in which God's own life and character are deeply engaged and put at risk."

So I have come to know all the *positive* references to gender-variant people in the Bible, and I rejoice. Speaking of putting God's own life and character "at risk," as Brueggemann says, I even lay claim to the sensitive topic of the references to the beloved disciple in the Johannine gospel. I recognize those references; they speak to me; I feel confident I know what they're talking about. It was in God's plan, I firmly believe, that the first church to welcome and celebrate gay people when their persecution began to ease ever so slightly, back in 1968, was named the Church of the Beloved Disciple.

My journeys with Scripture and with the whole concept of inspiration have brought me to a place where I do not see a fixed map, a rigid signpost, showing me exactly where I am located in the universe, but where a great many-winged bird that is not confined in a cage of printed words, but is waiting for me to climb aboard and soar beyond limitation, beyond dimension, to wonders too great for my imagining. I am grateful for the teachers who have helped me come to this place and for the guidebook they relied on to get us here.

CHAPTER 8

Reading the Bible in Search of Jesus and the Way

Ray Gingerich

Writing my "journey with Scripture" is writing my journey of life. These two—the journey with Scripture and the journey of life—constitute the warp and woof of a single cloth. To write narrowly about Scripture is like pulling threads out of a cloth that has a larger design. Placing my journey with Scripture into life's larger context illuminates the design of my life's tapestry.

The Clan

Although not the firstborn, being the oldest and only son in a paternally oriented, male-dominated society placed me into the family system as an oldest child. My twin sisters were older than I and another sister followed. But through childhood and youth it was known that I was the designated inheritor of the farm operation and the lineage of my father who was also the eldest son.

Seven years before my birth my mother, daughter of a Mennonite deacon, left the Conservative Mennonites and joined the Old Order Amish to marry my father. This is less a comment about any kind of romantic conservativism embedded in my mother than about theological and cultural proximity of the Old Order Amish and the Conservative (Amish) Mennonites in the mid-1920s. Technology—cars, telephones and electricity—had not yet created the divide that would later occur.

When I was three, my maternal grandparents built a nondescript little *Dahdy-Haus* (grandparents' house) onto the front entrance of a grand old Victorian farm house with ten-foot ceilings, a parlor, open oak stairway, and central heating. That is, it had central heating until it was ripped out to make it conform to Amish simplicity and frugality. For my parents, and undoubtedly for me, Amish simplicity—a euphemism for austerity—was a synonym for biblical simplicity. These were the lenses of my earliest reading of Scripture—a perspective shared by many people from the global South, but one that may be difficult to communicate to people who have not experienced that cultural-religious world.

On many a summer night my sisters and I sat on my grandparents' front porch and listened to my grandfather spin tales (true stories is what I thought they were) of his orphaned childhood days—half Native American Indian, half Irish. Only many years later did I realize that this wasn't quite what he said, and that he had really come from east of Goshen, Indiana, without a drop of "outside" blood. Yet there was something remarkably true about this slightly less than literal rendition of his past. And it is quite probable that my grandfather's romanticized version of the underside of his own past influenced how I would later understand the story of another marginalized people of God, a much more ancient people, whom I would claim as my spiritual family.

The bedtime stories my mother read were from *Hurlbut's Stories of Bible History* and from the *Egermeier's Bible Story Book*. The greatest hero was God, who early on seemed to have established a practice of drowning wicked people. Next to that were God's military heroes—Gideon, Joshua, David, and Solomon. Yet to my mother's credit—for I learned the Bible from my mother, not my father—she would wince a bit at the violence in the name of God and would wonder out loud how God, who called on his children not to kill, was left to do so much of the dirty work. By spring of my third grade in a country public school (all students of various stripes of Mennonites except for one family) I had memorized five hundred Bible verses and recited them to my teacher. With each fifty verses recited we received a small Christian fiction book from the Iowa Rural Bible Crusade.

When the shelves are cleared after I am gone, not my doctoral dissertation on Anabaptist missions but a little pocket-worn Gospel of John, carried with me for memorizing while I did my morning and evening farm chores, will be among the most precious memorabilia. The

Bible at that young and malleable age had become the *Word of God,* the Rock of Ages, the foundation, the source of all Truth. It was the keystone of my identity.

Though I probably respected my paternal grandfather as much as my maternal one (both grandmothers seem to have played only a secondary role), it was the deacon grandfather, staunchly certain that he knew what the Scriptures said, and equally unequivocal regarding its practical application, who early in life piqued my interest in the study of Scripture. Problematic passages and issues were usually referenced by prayer and the leading of the Holy Spirit.

And therewith the issue was resolved—at least for the time being. Certainly by the time I was twelve I sensed that scriptural interpretation for my grandfather, and the entire "bench" of fellow Conservative Mennonite ministers that on occasion met at our house, defied normal everyday reasoning and was given a special privileged status in our community. And, as I would later listen to my grandfather discuss their differences, I began to suspect that scriptural interpretation was less straightforward than he made it out to be.

Extending the Clan

It was summer 1955. I had just finished two years in "I-W service" (a pacifist alternative to military service) at the Lancaster General Hospital. That time was critical in introducing me, at a number of levels, to a more dominant community of Mennonites, Lancaster County Mennonites. Here I experienced a certain inversion of practice and theology: Those who lived in more closed communities possessed a communal humility (some might have called it an inferiority complex) and had a somewhat more pliable situational community theology. On the other hand, those whose self-identity was increasingly urban, who were in the process of rapidly moving away from the family farm, who were engaged in mainstream professions and endowed with rapidly increasing wealth and prestige, seemed to be compensating for all this "worldliness" with a theology that was more other-worldly, less relational, and placed greater emphasis on the certitude of individual salvation and doctrinal "orthodoxy." All this I later discovered was a phase of twentieth-century Mennonites moving toward a more mainstream Evangelical American theology that offered greater certainty for the soul and things invisible, while at the same time calling for less social differentiation and promising greater enjoyment while here in this world.

While I was in Lancaster, for the first time in my life those with whom I identified were in the "majority."[1] This spirit of expansionism, both psychologically and numerically, was most apparent in their missions emphasis. The Lancaster Mennonites who created a milieu of being in charge were missions-minded. Their calling was clear. Their roles as God's instruments were unquestioned. They possessed, for bounteous distribution, the knowledge of truth and the way of salvation for all peoples. Their call to missions, particularly overseas missions, provided perhaps the single greatest religious legitimation for wealth.

The Lancaster experience (particularly because I later served under the Lancaster Mennonite mission board) was and remains one of the social paradigms for my understanding of the Mennonite church and for the contrasting ways in which Scripture is read. Lancaster Mennonites were (and are) economically well-heeled, a people of power, a committed people who have traversed the world with a Bible and a theology that seemed to serve humanity well.

Not until over a decade after my I-W experience in Lancaster did I realize how closely my reading of the Bible was aligned with the "in-charge" ethos I had absorbed during my Lancaster era and the post-Lancaster college years. The realization came while I was in Europe with the mission of "bringing to the European Mennonites those parts of the gospel which they had lost over the past four hundred and fifty years"[2]— this during the time when the tax dollars of America Mennonites were supporting the war in Vietnam. The Lancaster-based theology and the way I was reading the Bible seemed to endorse the American ethos in its major tenets of imperialism rather than provide the foundation for an alternative community of love and nonviolent resistance with structures of mutual accountability. Slowly, very gradually, I began to realize how little my theology had kept me from becoming absorbed into the maelstrom of the world's Superpower Society.[3]

Comparative Cultures

The Lancaster experience provides a significant segment in my journey with Scripture. But it was what followed those two years away from my home community, rather than the Lancaster experience itself, that would be more immediately decisive. I "knew" that my life was surrendered to God and that God would lead me. But where? What? How? It was this sense of knowing *that,* yet not knowing *how* and *where,* that made me restive. I assumed that the answers to all of life's questions reside in the Bible. What was called for was insight under the direction of the Holy Spirit.

Following this two-year stint in the Lancaster General Hospital, I spent the summer months in New York City in several Lancaster Mennonite Conference mission churches. Inner-city New York contrasted sharply with the green rolling hills of Iowa, with cultivating the long rows of corn while memorizing Scripture or working through Howard Hammer's latest revival sermon (1951). In the morning on New York City's hot-tarred boulevards, I walked through trash-strewn alleys and entered the spaghetti-stenched, rat-infested apartments and high-rises, persuading the kids in the neighborhood to come to summer Bible school. I taught classes with African-Americans in the afternoon and Italians at night—while making my way through culture shock.

By the end of the summer there was a crack in my armor. I began to see how dependent on my cultural surroundings is my understanding of Scripture (and of life). The sensory experiences downloaded into my psycho-physical hardware during those summer months proved to be a significant subconscious motivating force for the next steps. I left New York City overwhelmed, not knowing what the larger contours of my life were to be.

What had become clear to me was that the world and its people constituted a phenomenon far greater and more complex than I was able to comprehend. For the first time, although I was still unable to verbalize this, it seemed to me as though the Bible had failed to provide the answers to life's most persistent questions. My next step was to acquire tools to discover myself in the context of my surroundings, as I sensed that where I stood determined what I saw.

College—Sorting Out the Pieces

Newly married, committed to missions, committed to the Bible, committed to the church: Wilma Beachy Gingerich and I, both from Kalona, matriculated at Eastern Mennonite College (EMC) nearly a thousand miles from home. Goshen College, a mere 350 miles, did not come into question. It was too liberal—so we were told. "EMC will make you more useful to the church." But most of our people in Iowa even had serious doubts about that. Why was I taking this interlude away from my farming responsibilities, or perhaps even leaving the farm? Sometimes in the tone of a warning, sometimes as a sincere encouragement not to leave the community, came the refrain: "You don't need an education to understand the Bible and serve the Lord. Only a humble heart and the Holy Spirit."

While at EMC I experienced different ways of reading the Bible. Should the Book of Revelation provide our hermeneutic keys? Or should we look rather to the Sermon on the Mount? Do we arrive at right ethics as a consequence of pure doctrine? Or do we understand doctrine in the context of culture and ethics? Does a somber form of worship with four-part singing best conform to the biblical model? Or is Appalachian Pentecostalism a more contemporarily fitting expression?

The real clincher for me came, however, in a course in *apologetics*. The text, Bernard Ramm's *Evidences of Christianity*, was an unusually clear and emphatic Fundamentalist book. I completed the course and for the first time clearly and definitively knew that I was not a Fundamentalist. Equally important, I knew that Jesus was not a Fundamentalist. It was doubtful that I could be a Fundamentalist and be Jesus' follower. But I knew that I could not be a Fundamentalist and maintain intellectual integrity. All this was a *freeing* but *frustrating* experience.

This experience of facing the solid rock wall of Ramm's Fundamentalism, his way of reading the Bible, and the "proofs" or evidences of Christianity that he provided is a landmark in a life-long pursuit in epistemology. I "knew" that Ramm believed himself to know things he did not "know." How is it that I "know"? And what is the peculiar nature of that knowing? Are certain ways of pursuing "knowledge" less prone to idolatry than others? Are some forms of "knowing" more faithful to the way of Jesus than others? And more life-giving than others? With the awareness of different routes to "knowing," some of them illustrated in the Bible itself, came a heightened recognition that there are different ways of reading the Bible—indeed, that in our Mennonite fellowship different ways, sometimes conflictingly different ways, are practiced but seldom openly discussed.

These socio-cultural questions of epistemology and their relationship to the nonviolent life of faith are what mark my interest in the Anabaptists of the sixteenth century and theologies of the disempowered on the margins of society. These people offer us a different way of knowing. The epistemological questions and the contrast they offer to eighteenth- and nineteenth-century Protestant missions, carried out hand-in-glove with Western colonization, is what so relentlessly piques my interest in Mennonite missions. But let me return again to my story.

The "aha" moment with Ramm was also painful and frightening. It challenged me to think and to act beyond the boundaries sanctioned by the communities to which I continued to be committed. It raised the painful dilemma that love is not passive, that to love my community of faith and to be loyal to it I must have the courage to challenge it. In my journey with Scripture I began to see Jesus as a person who had these qualities and used them to serve his community. I read the gospel stories and Jesus' conflict with the Pharisees in a new light, substituting "the Mennonites" for "the Pharisees"—a practice that I have continued throughout the years.

Missions and Anomalies

My years in Europe under the Eastern Mennonite Board of Missions and Charities (now Eastern Mennonite Missions) spurred a proliferation of further questions (e.g., the nature of the biblical text, the impact of cultural context on meanings and understandings, epistemological and theological orientations). Unfortunately, however, during this entire period far too often I found myself without a hermeneutical community with whom to share, to process, and to grow. In the framework of Thomas Kuhn's thought regarding paradigm shifts, it was a period in which theological anomalies grew larger and more complex, but with few genuine breakthroughs; much less did a new paradigm emerge. My professional role as pastor dictated not merely the content of my sermons but more and more the boundaries of my thought and the very way I dared (or was unable to dare) to read the Scriptures.

As I continued to listen to my American missionary peers in Europe and those stopping over in Luxembourg on their way to and from East Africa, I found none with whom I was able to explore faith questions in depth. Looking back, I find this astonishing and wonder whether I failed to be sufficiently open and transparent. Did my lack of courage cause me to fail to engage even the one or two Mennonite missionaries plagued by doubts similar to mine? For these expatriate peers local "native" customs were important for purposes of communication, for contextualizing the gospel, but cultural differences (be they European or African) offered no further hermeneutical insight. They provided illustrative materials but not the fabric of an alternative way to read the Scriptures.

My American Mennonite peers working in East Africa seemed to have an even easier path than my American peers in Europe. The customs of native peoples in Africa with whom they worked were so dramatically different that the expectations for the expatriate were limited to selective adaptations of cultural peripheries in contrast to the expectations of general conformity by our European hosts. More important for theological understandings, the worldview of the East African was much like the worldview of the first century depicted in the Bible. Hence the East African missionary experience—in contrast to the European missionary experience—seemed to reinforce the normalcy of a dualistic (this-worldly/other-worldly) cosmology of American Mennonite, Protestant-evangelical missions. "Mennonite theology" was evangelical Protestant theology appended with Mennonite particulars by North American Mennonites.[4] A serious faith struggle, one that moved beyond the application of "Christian practices," seemed seldom to ensue.[5]

The single factor that did make a theological impact was the great "East African Revival." That tended to push the American Mennonite missionaries into an even more pietistic, allegoric, "spiritualist" way of reading the Bible—one that corresponded with a premodern culture. But it was exactly in the opposite direction from the way that I was being pulled in Europe. I was struggling to find a political gospel that would be healing for a whole people.[6]

The "God" I had served I now surmised to be largely a human construct too puny, and too much fashioned after our American triumphalism, to be worthy of my loyalties—much less worthy of proclaiming to a needy and unjust world whether in Africa, Europe, or America. I could no longer go this route. If the Christian faith was worth my total commitment, there had to be more to it; it had to play a much more all-encompassing social role than I had seen or heard. So at age thirty-five, with a wife and four children to support, I left the "mission field" to find Jesus again for the first time, and to find God.[7]

A New Paradigm for Reading the Scriptures

At Associated Mennonite Biblical Seminary (AMBS), under John Howard Yoder, I experienced another conversion.[8] It was as dramatic and as Spirit-filled as any previous conversion. It happened, steady-by-jerks, over the course of a year or two. The anomalies which were as single threads now came together so that, with the help of Yoder as mentor amid a larger hermeneutic community, I began to weave together a new tapestry. I understood spirituality and faithfulness to be a quality of life, not a metaphysical perspective foreign to the primary mode of reality in our everyday lives. Ethics rather than doctrine, orthopraxis (right living) before orthodoxy (right doctrine), is what determines faithfulness.

Central to the gospel is the way of peace as both taught and practiced by Jesus. The model for understanding this gospel, and the community that gave birth to it, is Jesus of Nazareth. No longer was this Jesus one of the persons of the Godhead; were that the case, no logic would allow me to emulate such a "deity" as an ethical model. The doctrine of the Trinity was just that: a doctrine, a human construct debated and then sacralized and granted authority beyond Scripture by the pre-eminently Constantinian church. Whatever burdens such sacralized doctrinal constructs foisted on me, these were now of secondary or tertiary importance. For although institutionally I needed to lend these doctrines my respect, they could no longer be allowed to interfere with discipleship and with the necessary social constructs for faith. Life had new meaning and the Scriptures held new integrity and vibrancy.

My hermeneutical guideline for reading the Old Testament was to read it as Jesus did. He read it through the eyes of the prophets. They, not the kings, were his models. Jesus and his followers stood in that prophetic line. The earliest Christian movements were overwhelmingly simple people. Jesus was a "Zealot" who refused to hurt people or to use violence to gain kingdom goals. That is, Jesus actively embraced the Zealots' sense of justice (of sufficiency of goods, personal and ethnic dignity, participation in one's own destiny, and of solidarity with the oppressed), but rejected violence, which the Zealots unquestioningly assumed was essential as a means toward justice. And for this Jesus died.

Anabaptism as a Practiced Way of Life

At Associated Mennonite Biblical Seminary I developed a theological grid based not on dogma but on discipleship, not on supernaturalism but on the church as an incarnational presence in this world, not on salvation in the afterlife but on that which is life-giving and healing in the present life. And perhaps of greatest importance, a grid based on the nonviolent model of Jesus.

But it was in Nashville (where I did my graduate work) at Edgehill United Methodist Church that I experienced what Anabaptism and the Jesus way of life might look like if practiced as Monday's politics rather than Sunday's piety. The church was located one block away from a large urban renewal set of high-rises, one hundred percent Black, and five blocks away from a lily-White university. A dwelling house was converted into a Methodist "church" without a steeple; the "sanctuary" was a two-car garage used seven days a week for community services. Here was a modern version of "the church in thy house." I was being introduced to a politically active people of God whom I began to see as modern Anabaptists. Jim Lawson, earlier co-worker of Martin Luther King, was a sometime member of the pastoral team. This was in the early 1970s, before the days of the Metropolitan Church, but publicly posted—on Sunday afternoon it served as the worship place for Nashville's gay and lesbian community. This was also a congregation promoting women in ministry.

The lead pastor, Bill Barnes, with whom I continue a friendship to this day, had done an internship with Bill Stringfellow in East Harlem and was a pacifist. He introduced me to the Berrigan brothers, whose writings I read for my morning devotions during most of those years. And when, amid my doctoral studies, the *Politics of Jesus* (which I had received from John Yoder as class handouts while at AMBS) became available in published form, I began to see the possibilities of a pacifism that was linked to political action and social justice. Here was a kind of radical nonviolent revolution—quite different from the quieter pacifism of North American Mennonites which was the lens through which I had earlier read *The Politics*. I began to read the Bible again as though for the first time.

Back to the Beginnings

Two anecdotes must suffice. I was in the third or fourth grade when on one of those rare occasions the county superintendent of schools visited us. I recall nothing of what he said, except one line which he carefully wrote on the board: "The more you know you know you know, you know you know the less." This was before the postmodern era. He was not echoing the latest philosophical fad.

Here was the recognition that much of the certainty proclaimed is an illusion. What is not an illusion is the humble recognition that we do not know all that we are made to believe we know. Reading the Bible, even memorizing it, is no shortcut to the hard struggle of knowing and doing the will of God—to *hear* the voice of our Lord amid the cacophony of voices today, many of them believing themselves to know what we do not know, things that even Jesus never knew.

The second anecdote also comes from my very early years of school. On the report cards of the rural public elementary school I attended was a quote, all but forgotten, from Abe Lincoln: "I will study and prepare myself and perhaps someday my chance will come." I specifically remember my mother calling my attention to this. She, more than anyone else, intuited my gifts and anticipated my struggles. Somewhere long ago in the stream of life I learned that preparing myself—of which a saturation with the Scriptures seemed no small part—lies not simply in the studying but in the practicing. What I do I become; the company I keep determines the path I take; and those who seek in love to be instruments of redemption are of all people most likely themselves to appreciate the gift of redemption.

My mother did not quite realize it, but "my chance" was not some punctiliar, ultimate goal or some grand once-in-a-lifetime opportunity opening up to me for which all of my previous life was but a preparation. I was born into a home where the Scriptures were treasured and the way of Jesus sought after. My chance is the gift of participating in a hermeneutical community—sometimes weak and faltering, usually marginalized—that continues the struggle of searching the Scriptures amid dialogue and journeying together in the continued search for Jesus and the way. My chance is the gift of a community that allows me—and on occasion even encourages me—to read the Bible again for the first time, and in that context find Jesus again for the first time.

Notes

1. By this I am not saying that Mennonites constituted more than fifty percent of the larger society. That was obviously not the case. But among the many ethnic groups they constituted a critical mass, both numerically and culturally.

2. This is a quote from Amos Horst, Lancaster Conference bishop who preached at my ordination service in Kalona, April 1961. Though Horst stated this as the reason that Wilma (my spouse) and I were being sent to Europe, it was not an official statement from the mission board.

3. Here, if space would allow, a series of anecdotes, ranging from encounters on the MCC European Peace Section to my European peers' responses to the Cuban missile crisis, would best substantiate the point.

4. The two influential "classics " in this category are Daniel Kauffman's *Doctrines of the Bible* (Scottdale, Pa.: Mennonite Publishing House, 1914 and ff.) and J. C. Wenger's *Introduction to Theology* (Scottdale, Pa.: Herald Press, 1954).

5. Another factor that played a role in the very different expectations from the hosts was the different status of the American culture and the American way of life in the host cultures: In Africa the West (America) represented modernity, progress, and the promise of greater wealth. Europeans, on the other hand, often envied American wealth but saw their own culture as being superior—and certainly not pagan or in need of missionaries. Many of them were inclined to see Americans, particularly "missionaries" as "young upstarts," generally naïve.

6. During this time Paul N. Kraybill was Executive Secretary of EMBMC (now EMM). Paul was very perceptive and a personally empathetic administrator. But, assuming that he possessed the intellectual acumen and a sufficiently malleable personality, his location within the Lancaster Conference hierarchy and his understanding of administrative roles, did not allow him to be the bridge to a larger hermeneutical community.

7. Some of my existential evangelical friends would feel more comfortable if I would say, "to make space for God to find me." Who knows how it *really* is?

8. There were others on the AMBS faculty who were also very life-giving and helped me to find Jesus, the Jewish prophet. Among them was Millard Lind and the late Howard Charles. But I mention John Howard for two reasons: He was the faculty person in the small group to which I was assigned; and I found his social reading of Scripture combined with his horizontal theological constructs to be the most insightful and constructive, addressing my particular circumstances.

CHAPTER 9

Joining with the Energy of God

Roy Hange

Beginning the Journey

As I tell my story, I am sitting in a room with a group of people. We can hear water flowing in a nearby stream. We hear it through the open door like we hear words of faithfulness flowing through Scripture as the background sound and movement of our lives. To tell my story, I will use two different frames: First, my journey with Scripture has been a search for the energy of God to change, transform, and challenge in pastoral and prophetic ways. That energy appears as a "shimmering," as when you look into a waterfall and see those points where flowing water intersects with light. There is the shimmering presence of energy, movement, and light that we also can sense in worship and transforming encounter with people. Second, I will use the term *idolatry* at times in the simple sense of a diversion of energy. True faith then is when our human energies flow with the energy of God, as seen in Scripture, in a doxology of true worship and practice.

I was born in Canada where my father was a bush pilot with a mission organization. The first three years of my life were in the energy of nature with lakes, forests, and natural beauty. I grew up with these primal images informing the way I connect with Scripture. What is the

Great Spirit doing in these texts? How is the energy of God moving over time in history?

From my fourth year on, I grew up in a conservative Mennonite church in Franconia Conference. Conservative Evangelicalism and Anabaptism informed the manner of dealing with Scripture there. In this context I saw Scripture as a tool to turn souls toward God.

In about sixth grade and in our church library, our summer Bible school class met with our teacher. Daily the teacher opened the Bible and the *Martyrs Mirror*. We read and we discussed what we found. During that time a realization grew within me: These words are powerful. They change hearts and history. My journey with Scripture over the following decades has been an exploration of the depths and breadth of that power. I read many books and much Scripture in my youth.

On the Way from Reason to Beauty

At age sixteen, and at Christopher Dock Mennonite High School, I began to ask many questions about Scripture and the Christian faith. I had read Thomas Paine's *Age of Reason* and *Asimov's Guide to the Bible*.[1] Both asked many questions of the veracity of Scriptures. Both were rationalist critiques of Scripture. I discussed these questions with one of my teachers. She gave me two books that were to change the way I read Scripture: *Mere Christianity* by C. S., Lewis[2] and *The Politics of Jesus* by John Howard Yoder.[3] In these books I found a view of Scripture and faith that incorporates reason creatively and dynamically, and a faith that engages the whole world, not just the soul. My reading of Scripture was deepened in these two directions. In my late teens I went from reading the magazines *Moody Monthly* to *Christianity Today* to *Sojourners*. This movement represents my shift in perspective on reading Scripture.

I studied Bible and Christian Ministries at Eastern Mennonite College and appreciated what I learned about Scripture there. After graduating in 1982, I went to Egypt with Mennonite Central Committee (MCC) in part to better understand the Semitic culture in which the Bible emerged. I did not feel that I was getting in books the inner intuitive sense of the text. In Egypt I received many insights into how the Semitic world's sense of honor, purity, and family and tribal loyalties differ from those we assume in the West.

After three years in Egypt, I went to seminary at Associated Mennonite Biblical Seminary and enjoyed exploring the depths of Scripture's interplay of context, theology, canon, power politics, and true worship. I did in-depth work in Isaiah and found an editorial scheme related to the themes of the Spirit and justice and righteousness. In other courses I worked on a theology of a politics of the Spirit in the Hebrew Bible, which was for me both engaging and fascinating. Even though I did in-depth research on Scripture, I majored in Pastoral Ministries because my main concern was how to connect the energy of God with people. My focus was not on the text itself but how the message of the text connects with and transforms life today.

I pastored in the Goshen area for a few years during which I enjoyed bringing the Scriptures to life in preaching and teaching and, alternately, bringing life to the Scripture in discernment. I was then called by Mennonite Central Committee to work with churches in Syria. I did so for most of the 1990s. In Syria I first lived in a Syrian Orthodox monastery and seminary where I listened in on how a tradition that prays in Aramaic/Syriac, read and discussed the Scriptures in Arabic, all in a culture with similar assumptions to those of Jesus.

There I learned that in most Eastern Christian traditions Scriptures are most often chanted or reenacted liturgically. In fact in most religions Scriptures are not simply read but empowered by chant, song, or recitation that involves more than a casual reading voice. I discovered there the power of the chanted word to unite body, mind, and spirit and bring the Word to life in a way far more powerful than in the Western Christian reading. I found there as much a concern for beauty as proper understanding. I found a deep power in beauty to move the spirit toward acts of holiness, justice, and peace.

While there, my wife and I led a delegation of Mennonites on a tour to experience worship during holy week in a number of traditions. On Psalm Sunday we were in Aleppo joining in a liturgical reenactment of the triumphal entry. Children, each carrying a candle, were carried by parents past the bishop for a blessing, while the choir was singing Psalms of Passover in the balcony and the monks and priests were chanting Scripture around the altar. As we stood in that shimmering of beauty, movement, song, and glory I turned and saw a Mennonite from the delegation with tears streaming down his cheeks. We were all drawn into the beauty of Scripture coming to life before us. Later that person shared with the delegation the source of those tears saying, "Those were tears of grief. My childhood worship was so void of such a beauty."

I have come to feel that Mennonites have so often dishonored Scripture by the way we have treated it in worship. One of our Syrian Christian friends describes Mennonite worship as a courtroom with the "judge" up front making judgments and pronouncements on the Scriptures. In my thirties, in the Middle East, I began to ask many questions about the loss of beauty in my own Mennonite tradition's ability to communicate and interpret Scripture.

I have come to ask my tradition whether we connect with Scripture with our mind first or our heart first. In my journey through different schools and cultures I have sensed my mind and intuition engaging the text in deeper ways. This has led to a sharpening of my ability to discern the text and connect the energy of God with people in preaching, teaching, and pastoral care.

I have also had a strong sense of needing to listen to the voices at the edge of communities. I have seen truth in other contexts most often spoken from the edge of communities. I saw this also in Scriptures in the words of prophets, Jesus, and the apostles who spoke from the creative edge of communities. I began to see Scripture as the place where the Spirit of God was still hovering over the face of that which was to be created anew; speaking through those at the edge of communities; speaking into creation something new in the life of the faithful and history.

I have come to see Scripture not as an end in itself but as an invitation to a reenactment of God's energy in healing, in calling for justice, and in calling all to redemption and transformation. My conscience has been challenged from many angles and many times by messages of Scriptures. I have seen images from Scripture come alive in contexts of healing for persons and healing of nations like the truth and reconciliation process in South Africa.

Evangelical and Ecumenical Musings

I have seen Scripture forming and transforming other Christian communities. I cannot assume that the Word does not change and transform lives; I have seen it and in that sense I am evangelical. I cannot assume that others cannot find another way or tradition through which the Word transforms them, so I am ecumenical. The flexibility of my ecclesiology has drawn me to be both evangelical in an Anabaptist sense and ecumenical in a catholic sense.

I have also used Scripture more flexibly—seeing truth in Scripture resident in the style of the encounter of the Holy with the human, not locked in its original context. I have been willing to translate that style into many contexts unrelated to the original context. I have seen a person received back into a congregation at the end of a year of absence at a residential school to deal with issues from the past. This person was welcomed back to the church at the end of the year with a ritual of blessing in which Psalm 23 was read to her in the second person by the whole congregation: "The Lord is your Shepherd. . . . God restores your soul. . . . God leads you beside still waters. . . ." On the phrases went drawing the tears of the community's will for her well being, regardless of the fact that the original setting of the Psalm had to do with kingship.

I have moved beyond the conservatism of my youth when I held so close to literal readings of Scripture I missed the grand message of change in the original setting. I have come to see those who wrote Scripture as participating with God in a process of dynamic discernment over time. These were the people through whom God spoke in new ways and new contexts in a process of dynamic discernment that we are to replicate in our own time by changing hearts and history in a way in tune with the passion of God for healing hearts and history.

With regard to the controversial issues that the church has always faced, I have come to see that change that is too quick is often violent. I have come to think of change in terms of generations, which is how it often happened in Scriptures. In relation to difficult issues I encourage keeping the traditions but allowing openness for discernment over time in different communities to the degree change is possible when the community discerns that it is appropriate.

From Idolatry to Doxology

Now when I approach a text I attempt a generative listening. How can I hear with my being what the text says about the energy of God? That is, as the Word of God was willing to take on many cultural and literary forms, so now I assume the Spirit's willingness to generate in this context a new creation or understanding that connects the energy of God with people.

I have come to see Scripture functioning as a living memory of the presence of the Holy in times past with dilemmas and dynamics similar to those we face now. Scripture helps us truly see ourselves and see beyond ourselves to the reign of God in history. The dilemma of faithfulness has been how truly to see beyond personal and corporate delusions. Our false frames are our mini-idolatries and meta-idolatries—the ways we miss the energy of God and act in too-limited ways. I invite us to view these mini-idolatries and meta-idolatries through two images from Scripture: communion and the consummation of history.

On communion and the mini-idolatries in Scripture: The phrase of Jesus, "Do this in remembrance of me" at the Last Supper has always vexed me. What is the "this" we are to do? The following insight was aided by the fact that my wife and I pastor in a church as diverse as the broader Mennonite church. This is possible because we are the only Mennonite church in town that is part of Mennonite Church USA.

So what "this" did Jesus want us to do in remembrance of him? Jesus revealed a profound patience amid each of his disciples' self-absorption and missing the point of Jesus' message and mission. Jesus saw beyond their mini-idolatries, their delusion, to the potential for what the communion of the Spirit could do with them and for them over time. We cannot help but notice how many times the phrase "Now I see" is used by these same disciples in the beginning of the book of Acts. Jesus didn't reject these disciples at the time of the Last Supper even though the disciples were confused and deluded. After the Last Supper they all did what they thought was right or necessary according to their delusions.

Likewise we all live in faith with degrees of delusion and misunderstanding. I have walked with Scripture's call to be faithful, and pastored others long enough, to know that. Scripture's call for communion in the Spirit is the patience that calls each of us to do as Jesus did, to see each other beyond our delusions in hope of those times when we all will say, "Now I see." Doing so requires a holy patience called forbearance.

In looking back over the breadth of Scripture I see the text showing the delusions of the faithful . . . from Adam and Eve, to Abraham, to Moses, to David, to the apostles . . . and God's willingness to patiently transform their humanity. Their delusions come as a form of negative knowledge, a screen on which the greater glory and energy of God could be projected and played out. I have come to see Scripture as a dramatic interplay of human delusion and God's glory in ways that are always surprising, engaging, and hopeful. So, I have become very cautious about judging others' intentions or God's will in a given situation.

Turning to the consummation of history and meta-idolatries, we can see that the delusions of personal and corporate power shape the worlds in which we live. In Scripture the prophets and Jesus regularly reminded their listeners that they were not seeing the true nature and work of God in history. We can assume the same in our own time as Walter Wink and the disciples of René Girard have helped us imagine. These meta-idolatries are worked out through the foils of those whose power and passion are for themselves, their own people and the gods made in their own image—the pharaohs, Nebuchadnezzars, Pilates, and Neros of history. Their passion was for their own glory and power—a false doxology. The power of these grand illusions falls short of the greater power of God's passion. What then is God's energy and passion?

In Revelation 22, John sees an image of the river of the water of life flowing from the throne of God. The leaves of the tree growing beside this river are for the healing of the nations. Once I was with a group in prayer for someone in deep brokenness and a question came to mind: Where does this river of life for the healing of the nations come from? What could be behind God spiritually or spatially? I then saw this river formed from the tears of God, the great and continuous passion of God for the healing of the nations; that passion that has flowed like a stream through all of Scripture.

Can we see God sitting on a throne weeping tears of joy and sorrow, in the purest passion of a parent at the birth, marriage or death of a child? To the degree we all share in this passion we are all children of God in faith. We are the peacemakers who share in that being and journey that all of Scripture is pointing us to.

Notes

1. Isaac Asimov, *Asimov's Guide to the Bible* (New York: Avon Books, 1971).
2. C. S. Lewis, *Mere Christianity* (New York: Macmillan, 1952).
3. John Howard Yoder, *The Politics of Jesus* (Grand Rapids, Eerdmans, 1972).

CHAPTER 10

Getting the Steps Right

Nancy R. Heisey

Beginning the Journey

I awoke to the Bible by early illustrations of the fact that my parents took it seriously. My mother has read the Bible through for years. She and my dad encouraged us to read the Bible when we were still quite young. I recall my brother in an all-day marathon on December 31 when he had decided to read the Bible through during the year but had not quite gotten around to a regular reading schedule. I tiptoed into the bedroom with a tray-lunch for Dad, who was working on his Sunday afternoon sermon. We weren't supposed to bother him otherwise, as he sat there with Bible and notebook open. Sometimes, though, we'd be called in during those sermon-preparation mornings to be quizzed on our reading of a particular portion of Scripture he had assigned us. I know that it was this process that got me through the Pentateuch the first time.

My church experience from the beginning was either listening to sermons translated into Navajo or listening to Navajo preachers preaching in their own language. The expression *"Diyin God Bizaad"* carries the same weight in my mental home as Billy Graham's ringing tones, "The Bible says . . ." do for many other American Christians. I grew up hanging around missionaries who were Navajo language students, including those working on Bible translation.

Everyone talked in respectful tones of the legendary Faye Edgerton, an elderly Presbyterian missionary who was working on the translation of the Navajo Bible. We used the New Testament she and her Navajo colleagues had completed in 1956 and were waiting for the release of the complete Old Testament. Miss Edgerton died in 1968, and the complete Bible was released in 1985.

From the earliest stages I knew that there was more than one way to express biblical ideas, that figuring out the best way of communicating something in a different language was a struggle and a challenge. Hence I am always surprised when I have to force my students to recognize that the English Bible they use is a translation, and when they express a fear that they apparently never thought about before: "But what if they didn't translate IT [God's literal, exact word] correctly?"

Bible memorization played an important role in my childhood and teenage years. I dealt with my anxiety at my dad's frequent absences on church business by memorizing Genesis 28:15, "And, behold, I am with thee, and will keep thee in all places whither thou goest." I also would write this verse on a piece of paper and give it to my dad whenever he left. This promise had very little to do with Jacob and very much to do with me. My parents, during one period of time, devoted family devotions to the memorization of Isaiah 40. "Comfort ye, comfort ye, my people," became an important part of my picture of who God is, a picture that was not always able to sustain me amid the preaching about God's judgment that characterized the revival tradition in which I grew up (more about that soon).

When I was in high school, I participated in the Bible quizzing program that was (and still is) a big part of youth group life among the Brethren in Christ. The year we took on the book of Acts, our team won the regional playoffs and went to General Conference. Lots of high drama, and a little romance, as we met the nice young men on the other teams. Always the cadences of the King James were the ones that echoed in my brain. Today, when I want to look up a particular verse, I often have to go back to *Strong's Concordance*, because the words in the NRSV are not the ones emblazoned on my heart.

On the Way

My journey with Scripture was shaped by several crises, events, or periods of life that were critically important to me. The first of these was the crisis of getting faith right. In my Brethren in Christ community, influenced as it was by revival holiness and the child evangelism movement, I heard a lot of Bible verses used to urge me toward a right experience of salvation. By the time I was three I was being taken to children's meetings that concluded with invitations to come forward and accept Christ as my savior. Also from the time I was three, I was trying to get the steps right. Over and over throughout my childhood I found myself kneeling at some altar, trying to do the right things or say the right words, so that I would be sure I was saved. I accepted invitations at children's meetings, at revival meetings, at youth camps, and anywhere else I could find them. I accepted invitations to be saved until I was thoroughly sick of them.

Finally, as a first-year student in college, I sat in a spiritual life emphasis week, heard the invitation, and steeled my heart against it. I promised myself: "I will never go forward for another invitation." I wondered whether I had committed the sin against the Holy Spirit, but I persisted in this decision.

Yet my experience of the Bible at that point offered me no clues about how else to think about faith. It was a conversation with my great aunt, Annie Zercher, when I was still a college student and she was in her late nineties, that began to change this pattern. She told me that she had learned to stop seeking an experience (an amazing discovery in a church very bent on encouraging experience as central to faith), and instead to live the way Jesus wanted. I didn't think of this as a hermeneutical principle until much later, but the idea began to free me from the fear that my experience was not adequate to assure what I now call "being in right relationship" (Paul's being justified) with God.

Another crisis related to the Bible had to do with questions of women in leadership roles in the church. This of course should be no surprise—but it was a surprise to me, since I thought I had evaded the problem by working for Mennonite Central Committee (MCC). No one should be looking there, I thought, since administrative roles did not raise the question of ordination. MCC was, and probably continues to be, one of the more open Mennonite institutions for women in leadership. I received plenty of mentoring, affirmation, and opportunity. Once, when talking with a woman friend who was a pastor, she said, "If I have to choose between the Bible and my feminism, I'll choose feminism." I felt a little shiver of fear run down my back at her daring and the risk she was taking—but it was more the risk to her soul that I felt than the risk to her career in the church.

Then, while I was associate executive secretary, a constituent sent the executive secretary a book and suggested that he needed to think about it in the MCC context. My colleague passed the letter and the book on to me. I doubt it occurred to him that I would do anything other than laugh it off. I don't remember the title, the author, or the publisher. All I remember was that it went through all the old texts (1 Cor. 11, 1 Cor. 14, Col. 3, Eph. 5, 1 Tim. 2, 1 Pet. 3). I started reading, then within twenty pages put it down and never picked it up again. But I was shaken. Something in me said that I would have to choose.

As I wrestled, I decided, like my friend, to choose for the freedom of women to use all of our gifts, within the church if we could, and without the church if we could not. Over time, I came to a complex understanding of the text. In some cases I concluded it didn't mean what it said, but in other cases, when I believed it did mean what it said, it still did not mean that for me. Neither a very scientific nor a very theological approach. But one that has made me work, ever since, to take my experiences and those of the people I meet into serious consideration as I wrestle with the Bible.

I know strong voices in my faith community are condemning the place that experience has come to play in some Mennonite biblical interpretation, but perhaps here my faith heritage is offering me a gift. Rather than needing to continue to reject a form of experience that I couldn't reproduce, I am learning that the experiences we actually have matter. Where we live and how we seek, both faithfulness and abundant life matter.

Gaining My Bearings

My return to serious biblical study took place over the fourteen-year period during which I worked my way through seminary and graduate school. Seminary offered me the gift of entering into the biblical languages. But apart from a course on the book of Revelation with Gertrude Roten at Associated Mennonite Biblical Seminary, I found in biblical courses little more than a narrow focus on particular words and a limited entrée into the historical issues of the text. When I hit graduate school, I found myself better prepared than most of my colleagues to work with Hebrew and Greek but way behind in knowing anything about the worlds in which the Bible was written. My advisor, for exam-

ple, was shocked that I managed to get an M.Div. without taking a required course on the background to the Gospels.

It was exhilarating to dive into the "world behind the text." I discovered that my leanings were toward the historical, and that I wanted to
know more and more about authorship, compilation, social and political influences on the text. I became acquainted with the period when
Scripture as Scripture became the force that shaped the world of Jesus,
and found that my reading of the New Testament, and particularly Paul,
opened up again. Struggling with the notion that the text was not as ancient as it had always been assumed to be, I nevertheless found the exploration of how it was shaped, determined to be authoritative, transmitted, and canonized, in some strange way a record of God at work.

During my graduate school years, I was occasionally invited to
preach in my home congregation, and for one year I filled in on a regular basis. I found the process of preparing to preach an exciting and challenging one. I knew better than to try to dump everything I was struggling with in class onto my hearers. Yet the process of finding intersections with the life issues of my companions in faith and the texts in their
contexts was an invigorating experience. The text itself became a partner
in the struggle, for it made audible many voices. Voices proclaimed what
God had spoken to them and debated with other voices about how to
understand what God had spoken. Voices spoke back to God and called
on me to join in their prayer, praise, and protest.

I have not resolved in my own mind the tension between the idea of
varied trajectories in Scripture, which always require us to think carefully and to choose, and the desire to believe that Scripture offers one
clear way to understand God's will for the cosmos. As in the past year or
two I have begun to read critiques of some biblical scholars that historical study of biblical texts has failed in bringing life to the churches in the
West and the North, I find myself more and more willing to think in
non-intellectual ways about why this book still matters.

My most recent searching of Scripture has been in conversation
with partners from outside the global Western-Northern world, albeit
still with those trained in that world. I have begun to delve into some
postcolonial biblical criticism. My years of work with the Africa Department of MCC, as well as my cross-cultural childhood, probably oriented me in this direction. Yet when I first encountered South African
Itumeleng Mosala, with his critique of the oppression he found even in

Luke's gospel text, I found him extreme. Then when I cited Mosala's work in a paper at a conference of evangelical mission leaders, another biblical scholar told the gathered group that Mosala couldn't be taken seriously.

More recently, I have been intrigued by Musa Dube, a woman teaching New Testament at the University of Botswana. Again, her questioning of the power issues underpinning texts such as Jesus' encounters with the Samaritan woman or the Canaanite woman can make me uncomfortable. Not too long ago I presented some of her work to an adult Bible school class I was teaching. One class participant raised the question, "What right does she have to read the Bible that way?" My response then, and now, is, "Every right." It is not a question of whether I agree, but a question of whether I need to learn something by taking seriously the way Scripture sounds to those whose experience of my world has been one of perpetual violence and oppression.

Conclusion

I know I love the Bible but find it hard to explain why. In part, the Bible belongs to my cultural patrimony. In part, I love the soaring poetry and intense spirituality of certain sections. I don't often experience the Bible bringing me closer to God and almost never closer to other members of my faith community. These realities trouble me, because my intellectual theology says that both of those things should be part of the appropriation of Scripture. As I've said, I have found the most satisfaction and the greatest challenge when I am assigned to preach or lead a Bible study and sit down to do some serious study. I'm working on an article right now that describes how I work with the Bible in sermon preparation, and as I read what I've written, it's not as systematic as I was trained to think it should be, but it's a more holistic way of reading than most of my earlier experiences with the Bible were. Somehow, then, God's Word comes to me through Scripture, and I am humbled and, I hope, changed by the encounter.

I read longingly about others finding devotional meaning in Scripture through *lectio divina*, but I have never been able to do this often enough or with enough direction to find it helpful. When I read devotionally, I am always looking for honesty and for open windows. When I am praying for the world and my part in it, I read for justice. These days,

I am looking for hope—for hope that God is at work in the world, that we as God's people have a counter-voice to speak against the loud voices of violence. And that we continue our journeys with Scripture yearning for the completion of God's realm on earth.

CHAPTER 11

Scripture and Other Companions

John Kampen

The Canadian Prairies

I was born in Fiske in the province of Saskatchewan, Canada, six miles outside of a town with a population of a hundred. I like space.

I was raised in a Mennonite church where the members of my extended family also constituted the core membership of the church. The services were in German, my first language until I went to school, and the majority of the sermons were read by lay leaders without inflection from books of sermon collections.

My father and his mother had fled Russia in the 1923 emigration when he was two years old. His father, a schoolteacher, had been a fugitive from local Bolshevik and Ukrainian authorities, presumably for suspected *Selbstschutz* activities, and had perished there during those traumatic years. For the uninitiated, the *Selbstschutz* was the self-defense network that grew up in the Mennonite colonies largely in response to the rape and pillage of the marauding bands of Nestor Makhnov. My father was raised in this small church in this largely non-Mennonite community.

Through thrift, hard work, and the business savvy they brought with them from Russia, this extended family was in the upper half of the income bracket in that rural community. My mother had come from

Laird in Northern Saskatchewan from the same extended family and ethos that produced Mennonite leaders such as Peter and C. J. Dyck. Perhaps the best example to illustrate my home environment is a story I use in lectures on the book of Daniel.

Somewhere around sixth grade, I was caught smoking in the boy's outside toilet along with a number of other boys. The requisite note went home to each of our parents. That evening, when I arrived home from school, I was first of all summoned to my mother's bedroom, where she was resting. She gave me a lecture on Daniel and the lion's den. I was being a poor example and needed to resist the pressures to conform to the world.

When chore-time arrived, while milking cows by hand my father and I engaged in a discussion of the same subject. (This was years before health concerns about smoking were commonly discussed.) "I don't care what you do when you get older," said my father, "but it is illegal for you to smoke on the school grounds, and you are too young to engage in this activity." The immigrant was concerned about community standards and how we fit into them, while my mother was rooted in "religious" standards. I might add that this immigrant father was one of the few effective leaders in the community who could unite its elements to advance such causes as rural electrification and school consolidation and keep the sports organizations from erupting into internecine warfare. My psychoanalyst wife would say that those two forces have been engaged in combat throughout my life.

A second incident from my youth then changed my life. In the ninth grade I began to be bused to the consolidated high school about twenty-five miles from home. My mother recognized that I was somewhat unhappy there and began to suggest I might want to transfer to Rosthern Junior College, a Mennonite boarding school about 150 miles away. My father did not want me to go.

So one spring morning at breakfast I was given a choice. I could either get a car for myself once I had turned sixteen or I could attend Rosthern Junior College. To my father's and perhaps my own amazement, I chose to attend the boarding school favored by my mother. Those three years set the course of my future life and explain my commitment to Mennonite higher education today. Under the tutelage of Mennonite high school teachers, one a recent graduate of Associated Mennonite Biblical Seminary in Elkhart and one or two others who had spent a year there, I learned the excitement and the value of the intellectual pursuit of religious questions. It was probably their passion for both the questions and the institutions that promoted them that hooked me into a lifetime vocation.

My journey with Scripture began in high school with books such as Dietrich Bonhoeffer's *The Cost of Discipleship*, and an introduction to the historical-critical use of the Bible. These teachers convinced me that questions were not only legitimate in the Mennonite community, they were also essential for the Mennonite church of the future. Only many years later did I fully appreciate what a unique gift I had been given in that remote Mennonite high school.

After three years at a Mennonite school I was ready for a change, so I elected not to attend Canadian Mennonite Bible College (now Canadian Mennonite University) as some would have expected me to. Instead, I chose the University of Saskatchewan. I began in economics and graduated with a sociology major with a concentration in the social sciences.

Intellectually my attempt was to come to terms with the "other." How do we as peoples and communities with different backgrounds and experiences interact and relate to one another? How do we incorporate the insights and experiences of others into our own lives? Recall that Saskatchewan was the only province in North America with a socialist government and socialized medicine at that time, so the campus was imbued with an ethos of socialism and prairie populism. With professors from institutions such as the London School of Economics collected in this socialist environment, structural questions were of paramount importance. How do we build social structures that level the socioeconomic stratification of our modern world?

In 1967 I rallied in support of free tuition at a university where the annual tuition was $300 a year, so that all could have access to higher education. My senior research project was on the relationship between socioeconomic status and academic achievement at a university level. Religion courses were not a part of the university curriculum, even though a local Mennonite pastor met with Mennonite students on an infrequent basis to read books such as those of J. B. Philips, *Your God is Too Small*, and Harvey Cox, *The Secular City*. These works turned out to be influential in my life. I did work for both the Mennonite camps and the Saskatchewan Mennonite Youth Organization throughout those years. I emerged from university a committed socialist advocating the death of God and with a growing interest in the Anabaptist roots of my Mennonite heritage.

Seminary and the 1960s Counterculture

I went on to Associated Mennonite Biblical Seminary (AMBS) just as it was undergoing substantial development. I attended classes on both the Elkhart and Goshen campuses. Rev. J. J. Thiessen, a senior church leader in western Canada, had wanted me to go to seminary, then return to Saskatoon to lead a new suburban church, which he expected to be an important model for the future. Teachers and youth workers expected that I would return to play a leadership role in the western Canadian church as well.

However, shortly after arriving in Elkhart, Indiana, I was contacted about becoming the manager of a coffeehouse founded by seminary students, faculty, and others. This place—I hesitate to use the word *institution* in this case—was at the center of the local peace movement, interracial dialogue and discussion, artistic creativity, community development efforts, and the other social issues of the day. My involvement there proved to be at the center of a transformation in my life. This prairie boy who had developed certain leadership skills in the service of the church was suddenly put into the new role of countercultural (a word that dates me) leader and expert on drug use and abuse—not the normal career path for an aspiring middle-class Mennonite minister. Nor is it usually assumed that the prairies of Saskatchewan are a good place to learn the drug culture. But within one year of my arrival in the United States I had taken on this role. What had happened?

In this new setting I began to learn about what it takes to identify with and listen to persons different from myself. In this case, of course, it was easy for me because these hippies, who referred to themselves as "freaks," were frequently talking about and experiencing things that were also of interest to me. A certain alienation from the commonly accepted values of the day was a common bond. Much of this sentiment centered on opposition to the war in Vietnam. I found engaging "the other" in a deep personal way to be challenging and exciting in ways never experienced before. Along with the excitement, however, I quickly discovered that the process of getting to know "others" also has consequences. I will list three, the recognition of which I attribute at least partly to that experience.

First, I had to learn about the time and commitment required to develop deep relationships with those different from myself. Even when English is the shared common language, the communication of meaning has to be tested and learned, since language is an expression of culture. I remember once sitting in that coffeehouse with a woman of about twenty for half an hour. I suspect we exchanged a total of about six sentences of conversation. In most other contexts, times, and places such a "limited" conversation would have been meaningless. But when she left she thanked me for the conversation. Subsequent events showed that she had found the encounter meaningful. An exchange which would have been regarded as inconsequential in other contexts proved real and significant. Communication across cultures requires time and commitment.

Second, of considerable consequence is the fact that once we begin to see the world through the eyes of someone different from ourselves, our own world changes. And once it begins to change it can never again return to what it was. To echo the aphorism, "You can't go home again." I suspect this is most true for those of us who, in one way or another, are part of the majority culture and then begin to see things from the perspectives of the outsider, the alienated, the disenfranchised, the powerless, and the marginalized. Many decisions, activities, and ways of working take on whole new perspectives. I had not only begun to listen to the voices of the other, I had become willing to engage in a personal process of change and transformation.

Third, in getting to know the others we become drawn into their life circumstances and share in the consequences of their way of life as well as our own. In northern Indiana in 1969, this meant that I would call the ACLU lawyer in South Bend to come to Goshen, Indiana, when some elderly County Court judge was serving eviction notices on teenagers and young adults in "crash pads" because the residents of Goshen didn't like their lifestyles. The presence of an ACLU lawyer would cause the charges to be dropped immediately. Getting to know the others also meant going with people to the city court in Elkhart, Indiana, when the city attorney would charge people standing outside our coffeehouse with loitering because he didn't like them. Appearing with them in court again would lead to the charges being dropped.

I not only got to know people different from myself, I began to live with the consequences. In 1969 this meant arranging for young pregnant women left in very difficult situations to travel to New York to get abortions, then attempting to make sure they had adequate support and counseling upon return—because abortions were illegal in Indiana and there were only two of us in the city who were known to be engaged in making these kinds of arrangements. It meant shots through the front windows of an upstairs apartment in which I lived because we were willing to provide an environment that encouraged interracial gathering. The trust established in the process of getting to know someone and becoming friends had consequences. If one was not willing to live with those consequences, there was no sense investing the time to develop the relationships. Trust involves both time and consequences.

In the meantime I was a student at AMBS. There I had a faculty that guided and supported my activity, even though they must have sometimes shaken their heads while doing so. Even Leland Harder, a wonderfully supportive and encouraging presence, had his limits. After I read about some bar ministries in New Orleans and proposed that this could be a possible option for a supervised ministry experience in Elkhart, he wisely suggested another route might be more beneficial, indicating that appropriate supervision of bar ministry would be hard to establish. David Habeggar supported and guided my community involvements. But in the classroom it was the biblical studies classes that I found most stimulating. Jacob Enz and Clarence Bauman inspired me as much with their piety and humility as with their remarkable intellect. In my New Testament studies I was looking for the true faith that had informed those early Anabaptists to revolt and to begin something new. I gradually became convinced that this radical discovery was possible through a better understanding of the Jewish context of the life of Jesus.

More important than any one of these specific persons was the attitude of acceptance and encouragement that they brought to all interactions with me and which provided a context for the seminary community as a whole. The contributions of every faculty member should be listed, including such faculty as Gertrude Roten and Ross Bender. I don't think they were certain what directions the church would take in the future, but they were open to new possibilities. Gently they helped us sort out the possibilities we saw. In that process "death of God" thinking became less of an issue as we were drawn into a circle of belief and lifestyle whose purpose was to affirm life. We were experiencing it as we discussed it—the kind of education that changes lives.

Union Organizing

A year spent in factory work deserves a parenthetical comment. I left seminary without completing the degree and worked at Conrad Grebel College for a few years as Director of Residence and Chaplain. Still imbued with a certain naive idealism, however, I wanted to invest myself in union organizing as a way of meeting the grassroots needs of the common people. So I left Conrad Grebel to pursue this possibility. I invested my energies in an underground newspaper related to union organizing as I spent my days on the factory floor. This paper was eventually subverted by doctrinaire Marxist-Leninists who drove out all opponents of their viewpoints, a lesson in the dynamics of grassroots political organizing.

However, as I built custom windows on the factory floor and as I swept the floors of a cookie factory during the night shift, I had a conversion experience. I learned that I wanted a Ph.D. This was not because it would help me serve these people better. The fact was that my interests and aspirations were different enough from my co-workers that I had to recognize I simply would be a lousy union organizer. I had learned there were limits to my cross-cultural abilities that were a direct outgrowth of who I was. My multicultural abilities and aspirations themselves were shaped by my own experiences. The naive idealist had been chastened.

Graduate Studies, Religious Anti-Semitism, and Scripture

I then turned to the intellectual interests in biblical studies that had been fostered while at AMBS and returned to that institution to complete my work in preparation for graduate studies. Now two other persons emerged as central. Millard Lind began to prepare me for future work in Hebraic studies and has remained interested and supportive throughout my career. David Schroeder encouraged my exploration of the Jewish background of the New Testament, saw it as an important contribution to the life of the church, then stayed in contact with me throughout the years of graduate education.

In 1975 I went to Cincinnati to begin studies at Hebrew Union College, a Jewish school responsible for training rabbis for Jewish communal leadership and an intellectual center for the Reform Jewish movement. While my formal studies concentrated on Jewish history in the Greco-Roman era, I became deeply immersed in the stories and struggles of the Jewish people throughout history. I learned about the history of anti-Semitism and about the implications of Christian triumphalism which had condemned Jews to either outsider or lower-class status for the entire period of history shared by our two faiths. I learned about pogroms and concentration camps. I learned about the holocaust and listened to the accounts of survivors willing to share their stories. I learned about the manner in which the New Testament had been used to promote anti-Semitism, and I had to examine my own sacred texts to see whether they were at their essence anti-Semitic.

I began to see ways the Christian church had not dealt with these issues. And I began to see ways the Mennonite church had not dealt with these issues. I began to live with the consequences of my relationship with this new group of people and to work out the implications of this new knowledge for my own life and for the communities of which I was a part. In this process I also began to deal with some other issues.

In the interchange between Mennonite and counter-cultural identities which had characterized most of my life up to this point, I had understood myself to be a minority person, frequently labeling myself a radical Anabaptist. This identity served me well and provided a vantage point from which I could deal with the world and develop a response to the issues with which I was confronted. I now realized that this perspective perhaps was a too convenient way of dealing with the world. What I found on the Hebrew Union campus challenged this perspective. The arguments about the uniqueness of the Holocaust experience contradicted some of my own perceptions about connections I saw between that experience and the ordeals of my foreparents in Russia.

Even more importantly, I was now regarded as Christian and expected to be held responsible for the entire Christian experience in the same way other Christian traditions were. The Jewish students were holding me responsible for what Christians had done to their ancestors and for attitudes they continued to confront in the Christian world. I was being regarded as a member of the majority culture rather than a minority person. My gut response was to deny any responsibility—I was

Mennonite, even Anabaptist, not Christian. I now had to learn to relate to this new perception of me as a member of the majority. While in initial encounters I wanted to deny my relationship to mainstream religion and culture, I rapidly realized that this was not a tenable or responsible option within that setting. I needed to deal with my role as a member of mainstream religion and culture.

My journey with Scripture also faced new challenges. While I articulated my initial interest as exploring the New Testament's Jewish backgrounds, I rapidly realized such a formulation was inadequate. To remain true to the intellectual and religious commitments I had made up to then, I could not label the Jewish experience as background, even in antiquity. I rather began to develop myself as a Jewish historian of the Greco-Roman period, an identification with which I remain quite comfortable. I spent eight years in full-time study of Jewish Talmud and Midrash; the Jewish historians who wrote in Greek; Jewish apocalyptic writings; and finally the Dead Sea Scrolls. I established an intellectual and scholarly basis on which to build a modest scholarly and research career. Subsequently I began a program of regular research and contacts in Israel, so I could broaden my understanding of the "social realia" from the field of archeology to supplement my understanding of the texts.

Those one step ahead of me realize I created a problem for myself with regard to my journey with Scripture. As a historian of Jewish history of the Greco-Roman period, I had to make critical historical judgments about the New Testament and other early Christian documents in the same manner as I evaluated the writings of the historian Josephus or the Community Rule among the Dead Sea Scrolls.

My response to that challenge is to openly acknowledge that the New Testament is "my story." I developed a great love for probing the marvelous insights of Jewish Midrash. I am intrigued by questions of Jewish identity during this time period, how issues of assimilation and accommodation were dealt with in light of the pressures of Hellenization. But by religious choice I am a Christian, so in the final analysis it is the New Testament that is "my story." It is from that vantage point that I can enter into the theological discussions about the authority of Scripture. But I enter into that discussion based on a voluntary choice and not by any conviction of intellectual or even religious superiority.

Still there was one more complication. I had also learned about the manner in which sacred texts can be a source of oppression and discrimination. My original doctoral advisor, Samuel Sandmel, was the first Jew in the United States to get a doctoral degree in New Testament. One of the many books he authored was titled, *Anti-Semitism in the New Testament?*[1] I had to come to terms with the question of whether Christianity by its very nature and history is anti-Semitic. Even if not, how had this religion been able to foster and encourage so much anti-Semitism in societies where it was dominant?

These are not comfortable questions. To make matters worse, the radical Anabaptism I had grown to embrace was very christocentric: Jesus Christ was the center of the faith. So in Jewish eyes, that feature of Christianity which was the embodiment of what contributed to the growth of anti-Semitism was the same feature that had permitted me to build a satisfying personal faith. The fundamental challenge, however, was the fact that these sacred texts around which I had built my life were considered the source of oppression and even annihilation of another group of persons I had grown to love and cherish.

In the process of studying Jewish writings, however, I also learned one important thing about method. Let me state the conclusion first. In some senses this restates the classic Mennonite position: Scripture rather than theology is paramount. This insight grows out of my experience with Jewish Midrash and Halakah. In these exegetical traditions we find that Scripture (*Tanak*) is the eternal foundation and the starting point for endless inspiration, imagination, and engagement. And Jewish hermeneutical pursuits always return to Scripture. But Scripture is the source for opening up the world and human creativity; Scripture is not a means of confining world or creativity. Tanak is a source of identity, of defining who a Jew is. The Jews are the people connected with the Book. As a Christian that is what the New Testament is for me—my story. It is where I find my identity. It is to those writings that I point to with pride and say, "These are my people." My connections with these writings then are endless.

For most of us raised in the philosophical tradition of the West, the connections are theological. But having spent time in the Greek Orthodox churches of Palestine, I also know that for others the connections are iconographic. The ways in which the New Testament writings have impacted the art and literature of my world have a major impact on my faith and life. Tolstoy has impacted my appropriation of the New Testament for my own life. Such impacts are just as important as the theological formulations and just as crucial to my remaining a contributing member of my community of faith.

An exposure to Jewish reading of Tanak has also impacted my life in one other way that gets at the heart of a Mennonite appropriation of Scripture. The fundamental question is the development and nourishment of a way of life. The ultimate question for a Jew is always, "How do I live as a Jew?" This question is not merely an ethical one; it is a comprehensive approach that includes life's religious, personal, social, and ethical dimensions. Other questions then can be formulated: How do I pray? How do I believe? How do I treat my non-Jewish neighbor? I find it helpful to formulate many of the questions about my own life as a Mennonite in a similar manner.

Finally, my years in a Jewish institution permitted me to spend time in a community in which study is a religious obligation. Study is an act of piety, of religious devotion parallel to living a good life and doing acts of loving kindness. This brought a new passion to some of my studies that I had not experienced before. Study was not a way in which to achieve religious devotion; study was itself an act of religious devotion. Words cannot capture the sense of freedom and excitement such an environment brought to my work as an academic. I was able to begin to study the Jewish religious texts—Mishnah, Tosefta, Talmud, and Midrash—and even more importantly, learn the method for studying them as religious texts.

My work began with Samuel Sandmel. After his death I went on to work with Ben Zion Wacholder, the person who taught me the joy of study. In addition to class work and his supervision of my research, I was his research assistant, so I spent hours with him in his study at home, usually two full days a week over six years. When I arrived at his home each day, we would begin with the new things he had found in his reading of the texts the day or night before. His reading never was primarily in the secondary literature; he had been absorbed in primary texts such as the Dead Sea Scrolls, Josephus, rabbinic literature, and the Hebrew Bible. Sometimes he had been up half the night because he had grown so excited about what he had found. I learned the joy of study when one permits the primary texts to become the central focus of one's academic career. I also learned the continual excitement of a lifetime of study. This model for study sustains me to this day.

The Reality of Race in an African-American Seminary

In 1984 I went to teach at an African-American seminary, the third phase of my life important for the discussion of this topic. I learned again the importance of taking the time to develop relationships of trust and the difficulties one encounters on the way to achieving that objective. I learned again that building trust has consequences. I learned again that my world had been turned upside-down by a different context, a new set of contacts and experiences, and that I would never be the same again.

I learned again in this new environment the significance of my role as a representative of the majority—this time the majority culture rather than the majority religion. I had been drawn into the history of a people that is both sobering and inspiring, sobering with regard to the history of racism and its continuing legacy, and inspiring with regard to the determination and spirit which permitted this people to continue to survive and occasionally thrive despite the best efforts of the rest of us.

But my value to the African-American institution for which I worked was neither the fact that I was a Mennonite nor that I tried to lay claim to a certain kind of minority experience. My value was that I had a Ph.D. that I was willing to place at the disposal of the institution. Through a combination of education and racial privilege, I intuitively knew how to get certain things accomplished in the systems in which we live out our lives. So it was precisely my whiteness and my majority class status which made me valuable to this institution. From a Mennonite perspective, how ironic!

How did this experience affect my journey with Scripture? Note first an evolution in the titles and content of the classes I taught. I initially developed a course entitled, "Social Justice in the Bible." This was a valuable course that led me to construct in the middle 1980s a bibliography that relied heavily on liberal white male biblical scholars. It all sounded good, but something was missing from the educational experience of these aspiring African-American ministers.

It was at this point that I was able to spend time in the libraries and archives of Howard University and Atlanta University. There I began to look for primary documents that recorded in writing some of the manifold ways that African-Americans had used and interpreted the Bible. This permitted me to develop resources that moved my students into an enhancing of their knowledge of their own experience rather than a confrontation with outside perspectives. This actually led to an ability to more effectively integrate their learning with advanced techniques in contemporary biblical studies. So the new course was entitled "African-Americans and the Bible."

The development of this course, however, entailed one more challenge. I again had to come to terms with the manner in which the biblical text had been used as a source of oppression and subjugation. At a fairly general level, there are three primary challenges.

The first challenge is the most obvious: The biblical text was used to advance and support one of the most brutal systems of enslavement known in world history, with drastic consequences for the nation. How could this be true of a text with a message of liberation and salvation for the entire world? Again I had to come to terms with the limitations as well as the possibilities of my sacred text.

A second challenge was the recognition that our view of the historical context for our study and analysis of the biblical texts was distorted. We do biblical studies within the context of a world history which deemphasizes the role of Africans in world history, in this case particularly Egypt and Ethiopia. To build a credible historical context for an African-American study of the Bible, I needed to take more seriously the history of Egypt and Ethiopia and their connections with the remainder of Africa, not merely leave those two countries as step-children of a Fertile Crescent intellectually anchored in Mesopotamia. It was another challenge to my own view of how I had learned to know the Bible.

Finally I had been taught a set of biblical methods anchored in and sustaining a Eurocentric approach to faith. So this experience again challenged my use of my own sacred texts at the level of their content, their context, and the methodology of their study. Most fundamentally, it was a new exposure to the limitations of the sacred text.

I again learned a few things about method. In response to the narrative style of African-American preaching, I developed my own understanding of the literary approach to New Testament studies and incorporated it into both my teaching and my research. I developed modes for the analysis of the biblical story that would help these pastors on Sunday morning "tell the story" and then make it part of their own lives and the lives of their congregants for the remainder of the week.

Further engagement with the community brought other insights. I learned about critical engagement with a text that has been both the source of liberation and bondage for a people. The Bible was used to teach obedience to the master in all things. But then I learned about Howard Thurman's grandmother, who refused to read the writings of Paul because they had been used precisely for that purpose. I learned that any aspirations I might hold about a neutral and objective study of the text were unattainable. A social analysis of both the text and the interpreter were necessary to empower those African-American pastors to be sources of inspiration and liberation in their own communities as they confronted the formidable obstacles the rest of us had constructed to stand in the way of their success. A critical social analysis was necessary to unleash the saving word. A lifetime of study was suddenly relevant again.

My undergraduate degree in the social sciences was now crucial. The social analysis that had been absorbed in that environment of prairie populism could now be applied to the history of Judaism and the rise of Christianity in the context of the Roman Empire. In the twenty or more intervening years, I had acquired the skills required to master the literature produced by those Jews whose history and fate were dramatically transformed because they spent eight hundred years within the context of Persian, Greek, and Roman imperialism. I had begun to understand the religious perspectives they had adopted as a means of survival throughout that period of time. I could more adequately understand the impulses that impelled the origin of Christianity. I could bring all of those resources to bear on the social analysis of biblical texts that would help empower African-American church leaders to become forces of liberation within that racist empire for which Americans of European descent hold primary responsibility. It also seemed that my own community should become aware of these perspectives and this analysis.

Our Hermeneutical Task

I have argued elsewhere that the hermeneutical task with regard to the biblical materials for the development and nurture of a global Mennonite identity is formed around the interaction of the biblical text with the themes of struggle and survival.[2] In contrast to other approaches to the biblical text, here it is engaged as an ally in these experiences of struggle and survival. It is at this point that the interaction with Jewish and African-American experiences can be helpful. The history of Christian anti-Semitism provides ample evidence of how the biblical story can be used to support a triumphalism that oppresses and destroys.

Anti-Semitism provides an important point of caution for all those using the text as basic formative material. Given the pervasive manner in which anti-Semitism has been woven into Christian theology, the disentangling of that element from Mennonite use of this material that has relied so heavily on basic Christian formulations for the justification of its own positions points to the difficulties in the use of biblical materials for identity formation. The biblical record as an account of struggle and survival need not support a history of Christian triumphalism. But a good deal of critical evaluation and creativity is required for it to function in a manner that supports the liberation efforts of people around the world engaged in struggle and survival. A critical disengagement from triumphalist Christian theologies, coupled with a heightened appreciation for the stories of struggle and survival from peoples around the world, is necessary for an appropriation of the biblical materials that supports such a formative endeavor. A greater understanding of the stories and hermeneutical techniques that have permitted the Jewish community to construct a basis for life and community from those same texts could be helpful. The African-American experience also can be instructive.

African-American history challenges any claim by groups of European origin to a comparable minority status in the United States. The history of Christians of African descent is a story of such tragic proportions that comparisons pale in the telling. Precisely for this reason this history is crucial for a discussion of the use of the Bible as a foundational document for the identity of a people. Significant benefit can be derived from a critical appraisal of how the biblical materials were appropriated to support a system of subjugation and oppression. Continuing analysis of the biblical materials is important to free them for use in the formation of an identity that supports persons around the world in their struggles for survival.[3]

Also instructive is a greater understanding of the use of the Bible in the African-American community. How did the Bible, forced onto the community as a document for the purposes of social control, become adopted by African-Americans as a source for liberation? What in their foundation myth permitted the Bible to function in such a manner? This is important to understand for other communities that use this document as a foundation myth. Continued research and a heightened awareness of how this document has continued to function as a source of support for the survival and struggles of the African-American community could be instructive in helping a global Mennonite community evaluate and develop the use of this foundation myth as a support for its own struggles and survival. The hermeneutical task employs a biblical text chastened by a history of Christian triumphalism and empowered by struggles for recognition, dignity and liberation.

So here I stand the product of Mennonite, Jewish, and African-American encounters with Scripture. In this short chapter I cannot begin to weave all of the strands together. That is a book-length project. I do not have final answers, but I do know that the most important choice is the selection of the companions. I speak from a sense of gratitude for the companions I have been blessed to have. I cannot imagine my life without them. But I have chosen to live "my life" in partnership with that text and experience that I have adopted as "my story." It continues to give my life coherence and meaning as it witnesses to the saving God who offers myriad ways of salvation for the wonderful array of human beings that attest to that same God's creative activity.

Notes

1. Samuel Sandmel, *Anti-Semitism in the New Testament?* (Philadelphia: Fortress, 1978).

2. John Kampen, "The Mennonite Challenge of Particularism and Universalism: A Liberation Perspective," *Conrad Grebel Review* 19 (Spring 2001): 5-28, with responses 29-51. Note the similarities to the conclusion offered 21-22.

3. Examples of this type of analysis from a variety of cultural perspectives include the following books: Daniel Smith-Christopher, ed., *Text and Experience: Towards a Cultural Exegesis of the Bible* (Sheffield: Sheffield Academic Press, 1995); Fernando F. Segovia and Mary Ann Tolbert, eds., *Teaching the Bible: The Discourses and Politics of Biblical Pedagogy* (Maryknoll: Orbis, 1998); Vincent L. Wimbush, ed., *The Bible and the American Myth: A Symposium on the Bible and Constructions of Meaning*, Studies in American Biblical Hermeneutics 16 (Macon: Mercer University Press, 1999).

CHAPTER 12

Beyond Criticism:
My Life with the Bible

Richard A. Kauffman

Although I was not quite five at the time, I remember the first time the Brunk brothers from Virginia brought their tent revival meetings to Lancaster, Pennsylvania, my home area. I still smell the sawdust aisles and the canvas tent. Although my memories probably come more from later encounters with the man, I can vividly picture George R. Brunk II, that towering preacher man with the booming bass voice, who implored his audience to repent of sin and turn their lives over to Christ. Despite the fact that I was too young at the time to respond to the altar calls, I knew it was serious business. In fact, more than any other one event, these Brunk Revival meetings shaped my spiritual and theological upbringing and indirectly how I came to view and use the Bible.[1]

After the revival meetings in summer 1951, my parents became part of a group of members at the East Chestnut Street Mennonite Church who were already dissatisfied with the legalisms of Lancaster Mennonite Conference and conflict in the East Chestnut Street congregation. Having their "hearts strangely warmed" through the Brunk revivals, some of these men formed a Saturday morning prayer group. Eventually this group, largely consisting of young men with families, left the East Chestnut Street congregation. At first they attended the Monterrey Mennonite congregation, a member of the Ohio and Eastern Mennonite Conference that was more progressive than Lancaster Conference. But this renegade group from East Chestnut was encouraged to start their own congregation, so they eventually founded the Neffsville

Mennonite Church, which became my spiritual home for the rest of my childhood and youth.

Neffsville too joined the Ohio and Eastern Mennonite Conference. But since most of these congregations were miles away in the state of Ohio and the Neffsville group had alienated itself from the Lancaster Conference, Neffsville developed an independent spirit. Thankfully, it kept its ties to the Mennonite church and maintained commitment to what was then called the nonresistance tradition, yet in other respects it theologically reflected the dominant fundamentalist and evangelical character of Lancaster County churches. My parents both attended evening school at the Lancaster School of the Bible, which was not only fundamentalist but also dispensational, following the teachings of Charles Darby, the Scofield Bible, and Dallas Theological Seminary.

The director of the Lancaster chapter of the Child Evangelism Association was a charter member of the Neffsville congregation—an ironic twist for a tradition founded on the principle of adult baptism, among others. Indeed, the first time I responded to an altar call was at a Child Evangelism Rally, after which I was baptized at Neffsville at the young age of eight. In high school the Youth for Christ chapter in my public high school was my primary social group, more than the youth group in my church, but that was an acceptable and common pattern for Neffsville youth. Neffsville also found itself caught up in the conservative political milieu of the area. For instance, while many other Mennonites became increasingly troubled by and vocal about their opposition to the Vietnam War, Neffsville was quiescent at best and many members were upset by the antiwar movement because it seemed so anti-American and unpatriotic.[2]

The view of the Bible that I picked up through teaching and osmosis—although I didn't know what to call it then—was that it is inerrant in all its details. That is, the Bible is without error, even in matters of history or science. As I began to gather back then, if modern science seemed to contradict Scripture in some way, it was due to the naturalist bias of many of its practitioners and had to be wrong. Further, the whole Bible was inspired by God. Indeed, it was God's Word presumably dictated to the "authors" to whom its different books are attributed.

One Sunday afternoon when I was about twelve I was bored, so my parents encouraged me to read a book. I wasn't much of a reader until college. So I told them the only book I liked to read was the Bible—but

I didn't want to read it just then. It was an effort to please my parents, to tell them what I thought they would want to hear, to show them my reverence for the Bible. Actually I didn't enjoy reading the Bible either, although by the time I reached high school I started to "mine" the Bible for theological truth and devotional inspiration. Still, I found it a boring book and didn't understand much of it, even though I felt compelled to defend its veracity. Of course the fact that we used the King James Version exacerbated the situation. It was a delight, however, to discover J. B. Phillips' paraphrase of the New Testament while in high school.

It is neither inaccurate nor unfair to say, then, that my upbringing was more shaped by fundamentalism, revivalism, and pietism than it was by Anabaptism. Nevertheless, I was "saved" for the Mennonite church and ultimately the Anabaptist tradition by several factors. One, my mother had a keen interest in extended family and genealogy. Through that, I became aware that there was a broader Mennonite social world out there to which I belonged. Also, during high school our youth group attended several youth gatherings of the Ohio Conference of what was then called the (Old) Mennonite Church, which gave me some sense of connection and curiosity about what this larger church was to which our congregation belonged.

Then when it came time to attend college, although I considered a local college and the Philadelphia College of the Bible, I chose to attend Hesston College in Kansas. At Hesston I joined the touring choir, singing in Mennonite congregations across the United States and staying with Mennonite families along the way. Through this exposure, I discovered there were other ways of being Mennonite besides the legalisms of Lancaster Conference or the fundamentalism of Neffsville congregation.

Still, Hesston didn't challenge my conservative theology or politics. That would come later, when I transferred to Goshen College in Indiana. Goshen at the time was caught up in an antiwar fervor, which at first distressed me. Even though I had registered as a conscientious objector when I reached draft age, I thought *someone* had to stop the spread of godless Communism in the world, lthough my conscience kept *me* from doing it. By the time I graduated from Goshen College, however, I was frustrated with people from my home congregation who supported American intervention in Vietnam while paying lip service to nonresistance. At the same time, I got into theological debates with some of my professors, not only because I thought they were too liberal theologically but also because I even questioned their Christian commitment.

Because of this ambivalence, I chose not to go to Goshen Biblical Seminary at the end of college. Instead, I enrolled at Eastern Baptist Theological Seminary in Philadelphia. Those years were formative in several ways: I discovered there were ways of taking the Bible seriously without taking it literally through a professor who introduced me to Emil Brunner and Neo-Orthodoxy. I also encountered historical-critical methods of the Bible in a seminary that touted itself as evangelical! For once, when I began to understand the historical contexts out of which the biblical texts emerged, the Bible started to make sense. I also was one of two leaders in a small antiwar group at Eastern Baptist.

Just as important for my faith development, my wife Suzanne and I became connected to the Franconia Conference in eastern Pennsylvania during my seminary years and following. Franconia Conference at that time shared many of the cultural vestiges that reminded me of the Lancaster Conference my parents had left, but there was a difference: the core congregations and leaders in Franconia had an unwavering commitment to Anabaptism and to Christ's way of peace. Indeed, their conservatism served as a "carrier" that kept alive a view of the church as an alternative community with a commitment to discipleship and Christian pacifism. And the leaders in Franconia Conference, thankfully, were wary of American fundamentalism and evangelicalism, despite their conservative theology.

In my senior year of seminary I was selected to participate in an inter-seminary seminar involving four students and one professor from four seminaries in the Philadelphia area: in addition to Baptists, other communions represented were Lutheran, Episcopal, and Catholic. Half of the students from Eastern Baptist Seminary were Mennonite! For that interfaith seminar I wrote a paper entitled "The Anabaptist Conception of the Church." There was nothing original about it, but the process of writing it and even more defending it in a context where most of the other students represented infant baptism traditions sealed my theological identity: I'm Mennonite, I'm Anabaptist. How ironic, I thought, that all the students from infant baptism traditions agreed, running ahead of their own traditions, that personally they could accept each other's baptisms. But they couldn't accept mine!

A Critical Perspective

All of my graduate school training convinced me that we can't ask how the Bible is a divine word for us today before we ask how it was a divine word in its original contexts. Hence the need for understanding both the historical contexts from which the disparate texts emerged and the means by which the texts were written, edited, and compiled. But I also realized that higher criticism isn't the whole story. Indeed, after slicing and dicing the Bible into its disparate parts, I struggled to put the whole thing back together again, to see a coherent story line in it, to see, yes, the story of salvation history.

By the time I was asked to join the administration and faculty at Goshen Biblical Seminary, then one of two seminaries comprising Associated Mennonite Biblical Seminaries (AMBS), I was a long way from the fundamentalism of my youth. But I hadn't let it go either. In fact, when I taught the Introduction to Theology course at AMBS, which I did for eleven years, I frontally attacked the plenary-inspiration and inerrant views I had absorbed as a young person. I argued that the theology behind this fundamentalist perspective on the Bible was foreign to Mennonites, largely having come from nineteenth-century Reformed theology. Besides, in the final analysis, the real job of dealing with Scripture is to interpret it in the context of a Spirit-led community of faith, apply it to life, then live it out. The truth of Scripture, in other words, is in its embodiment in life.

Although I persisted until the end of my teaching days at AMBS to confront the fundamentalist view of Scripture, I increasingly became aware that I was fighting the wrong battle with students. It was rare that students came to AMBS with the assumptions I was attacking, so I was trying to deconstruct a nonexistent construct. It also seemed instead that students had the same difficulty I had had after being steeped in critical biblical studies: how to have an appreciation for the Bible as a whole, how to see it in some way as God's Word for humanity.

What I tried then to positively affirm—and still affirm—is that in this book we encounter the living God, not just facts about God but God's own self, most preeminently in the person of Jesus Christ. The Bible is trustworthy in relation to its aim and purpose: namely, to bring people into a saving relationship with Jesus Christ and his body, the church. The Bible, to be sure, is viewed and used variously by Christians as a source of truth about God and about how we humans should live (theology and ethics); or as a sourcebook for worship and personal piety; or still yet as a sourcebook of stories and history about the people of God. But what matters, ultimately, is that in and through its many forms and genres, contexts, and situations, the Bible is a people-forming, identity-shaping, life-orienting book. From this book, in other words, we as the people of God discover who we are and to whom we belong.

We belong, first of all, to God through Christ, and secondarily to Christ's body, the church. This relativizes all natural affinities such as race, nation, gender, or socio-economic class. But the Bible also gives us orientation in life and living, both corporately and individually. The root meaning of orientation relates to the Orient, from whence comes the sun. By the sun the ancients could get their bearings both spatially and temporally. Likewise, the Bible, the charter document of the Christian faith, gives us our bearings in time and place and suggests direction for our lives. It is not an answer book for life, and it certainly doesn't address every issue that arises in history. But it does suggest a direction, and through being formed by this book and inspired by God's Spirit, we can discern what God's will is for our lives in the present.

While teaching Introduction to Theology at AMBS, I also introduced another concept I had picked up from the Wesleyan tradition—the Wesleyan quadrilateral. It had seemed to me that the Reformation principle of *sola scriptura* (Scripture alone) was not adequate; in fact, to say that Scripture is our only source of authority for Christian faith is even dishonest. At the very least, we filter Scripture through our own lens of experience. What we see in Scripture has much to do with what we bring to Scripture, even when at our best we keep open minds and hearts to discern what Scripture has to say to us.

Scripture doesn't come to us unmediated; it has no meaning apart from our interpretation of Scripture, which in itself is an exercise in the use of our minds—our reason. Additionally, we are not the first to read and interpret Scripture. Others have interpreted it before us; from them we receive insight about its meaning. It was a relief, then, to discover that the Wesleyans talk of a four-fold pattern of authority: Scripture itself is the primary authority; indeed, it is the one by which all other sources of authority are judged. Nevertheless, tradition, reason, and experience are also recognized as being legitimate, even necessary sources of theological authority.

Take tradition, for example: It is arrogant to think our forebears have nothing to teach us about interpretation of Scripture and its meaning for Christian discipleship. While I believe that the local Christian community is the proper place for biblical interpretation and application, the hermeneutical circle must be enlarged to include the insights of those who have gone before us and expanded outward in "space" to include those from other cultures and traditions. As for reason, who would argue that the simple acts of reading or listening to the words of Scripture demand the use of our minds, not to mention its interpretation and application to life's circumstances? Indeed, the process of interpreting the Bible is both rational (using our best mental capacities) as well as spiritual (listening to the Spirit of God through the words of the text).[3]

Finally, our experience comes into play in two ways: when we come before Scripture, we bring all of who we are—our past, our commitments, our context. We cannot and must not avoid it. What is necessary is more transparency, not less, about how our experience shapes our perspectives, not least on the interpretation of Scripture. But the reading and interpreting and applying of Scripture should, in turn, shape our experience. Indeed, it doesn't merely shape what we do in the future but also shapes how we look at our past experience. Experience, in other words, doesn't have to do with brute facts alone, but experience is both what happens and how we understand what happens, what meaning we attribute to it, how the events of our lives are woven into the story of our lives. We bring our experience to the Bible, but used rightly Scripture also shapes our experience. Our different experiences account, in part, for our differences in the interpretation of Scripture.

The Laurelville conference that generated this volume gave ample evidence of this truism. We told our stories about Scripture; our stories reflected our uniqueness, which in turn resulted in differing perspectives on Scripture. Yet, having been shaped by a similar tradition—Mennonite and Anabaptist—we also shared many commonalities. It might be prudent when we find ourselves reaching very different conclusions about the meaning of Scripture in group settings to take some time to "tell our stories." It doesn't necessarily resolve the differences, but it helps us to understand why we reach difference conclusions and to respect and listen more carefully to alternative perspectives.

It seemed to me, then, that the Wesleyan quadrilateral helps the Christian community to be more fully aware of what is happening in the process of interpreting the Bible. It also provides a bridge for moving from interpreting individual texts in Scripture to thinking more holistically (that is, theologically[4]) about Scripture, about how we think of God, humankind, sin and salvation, the church, discipleship and mission, and a host of other topics.

The quadrilateral also provides a grid for looking at such controversial topics as homosexuality: What does Scripture itself have to say on the subject? What does reason bring to bear on the topic? What light do modern, scientific perspectives shed on the subject? What about our own experience? What in our experience shapes how we interpret what Scripture says on the subject? What in our experience determines even what we think is relevant from Scripture on the topic? Is it just the few texts in Scripture that specifically mention homosexual acts? Or do the grand themes of grace and mercy, holiness and justice have some bearing on how we deal with people of same-sex orientation? Does Jesus' apparent silence on the topic or his model of relating to the marginalized of the faith community have any relevance?

Of course, awareness and use of the quadrilateral doesn't finally resolve the issue for us. What does it mean, for instance, to say that Scripture is the "norm that judges," while tradition, experience, and reason are the "norms that are judged"? What, in other words, does it mean practically to say that Scripture is the final and ultimate authority when Scripture itself needs to be interpreted and is therefore filtered through tradition, experience, and reason? What happens, for example, when social conscience comes to contradict Scripture, as it has for slavery? Do Bible-believing Christians still insist that Scripture trumps all? Or do they come to understand that the Spirit has still more light to show us from God's Holy Word, to paraphrase the Puritan John Robinson? While the Wesleyan quadrilateral doesn't resolve controversial issues, it makes our sources of authority and our assumptions more transparent and open for discussion and debate.

Presbyterian theologian Bill Placher makes a helpful distinction.[5] The biblical authors intended to teach something to those for whom they were putting down words; but as children of their time, they expressed things we recognize as culture/time-bound and which should not bind successive generations of biblical people. For example, biblical writers assumed and reflected certain cosmological understandings which have long since been superseded by Copernicus and Galileo. But it wasn't their intention to teach us science as such but rather to teach about God and God's relationship with the world and us humans.

Most thinking people today can understand the distinction Placher makes, even accept it. Still, there is a debate over where you draw the line between what the Bible intended to teach and what it unintentionally conveys by its own time-bound cultural assumptions. For instance, most Mennonites today would agree that the apostle Paul's teaching on head coverings for women (1 Cor.) represents a time-bound, culture-based practice, not to be taken as universal principle or practice. But not so long ago many Mennonites would have argued otherwise—that the injunction for women to cover their heads was intended for all times and all places, indeed for all occasions, not just worship and prayer. So, the question remains, for instance: Are the few texts which deal with homosexuality what the Bible intended to teach us? Or are these texts part of the biblical cultural baggage reflected and assumed in the effort to teach us something about human relationships under God? That is part of the ongoing conversation and controversy. And while Bible-believing Christians might be able to reach agreement on what the Bible has to say about homosexuality, they still could disagree about what it means for us today practically.

Post-Critical Perspectives

As an undergraduate student I majored in music. I chose this field for a number of reasons, but certainly the most important was my love of music, especially vocal and choral music. My formal training in the field helped me to think critically about music and to analyze what was going on in a Handel oratorio or a Bach chorale. One result was that, for a time, I couldn't just listen to music for the simple pleasure of it; I had to think about what was going on in the music. Indeed, "background music," even if good music, nearly drove me nuts. I couldn't read or study while music was playing because I found it too distracting. Eventually I had to find my way back to what drew me to music in the first place, the simple pleasure of listening to or performing good music—without ever fully giving up the critical perspectives I had learned to analyze and judge what makes for good music.

Something like that had to happen for me in relation to the Bible as well. As I've already said, the Bible didn't really make much sense to me until I began to understand it in a historical, critical perspective—to learn to see how texts emerged, in what contexts, under what circumstances, through what agency. But a historical-critical perspective on the Bible not only seemed to slice and dice the Bible into a myriad of disparate parts which often seemed disconnected; it also seemed to drain the life out of the Bible, one might even say take the spirit (or Spirit?) from it.

Like so many others trained in the historical-critical perspectives, I needed to discover what Paul Ricoeur has referred to as the "second naiveté." Indeed, a three-fold process is involved: One first moves from a naïve stage (pre-critical understanding) to an analytical stage (critical explanation), but then one must move on to a post-critical stage, Ricoeur's second naïveté (understanding through appropriation of text). Whereas much of modernity languishes in an "analytical 'desert of criticism,'"[6] we can't take a detour to a post-critical understanding, bypassing the critical stage; nor can the gains of a critical perspective be lost in the third stage. A post-critical stance absorbs a critical stance while at the same time going beyond it.

My first step toward a post-critical appropriation and appreciation of Bible came through a discovery of cross-cultural understandings of the Bible. As I said before, the hermeneutical circle (that is, community of interpretation) must be drawn larger than just our own congregation or community; just as we should incorporate voices that have gone before us, we should also include voices from other cultures in our own time. I first realized this existentially when I audited a graduate seminar at the Catholic Theological Union in Chicago while on a sabbatical leave from AMBS. The course was taught by Robert Schreiter, who is noted for what he calls "local theology,"[7] or what others call "contextual theology." It is, in other words, a theology that takes seriously one's own cultural, political, and economic context.

Such an incarnational perspective on faith and the Bible assumes that the Word must take root indigenously, rather than simply involve transplanting perspectives from other cultures. A surprising aspect of this seminar for me was that it turned out to be an exercise in cross-cultural theology. Everyone in the group, except for one white priest and me, was either from some other culture or had spent significant time in other cultures, mostly in the Third World. This opened up for me a whole new horizon in biblical interpretation—not just coming to terms with the multiple contexts of Scripture itself, but also the multiple contexts in which Scripture takes root and bears fruit. My own white, Western, and largely Enlightenment biases and perspectives weren't challenged so much as they were broadened and absorbed in a larger panorama. It was like focusing a telephoto lens on many other contemporary contexts, whereas heretofore I had been mainly focused on my own context.

One story will have to suffice: Some representatives of the Church of Canada met with representatives of some aboriginal groups. But the conversation went very poorly at first, in part because the latter were reticent folk and not accustomed to this kind of ecumenical encounter. In a moment of painful silence, at least for the Church of Canada folk, someone brought up the Exodus story, thinking that the aboriginal peoples could identify with the paradigmatic story of liberation. But as they began to talk about this story, it became apparent that the aboriginals did not identify at all with the Hebrew experience of freedom and liberation, as the Church of Canada representatives assumed; instead, they identified with the Canaanites whose land was taken from them by the Hebrew occupation. The aboriginal perspective turned out to be a word of judgment!

The other personal development leading to a post-critical perspective on the Bible grew out of my spiritual pilgrimage of the last ten years or more. Having been taught to think critically in higher education, I had long abandoned the conservative pietism and revivalism of my childhood and youth, which seemed to me excessively emotional, individualistic, non-critical, and lacking a social ethic. The piety of the first twenty-five years of my adult life, if it could be called that, was largely intellectual and volitional. Indeed, it was mostly informed by what many would refer to as neo-Anabaptism, the renewal of Anabaptist theology in the middle of the twentieth century, led by such intellectuals as H. S. Bender of Goshen College and Goshen Biblical Seminary.

What stood out for me was an emphasis on discipleship: Christian faithfulness entails neither thinking the correct thoughts about theology (orthodoxy) nor having the proper inner dispositions or religious experiences (pietism), but rather following the teachings of Jesus at all cost. Over time, however, I came to see that what comes through in much of neo-Anabaptism is a joyless, duty-bound form of discipleship. Not only did it underemphasize the empowering work of the Holy Spirit, it seemed to also downplay the human affections. But I came to sense that, whereas faith cannot be reduced to the affections or emotions, a holistic faith will work toward the transformation and expression of our affections.

Hence, like Ricoeur's third stage of biblical appropriation that goes beyond a critical perspective without abandoning it, I needed to go beyond neo-Anabaptism without abandoning it, while incorporating it into a larger framework of understanding and experience. Several things happened to help that. One was that in a span of a few short years I went through a number of personal crises, not the least of which was being in the hospital four times in less than twelve months, culminating in open-heart surgery when I was only fifty. That experience not only put me in touch with my mortality for the second time in my life (the first time was when I was in a serious car accident at age fifteen and nearly killed); it also put me in touch again with my emotions. I had to have heart surgery to rediscover I had a heart.

The second development was the discovery of the contemplative tradition of the Christian faith through reading Thomas Merton, Henri Nouwen, Joan Chittister, and Roberta Bondi, who introduced me to the early desert fathers and mothers and some of the Christian mystics. Through them I'm learning to read the Bible in a new way, to see that at one level the Bible is speaking to me: God's Word is God's personal address to me personally, but not individualistically. I also discovered a slow, meditative, and contemplative reading of Scripture called *lectio divina*, which restored a "devotional" reading of the Bible to me without being individualistic, anti-intellectual, or lacking in a social ethic. But even more important than the reading of Scripture in this new way, this contemplative stream in Christianity has helped to speak to a deep longing that all humans have: to have a personal relationship with God, to know God and to be known, personally, by God. It is through this personal relationship with God that I am being transformed, so that discipleship is not something I do because I must but is something I am becoming because of whose I am—God's beloved child.

Still, I can never hold to a faith that focuses on the personal apart from the communal. While we are made for personal relationship with God, for God that intent fits into a larger agenda. God is, in fact, calling out and creating a people in the world, a people that, despite all its flaws, we call a holy people, a set-apart community. A happy corollary development to this discovery of the contemplative tradition was the rediscovery of the joy of being part of a worshiping community that sets time aside each week to be together, to remember what God has done in history, to praise God, and to call and energize us for a ministry of reconciliation, peace, and justice in the world. At the center of the community is the Bible that it reads, interprets, applies to life—and argues over. Better to have disputations over Scripture—indeed, disputations with the Bible—than to benignly neglect it.

Karl Barth once said that talking about God is like painting a bird in motion. That is how it's been for me to chronicle my journey with the Bible. It's a journey that is intrinsically tied to my faith pilgrimage, a journey that keeps changing and, hopefully, transforming me. May it continue to be so.

Notes

1. The tractor-trailer in which the Brunks hauled their tent and other equipment had painted on the side Mennonite sounding words: "The Whole Gospel for the Whole World." But on the front it carried a slogan which sounds like civil religion, "Christ for America." The latter slogan didn't keep the Brunks from responding to invitations to take their revivals north of the border to Canada!

2. For the history of the Neffsville Mennonite congregation, see Roy S. Burkholder, *Pathways to Renewal: A Narrative History of Neffsville Mennonite Church, 1952-2002* (Neffsville, Pa.: Neffsville Mennonite Church, 2002). Burkholder casts the history of the congregation as an ongoing struggle between two forms of church renewal, fundamentalism and Anabaptism. While this is a very capable congregational history, Burkholder, as a long-term member of the congregation, seems to me overly magnanimous toward the fundamentalist element there. I also think fundamentalism is better understood as a reactionary movement than as a renewal movement.

3. It is theologically proper, it seems to me, to refer to the Bible as the Word of God, and to maintain that it reveals God to us. But the Bible also reveals to us much about human nature and affairs. It takes some discernment to be able to know the difference between what God intends and what instead is a reflection of unredeemed human nature. Another way to put this is to say that not all the Bible is life-giving; or at least not all interpretations of the Bible are life-giving. One need only look at the Bible used as justification for religious and other kinds of wars. But the still stronger claim can be made: There are some parts of the Bible that if taken literally can be used to justify the use of lethal force for a righteous cause, but since the life, death, and resurrection of Jesus, we need not accept that the former ways of thinking and acting were or at least remain God's will. But this is a debatable perspective involving *theological* discernment, not just exegesis of scriptural texts.

4. I think that often we disagree on the issue of homosexuality because we are working from different theological assumptions that are largely implicit and unexam-

ined. Indeed, we have different theological paradigms: stated simplistically and too much in a bipolar manner, conservatives tend to emphasize the holiness of God which calls for righteous living on the part of disciples of Jesus and tends to yield a church that is exclusive; progressives, on the other hand, emphasize the love of God which calls for justice within the human community and a church that is inclusive. But aren't both perspectives on God necessary? If so, we need to continue to be in dialogue and fellowship with each other, despite our differences on this and other issues. Our theological fidelity is at stake!

5. William C. Placher, "Struggling with Scripture," in Brueggemann, Placher, and Blount, *Struggling with Scripture* (Westminster John Knox Press, 2002).

6. Dan R. Stiver, *Theology after Ricoeur: New Directions in Hermeneutical Theology* (Westminster John Knox, 2001).

7. Robert J. Schreiter, *Constructing Local Theologies* (Orbis, 1985). Any bibliography on either contextual or cross-cultural theology could be nearly endless, but one book particularly apropos is Priscilla Pope-Levison and Jon Levison, *Return to Babel: Global Perspectives on the Bible* (Westminster John Knox, 1999) which features Christians from different cultures interpreting the same biblical texts with interesting results.

CHAPTER 13

Scripture as a Mirror

Paul Keim

Resistance to Stories

I resist telling the story of my journey with Scripture for a number of reasons. To tell a story is to spin a yarn, to create order out of the chaos of our experiences and our selective memory. I believe in stories and the truths embedded in narratives. But the truth of stories is a kind of verisimilitude, a partial truth. So I have suppressed the urge to render my journey into a coherent narrative that appears to make sense, that implies, or worse, claims to know the elements of cause and effect that have produced these constructs I glibly assume to be "myself," "my journey," and "with" Scripture.

A narrative account of my journey with Scripture would require a beginning point, an origin of some kind. I don't think I am able or willing to arbitrarily designate a particular time or experience as such. But I will attempt to describe elements of my experience with Scripture and the formative influence it has had on my life. These descriptions will proceed more or less chronologically. The result is not a coherent narrative but rather an impressionistic montage, one with texture rather than plot.

German was not my first language, but in a sense it was my first biblical language. It was my mother's mother tongue, and Luther's Bible was the "original text" in that child's imagination, a text rendered, at some point, into the not exactly comprehensible English of the King

James Version. How many times did I hear recited, before I began to listen, then murmur its cadences, then recite, along with the rest: *Our Father which art in heaven. . . .*

Yes, that's the way to pray, and mean it, and belong. Even a child could understand that it was all about belonging. And the biblical text was at the heart of what it meant to belong, to have an identity. Biblical truths seemed inherent in the life of the community and were passed along almost by osmosis. Bedtime Bible stories. Bible memory. Worship on Sunday morning, Sunday evening, and Wednesday evening. Sermons, Scripture readings, hymns, Sunday school lessons, and of course the interminable prayers (most torturous before big meals). In each setting the words and world of the Bible were evoked. There was Scripture on the lips of virtually every adult who mattered in that child's world.

As a professional biblical scholar, I spend considerable time trying to figure out what texts "really" mean. Yet my earliest encounters with Scripture had less to do with referential meaning and more to do with the function of Scripture in my family and community. It was the ubiquity of the Lord's Prayer and Psalm 23, more than the content, that impressed and endeared me to Scripture—and that continues to evoke deep responses. Now that I can chase the meaning of each Hebrew and Greek word, and of each verse, and of the whole, in its biblical and Ancient Near East context, I can see how significant the other levels of meaning are—the sounds, the verbal and visual imagery, the look and feel of the Bible in the hand. In Christianity, as in Judaism and Islam, the phonology of Scripture is laden with theological significance, independent of interpretation.

Inherency and Osmosis.

My journey has no discernable beginning in an individual sense because it has been intergenerational, inseparable from the journey of my parents and the journey of the church. Mennonite family, Mennonite congregation, Mennonite college. Differences, but also deep continuities. Favorite verses. Oft-repeated phrases. Movingly spoken with a catch in the voice. The words of Jesus—offered in solace, in salutation, in service; self-evident, sentimental, sermonic, sonorous, simple, solemn, sustaining, symbolic, significant.

Scripture from Genesis to Revelation, with a whole lot left out in between. My conscious interaction with the Bible was characterized by a fascination with those vast areas of Scripture that were not referenced in my childhood. This included much of the Old Testament. I once heard a radio preacher claim, either oblivious to or conscious of its self-congratulatory tone (I don't even know which would have been worse) that reading his Bible daily, he could even get a blessing from the book of Leviticus. *Even* the book of Leviticus! That's where I was drawn—to the rituals and the law and the language most foreign, seemingly, to the "Jesus meek and mild" of our canon within the canon.

Another reason why it was difficult for me to be content with a narrative rendering of my journey with Scripture is that some of my current attitudes toward Scripture lend themselves less well to a narrative approach, one with an inevitably and unambiguously redemptive outcome. More and more, I find the content of revelation in Scripture having to do with the right questions rather than the right answers.

There came a time when I was confronted with the specter of historical and critical methods of understanding the Bible and religion. Sitting in a college classroom, awash in the enthusiasm of the just recently en-doctored Dennis McDonald, and the mesmerizing eccentricity of Stanley Shenk, I struggled with Van Harvey's *The Historian and the Believer.* I fought with him throughout the semester, holding out for what I thought was the integrity of faith and the inviolability of Scripture, trying to avoid what seemed like a slippery slope. Then, in the following semester, walking across campus, it hit me, like a revelation: I don't have to give up faith! I don't have to give up the Bible. I can embrace the Bible and pursue its truths wherever the text might lead. The key, so I thought at the time, was language.

I began studying biblical languages, first Hebrew, during my general education biology class (where I richly deserved my low B, or was it a C?), then Greek, then Syriac, then . . . , well it never really stops. Teachers became mentors, guides into a language and culture and world of Ancient Near Eastern religion so rich it seemed impossible to take it all in.

I have weathered a number of critical episodes in my life, but none that questioned the Bible as a source of light and life. The more I came to know it, the more I came to appreciate it in all its aspects. I rediscovered and embraced the King James Version for the majesty of its language—not as a study Bible, but as a monument to the efforts of a community of faith to render both the meaning and the majesty of the text from one language to another.

Over the years, texts have become familiar and new—the power of two of the most dramatic words in the Old Testament: *'attah ha'ish* from 2 Samuel 12. There's truth in there that goes to the heart of what it means to be human—to stand, to fall, to accept the fallen part of one-self, to turn, to receive forgiveness, to continue the journey.

This growing awareness and appreciation of Scripture has included, on some kind of parallel track, appreciation of other scriptural traditions, starting with the Hebrew Bible as a coherent story of salvation in its own right. But especially of the Old Testament as part of a longer story that includes the testimony of Jesus' life and teachings, Jesus' self-sacrificing love, Jesus' defeat of the powers of vengeance and hatred. The Bible has become a mirror in which I find analogies for my own thoughts, feelings, and experiences.

I haven't felt the need to locate my understanding of and interaction with the Bible theologically—to systematize a doctrine of Scripture. My current orientation to Scripture is the sustained assumption that there is redemptive life in its pages. Its texts point the way. A way of faith. A faith that must be nurtured. A way that leads toward the divine.

The role of the Bible in the life of the community seems to be changing. It is troubling to perceive growing biblical illiteracy in the church, a lost sense of the relevance of Scripture to real life. Authoritative appeal is made to proof texts lifted out of context to support doctrinally determined positions. Interpretations of selected biblical texts provide sanction for separation instead of invitations to build each other up. But the Bible I know gives a broader view of religious experience than that contained in confessions and doctrinal litmus tests. Therein lies my hope—and some confidence that no matter how far we stray, our journey with Scripture can help us find the way back.

CHAPTER 14

The Journey Is My Home

Marilyn Rayle Kern

I didn't start out as a Mennonite, but I always felt Anabaptist. My father and mother were editors of Sunday school literature for the Churches of God, General Conference—a denomination based on Anabaptist values. John Winebrenner, its founder, never intended to found a new church. He only wanted to reform his German Reformed Church to be more like his understanding of the New Testament model. He was greatly influenced by Church of the Brethren and former Mennonite pastors in Pennsylvania.

From earliest childhood, I was taught to respect the Bible. Mother made sure I never put anything on top of a Bible because it was so special. Imagine then my horror when at age eight I came into the kitchen after supper one evening to find my own parents cutting Bibles to shreds! I was sure something terrible was about to happen. When they finally noticed I was speechless, they explained that it was okay. The Sunday school quarterlies which they wrote printed a Scripture passage for each lesson. Because they might make mistakes if they typed out the verses to be studied, they got cheap Bibles from the American Bible Society, cut out the passages for each Sunday, and pasted them up for the linotypist. Because the linotypist might also make mistakes, when the galley proofs came back one editor read the paste-up out loud—with all the punctuation marks—while the other made corrections.

I learned a lot as I began to participate in this part of the family business. I found that some sections of the Bible were never used. Since Christmas and Easter texts were used every year, the Bibles got more "holey" sooner in those sections. I learned to find the passages to cut out long before we memorized the books of the Bible in Sunday school. I loved to be the copy reader who read all the commas, colons, and semicolons and got to call the exclamation points "screamers." I learned many words that weren't in my readers at school.

Most of all I was learning the difference between the spirit and the letter of the law. The letter of the law said "never deface a Bible." The intention of that rule was to show respect for God's word. Making sure that Sunday school students had an accurate copy of the text was actually a way of showing profound respect for Scripture. The power of the Bible was not something magical; it came from faithful application of the most accurate text available.

Obviously the Bible and its interpretation were central to our family's life as I grew up. I was fascinated by my father's big heavy Hebrew Bible and thin little Greek testament and his explanations of how a word in one of those languages could carry a richness of meaning that went way beyond what was obvious in King James English. My father told me that Professor Bruer, his Greek professor at Findlay College, had taught him that "you never have to be afraid of searching for truth because God is so much bigger than all that we understand. God will always be where truth is found." When my dad went to Yale Divinity School in the 1920s, he saw many seminary students who lost their faith when they encountered historical-critical methods of studying the Bible. Professor Bruer's words saw him through. My father processed and integrated much that he was being taught, and held the rest in reserve in case he ever needed it. He was probably as conservative as his classmates who fell by the wayside, but he continued to learn and to grow in faith all his life. I wanted to be like him.

If I had been a boy, I know I would often have been asked, "Are you going to be a preacher like your daddy when you grow up?" Nobody ever asked me that. In my teens I became increasingly interested in science. At the same time my faith was deepening. The vocational call I heard was to be a high school science teacher who was a Christian. When I won an award for being the outstanding science student in my graduating class in high school, I felt the need to put the money aside to do something symbolic with it. By the end of my first year of college I knew what it was for. That was the year the first Revised Standard Version (RSV) translation of the Bible was printed. Carl McIntire was rampaging across the country condemning the RSV as the work of Satan. I used my prize money to buy a new RSV Bible and was delighting in the new insights it gave me.

In college introduction to Bible classes, and many years later in seminary, I encountered professors who seemed to delight in ridiculing the naïve beliefs of ministerial students. Like my father at Yale, I grieved for classmates who lost their faith. I know the professors justified their actions by saying, "If they can't take the truth, they don't belong in the ministry." My problem was the gleefulness of these learned men when another would-be preacher bit the dust. What was Christian about crushing the sincere faith of someone who had come to college in response to God's call to serve? Maybe some weren't cut out for pastoral ministry, but when they dropped out, the church lost what could have been a core of educated laypersons. It seemed so wrong and unnecessary.

I decided that even if I were sure I knew more of the truth than someone who disagreed with me on a biblical interpretation, I would never knock the props out from under that person's basic beliefs. I wanted to help people build a more adequate foundation to support a faith that could continue to grow. I practiced understanding how the world looks through another's eyes. I married a minister, taught science for a couple of years, then became a lab technician for a research endocrinologist while my husband worked on his Ph.D. As a University of Chicago employee, I could take courses for half tuition. I already had two years of Hebrew, so I took Exodus from Hebrew text, Ugaritic, and Near Eastern Linguistics—all just for fun.

After a stillbirth, we were blessed with four healthy children. I became a stay-at-home mom, taught Sunday school for various ages, and kept on learning from Scripture.

One Sunday, on the way home from church, I noticed four-year-old Kathleen seemed upset. When I asked what was wrong, she said, "My Sunday school teacher read the story about Noah. The picture showed giraffes and people in the water. They couldn't get into the boat, and they died. He said it was because people were very bad and God had to punish them—but what about the animals?" Her eyes widened, tears gushed, and she said, "And what about the babies? They weren't bad!"

I knew that the story is about preservation of the righteous and involves several strands of Near Eastern mythology. It is the etiological explanation of the rainbow as told to the differing audiences of the Yahwist and the Priestly writers. This isn't the only place in the Old Testament where the wrath of God is portrayed.

I also knew that my little girl was four years old, and none of that had anything to do with her heart breaking with the injustice of it all. What she needed to hear was, "No, I don't think God is like that. God cares about the animals and loves every baby. The Bible tells us that even when we're bad, God still loves us." I knew that I had Hosea, Deutero-Isaiah, the book of Jonah, and Jesus on my side for right now, and she could get to theodicy when she was good and ready. As far as I was concerned, she was intuitively closer to the truth about God's justice than her Sunday school teacher and the artist who drew that awful picture. Kathleen has taught me a lot about what's important in the Bible.

I finally recognized my long dormant call to ministry through a marriage counselor's question. I returned to school to earn an M. Div. degree—learning Greek at last! I was ordained and became Assistant Pastor of First Mennonite Church in Bluffton. I went to Iliff School of Theology, where I learned much about interpreting the Bible and proclaiming it. For me, John Spangler's word of truth was, "Remember that church people are a lot more ignorant and a lot less stupid than you give them credit for." That rang true then and continues to be my experience in a variety of church settings.

Ignorance about the Bible grows at an alarming rate, but fortunately there is a cure for ignorance. At Iliff, one of the ways they helped students lay a more adequate biblical foundation for their faith was through what they called the "Dialogue Model of Interpretation." I've used this tool with high school and college classes, where most were totally ignorant of the Bible, and with pastors and Sunday school classes who thought they knew it all. We all learned new things every time.

Using the dialogue model, we basically ask, "What did this text mean to the original writer and the audience which first heard it? What was its setting? What life situation did it address? From all we can find out about this time and place, what was the author's intention?" Then we ask, "What does this mean to me, to us, to our class, our church, our community, our nation?" This can lead us to additional questions and answers about what the text meant to its original audience which may give us more insights about what it means to us.

It's not fair for a pastor to fling at a congregation a biblical truth she knows will be disturbing then leave people to digest it, spit it out, or choke on it. Some truths need to be studied and discussed in the community of faith. Rather than abusing our power or showing off our scholarship, working with people around the hermeneutic circle offers the possibility of their discovering a more adequate understanding for themselves.

People who say they aren't interested in Bible study because, "We know all that stuff," have often not gotten beyond a flatly literal reading. The dialogue model offers people tools for interpreting themselves as well as the text, and applies historical, geographical, and cultural concerns to what a passage may have originally meant. This may be very different from what seems to be the obvious meaning to a modern reader or from what we want to hear.

The dialogue with self and text helps the scientist in me to be more objective about both, and to keep them from blurring together. Each time I come to a familiar passage there are new things to learn, because I have had new life experiences. It's never just ancient history that has nothing to do with me. I remember visiting the Tomb of the Patriarchs in Hebron—a building which houses both a synagogue and a mosque built over what is alleged to be the Cave of Machpelah (the ancient burial place that Abraham bought). There were watchful Palestinian guards in the mosque, and we went through two Israeli checkpoints to get into the building. I had to be searched because the zipper in my coat set off their very sensitive alarm. Now I am drawn to the simple account in Genesis 25:7-10 where we read that after prolonged estrangement and alienation, Isaac the ancestor of those Israelis and Ishmael the ancestor of those Palestinians together buried their father Abraham in that cave with his wife Sarah, in the only piece of the Promised Land Abraham ever owned. That story is as current as CNN Headline News for me. There is truth there we have yet to grasp. This shines a flickering hope into a future worth imagining.

A book I return to again and again is *Slavery, Sabbath, War, and Women* by Willard Swartley.[1] It provides an excellent example of how the dialogue model of interpretation can lead people to discover new understandings of biblical teachings which are evoking controversy in our time. Another book which has energized my study of the Bible is *The Prophetic Imagination* by Walter Brueggemann.[2] I remember buying it at a Society of Biblical Literature meeting and staying up all night reading and highlighting it. I was serving the Oak Park Mennonite Church in Chicago by this time, and Brueggemann's model clarified much that I had been experiencing.

Brueggemann has done a number of variations on this theme, using various labels, but essentially he sees two apparently contradictory trajectories of thought which sweep from the Old Testament to the New Testament, and into our own day. There is truth in both, which I need to remember when I encounter other paradoxes in the Bible. On the one hand we have what we might call the Purity Party, which takes seriously the call to be a Holy People, as we all should. It can lend itself to top-down hierarchy enforcing the old laws and trying to keep people in line by making more rules. It's very concerned about enforcing the boundaries—who's in, who's out. This was the mindset of the Pharisees ("pure ones") which Jesus was challenging with the parables of the Good Samaritan and the Prodigal Son.

On the other hand the Prophetic Party reinterprets the Law for new circumstances. It looks for the spirit, the intention of the Law to apply to new situations. That's why the Pharisees were outraged at all the rules Jesus broke, while Jesus claimed he was fulfilling the Law. The prophets see reaching out to the poor, the oppressed, and outsiders as doing God's holy work. It's what we see Jesus doing all the time.

In my experience, putting the Prophets and the Purists in the same room to duke it out has been less than helpful in changing minds—even if we call it dialogue. I know that "the word of God is . . . sharper than any two-edged sword" (Heb. 4:12), but I don't believe that it was ever intended to be used as a weapon against fellow believers. That verse from Hebrews speaks more to the experience of being pierced through by a command like "love your enemies" as I open myself to what that means to me as I deal with a very particular enemy.

I have found the Holy Spirit-guided community of faith vital in keeping me from going off the deep end with my own strange interpretations, but that doesn't mean we should take a vote to determine the correct understanding of a text. Prophets tend to be in the minority, especially in their own age. It may take centuries before their truth is vindicated, but then we realize it was true all along. At this stage of my life, I feel the need for more work on seeing the whole picture. Without some sort of regular attention to the great themes in the Bible and the contexts of our favorite verses, we concentrate on bits and pieces and remain ignorant of how they fit together, or challenge each other.

That's why I think the Prussian Union statement is helpful. I learned it from hearing so many General Conference Mennonites quoting it: "In essentials unity; in nonessentials liberty; in all things charity." But what are the essentials? Jesus and Paul agreed on the two commandments from Deuteronomy and Leviticus: "Love God with everything that's in you, and your neighbor as yourself." If we were to have a litmus test for who's in and who's out, wouldn't that be it? Can't most of us agree to focus on God's incredible love, peace based in justice, the life and ministry of Jesus, costly discipleship, and the church in mission? If we keep centered on these things, our differences over the nonessentials won't have power to divide us, especially if we maintain love "in all things."

So where am I now after sixty-some years of Bible study? I believe the Bible is the inspired word of God and the evidence of searching souls through the ages trying to make sense of the world and their place in it, of how to live with God and with people to whom we are called to be neighbors. In retirement I enjoy venturing into parts of the Bible I haven't studied before and always find something of interest. I hope to continue to learn new truths as long as I live. I turn to the Bible for inspiration and comfort, often with our hymnal as its companion. I also need the challenge of studying with others who are open to the Holy Spirit's surprises.

My walk with the Bible is what has led me to a Mennonite church where concern for justice is expressed in Victim Offender Mediation Programs and support of Ten Thousand Villages artisans from around the world. This is a church that doesn't only pray for peace but actively works at conflict transformation and supports Christian Peacemaker Teams as well as conscientious objectors to war. This is a church where people of all ages are coming and going from short- and long-term service projects in nearby cities and around the world. This is a church where Purists and Prophets labor together through Mennonite Disaster Service to do the dirty work of cleaning up following a natural disaster. The Bible is alive in the actions of our members. By the grace of God, we are able to live the good news that so many people need to hear.

Notes

1. Willard Swartley, *Slavery, Sabbath, War, and Women: Case Studies in Biblical Interpretation* (Scottdale, Pa.: Herald Press, 1983).

2. Walter Brueggemann, *The Prophetic Imagination* (Philadelphia: Fortress Press, 1978).

CHAPTER 15

Making Scripture Dance

Phil Kniss

My conscious journey with Scripture begins in St. Petersburg, Florida, one of the wealthiest and whitest retirement communities on the Gulf Coast. We worshiped, however, in a small Mennonite congregation located in the middle of an African-American community. With all good intentions, we referred to our church as the "colored mission."

My first memory related to Scripture was around age four, when I attended a Children's Bible Club in the all-white neighborhood where our family lived. There I memorized a whole Bible verse and proudly recited it to my big brother and other playmates. I have never forgotten it: "The heart is deceitful above all things, and desperately wicked: who can know it?" (Jer. 17:9 KJV). In my adulthood I have pondered how it was that the very first Bible verse I memorized honed in on my wicked and deceitful four-year-old heart, rather than on God's unlimited love for me. That verse is still one of only a handful that I can quote with chapter and verse.

Nevertheless, I have nothing but appreciation for the vigor with which my church community taught me the Scriptures. Tirelessly, my Sunday school and vacation Bible school teachers taught us stories and truths from the Bible, insisted that we work hard to memorize individual Scripture verses, and called us to name all the books of the Bible in order. One day, years later, I sat with several other Mennonite teenagers in an adult Sunday school class in a non-Mennonite church. We contributed a few short and simple comments. These adults were astounded at how much Bible knowledge we Mennonite boys displayed. It was the first time I realized that biblical literacy was not the norm for all Christians. I then became, and still am, deeply grateful for the rich gift of biblical knowledge my church gave me.

At the same time, I have since become aware that this Bible knowledge was quite limited in scope. Oh, I learned the many details of the Bible well. In Bible quizzes and "sword drills" I was nearly unbeatable. I majored in minutia. At age thirteen, I wrote on the inside front cover of my King James Bible, for easy access, the references of various verses, and their significance. Not only John 11:35, which we all know is the shortest verse in the Bible. But also Esther 8:9—the *longest* verse. And (get this!) Psalm 119:8—the *middle* verse. On the inside back cover, I started a list of strange Bible cities or places—Adaminekeb, Bethjeshimoth, Ham.

I also learned all the doctrinal affirmations *about* the Bible: it is inspired, it is the voice of God himself, it has no errors, it is literally true, it must be obeyed in every way, and it contains clear and ready answers to all of life's questions. One feature of my particular edition of the Bible was that in the appendix was a list of all kinds of life situations and which Bible verse I should turn to in each situation. "When you are afraid, read Isaiah 41:5-13. When you are depressed, read Ephesians 3:14-21. When you are experiencing peer pressure, read Proverbs 1:7-19. When you start a new job, etc., etc." It had all the bases covered, which I appreciated as an adolescent with lots of emotional ups and downs. I turned to these "answer" verses in much the same way I now look for a pill in the medicine cabinet when something ails me.

Another dimension of Bible reading opened up to me when the *Living Bible* paraphrase was first released in a New Testament-only special youth-oriented edition called *The Way*. Not only did the text read more easily and naturally, but each book had an interesting introduction written up with a modern photo illustrating the theme of the book. During long sermons, we teenage boys especially enjoyed studying the introduction to the book of 1 Peter, which featured a photo of a beautiful young woman with an alluring smile, wearing a white knit sweater. Ah! Until then, we had no idea we could find those kinds of pleasures *in the Bible!* Seriously, though, the arrival of the Living Bible made it possible to actually read large portions of the Bible, understand it, and enjoy it. That was a good thing.

At age twenty-one, newly married, I pulled away from the spiritual bosom of family, church, and Sunday school. I began to drink from the streams of Mennonite academics. I took all the Bible courses I could, and a whole new world opened up to me. I learned that the Bible not only contained stories—it *was* a story. My natural love of history whetted my appetite for learning more about the story behind the stories. I was fascinated with the very human world that shaped how the Scriptures were formed and transmitted to us.

At the same time, my love of the arts opened up the aesthetic side of the Scriptures—the sheer beauty of the language, the drama, even the humor. The fact that these writings were first an oral tradition helped me see how the Scriptures might live anew in the telling of them. I discovered, quite by accident, a whole new way to memorize Scripture. In my Old Testament survey class at Eastern Mennonite University (EMU), I jumped at the chance to do an alternate term project and memorized the first four chapters of Genesis. I recited those chapters to the class—including the "begats" — with a theatrical flair all my own. At that moment I realized I had found a new door through which I could enter the world of the Bible.

However, the sturdy framework my church gave me for understanding the Bible began to tremble. Was this book as God-breathed as I had been told and had come to believe? Was all of it true? Could I still bank my life on it? When we examined the human dimension of Scripture—the oral traditions, culture, and literary practices of the times—some of the supernatural acts of God revealed in the Bible were easily given other explanations. I allowed myself to wonder where this logic might lead. Perhaps, I hoped, it was only parts of the Old Testament that were historically suspect. Certainly I could trust completely in the deeds and sayings of Jesus recorded in the Gospels. But then I discovered that some sincere Christian scholars had other ways of talking about Jesus, about how the Gospels were formed from multiple traditions and shaped by the experience of the early church.

On the one hand, I found myself rejoicing in the rich new insights about the origins of Scripture and the culture that gave them birth, and how those insights added to my appreciation of the Scripture. On the other hand, I was slightly unnerved by the level of skepticism I had allowed to enter my thinking process. Was this way of reading the Bible compatible with a vibrant, personal, and growing faith? For quite a few years I wrestled with these polarities—and to some extent, I still do. After finishing my undergraduate studies at EMU and taking a smidgeon of seminary training, I became pastor at the tender age of twenty-four. In my sermons, and in discussions with other church members, every now and then I pulled out some historical-critical piece of information from my EMU Bible courses that I had found meaningful, and I discovered it totally failed to connect.

What was I, as a Mennonite pastor, to do with this way I was reading the Scriptures? Was I supposed to keep my measure of skepticism (which I considered healthy) purely to myself, as a dark secret, lest my parishioners question my faith and stop listening to my sermons? Should I publicly preach about Adam and Eve as if they were actual historical characters or about the parting of the Red Sea as if the wind literally cut a dry path through the deep water? Could I honestly do this, while in my private thoughts, I contemplated that *Adam* is a generic Hebrew word for humanity, that the exodus stories were likely a compilation of various oral traditions not actually written down until long after Moses' death? I resolved this by telling myself that ultimately, the only important thing is what these Scriptures tell us about God—not whether they meet a modern scientific standard of historical reliability. So in my public preaching, I have for the most part ignored the critical questions and simply preached the story as presented.

Now, as a seminary graduate and experienced pastor, I have made peace (mostly) with my approach to reading, interpreting, and preaching Scripture. I read it first as narrative. To me, the whole canon of Scripture is a narrative of God's love and longing for humanity and all creation, and of humanity's bumbling attempts to respond to God's initiative. The bottom line is the good news that God never gives up on us—*never!* I can easily find myself all through the pages of Scripture, Old and New Testament. I am Moses, who is afraid to take a risk in leadership. I am Elijah, who God uses despite my struggles with self-doubt and occasional despair. I am Martha, who would rather stay busy working than sit still and listen. I am a member of the church at Corinth, who needs Paul to remind me to act like a servant to those I have trouble getting along with. And God still loves me and pursues me!

I say I have *mostly* made peace with this narrative approach, because I have not let go completely of a more didactic, prescriptive, and doctrinal way of reading Scripture. I am still a product of the church of my childhood, and I do not disparage that. Yes, that approach was incomplete. And yes, I am grateful for the broader horizons I now enjoy. But it did provide me a firm foundation to build on. Since then, I have dismantled some of the structure, but the foundation remains. I have a deep belief instilled in me that the Scriptures can be wholly trusted, that they are worthy of the authority granted them by the church. I can still say without hesitation that I want my life to be shaped by the Scriptures, not the other way around.

If I had *begun* my journey with Scripture by simply seeing it as a wonderful story that I could learn from, identify with, and be inspired by, I wonder whether I would still be so willing to grant this kind of personal authority to the Scriptures. I have benefited immeasurably from my conservative upbringing, as well as from my freedom to depart from it.

I have recently adopted a new metaphor for my spiritual life, and I think it applies equally well to my journey with Scripture. I want my life with God to dance. I also want my journey with Scripture to be a dance, not a plodding path from point A to point B. Maybe because of my Mennonite upbringing, maybe because of my personality, I have this inhibition about dancing, about simply letting go, and letting the music fill me and move me. I was taught by my family and my church to walk straight—in life as well as in biblical interpretation. It was always emphasized how important it was to know where and how to step. I needed to be diligent in watching my feet, making sure I put my right foot precisely where it must be, followed immediately by the careful placement of my left foot. And on and on I went, persistently plodding forward in a straight line.

Much later, I learned to dance with Scripture. Beginning with my dramatic recitation of Genesis in an EMU Bible class, I began to let the Scripture get into me in new refreshing ways, which I could then express not only with my mind but also with my emotions and my body. My dance with Scripture continues to be immensely freeing for me.

But if a dancer in training learned *only* how to let the music get inside them and how to let it move their bodies, it would not be enough to make them truly great dancers. They also need to put in the grueling hours of classroom instruction and practice. They have to do their stretching exercises. They have to learn precisely how to place their feet, position their arms, hold their heads, and turn in just the right way.

Once they have mastered the fundamentals, they can then be free to let the music within them decide how to express itself in dance.

I am grateful to the Mennonite church of my childhood for teaching me the right steps, for showing me the necessary disciplines. And I am grateful to modern scholarship for giving me the freedom to depart from those traditional steps and maneuvers. But ultimately my journey with Scripture is not to get safely from point A to point B. I want to make the Scriptures dance, to communicate with both power and passion, so that all persons, from the oldest to youngest, are filled to overflowing with the realization that they are loved by God. And to make sure no child ever memorizes Jeremiah 17:9 before John 3:16.

CHAPTER 16

Receiving, Researching, and Revisiting Scripture

James R. Krabill

My journey with Scripture has taken me through three rather distinct phases of my life: *the early years* (1951-1971), when I more or less received the Scripture; *the academic years* (1971-1976), when I found myself in upper level college and seminary programs researching Scripture; and *the international, cross-cultural years* (1976-1996), when my assignment with Mennonite Board of Missions in Europe and Africa forced me to revisit Scripture with the help of sisters and brothers whose different cultural filters offered new and fresh insights to my Western and largely sectarian understandings.

Receiving the Scripture (1951-1971)

Scripture was so central, so much a given in my early years that I can't imagine what life would have been like without it. Food, family, sleep, school, play, church, Bible—these were the inseparable components of daily childhood life growing up at 409 Middlebury Street, North Goshen, Indiana. As I think back on those years, three influences come immediately to mind as playing particularly significant roles in shaping my early experience with the Bible: Russell Krabill, my pastor-father; Harvey and Prudence Birky and their "Bible Memory Program"; and a third character, less obvious but no less important, King James I of England.

I recently saw a car with a bright and bold bumper sticker: "Angry? Need a weapon? Pray the Rosary!" For my father, that would have been, "Read the Scripture!" The Bible was at the center of my father's life. He led family devotions each morning; went to bed each night reading the Bible until sleep overtook him; memorized large portions of Scripture (most notably the Sermon on the Mount, which he has recited in public on numerous occasions). He taught Bible in local northern Indiana public high schools and sold Bibles as a part-time job in college plus later as Goshen's Gospel Bookstore manager. He prepared at least two sermons weekly for seventeen years at the North Goshen Mennonite Church and one sermon weekly for another twenty-three years at Prairie Street and Holdeman Mennonite churches. In addition, he held several annual series of one- or two-week meetings in various Mennonite communities across the country for all of my growing-up years. For the past fifty years, he has either read the entire Bible or listened to it on cassette at least once annually.

My father speaks in King James. Biblical characters are his friends and mentors, not people to deconstruct, dissect, or analyze. I'm sure he knows more about biblical life and times than about any living culture in our world today. My father regularly reads the Bible—but more importantly, he lets the Bible read him. He takes its counsel with utmost seriousness and is constantly seeking ways to apply its meaning to his own life and to the life of God's people. The Bible is not a tyrannical rulebook; it is life and breath, the way God wants us to live because it is best for us and for our world.

Not surprisingly, my father has always been troubled by people who treat the Bible lightly or who throw it off as archaic, outdated, chauvinistic, or unhelpful for issues facing the church in our time. He is equally concerned about those who seem to be deliberately looking for flaws and contradictions in the biblical content, who study it "like any other book," or who construct theories *about* the Bible which take on a life of their own and ultimately become more important than the biblical text itself. He understands "higher criticism" but is suspicious of it. Critical methods, he would say, come and go, "but the Word of our God shall stand forever."

I lived for twenty years in my parents' home, attending churches where my father served as pastor throughout all of those years. During that time, I would guess I sat through at least 1,500 of his sermons and participated in 5,400 morning devotions over which he presided. Throughout the years, we have had many debates about Scripture around the dinner table and often late into the night. Needless to say, the two of us have not always seen eye to eye. But my father's deep love and respect for God's written Word has become my own. His daily determination at age eighty-five to let it "speak a word into his life" continues to be a constant challenge and inspiration for me.

Harvey and Prudence Birky were a Mennonite couple living in our community who had a passion for the Bible. In the 1950s they developed a regional ministry focused on Scripture memorization designed to encourage local Mennonite children and youth to take the Bible seriously in their daily lives. The centerpiece of their ministry was Bible Memory Camp, a weeklong camping experience spread out over a several-week period each summer to accommodate different age groups, ranging from elementary through high school.

To qualify as a first-time camper, each participant was required to memorize 300 Bible verses—carefully selected and compiled in a handy little booklet—and recite them to designated monitors scattered throughout the various participating congregations in the Great Lakes area. In the second year, fewer verses were required, but Bible correspondence courses were added. They were mailed to individual campers during the school year, personally corrected by Harvey and Prudence, and returned to participants to monitor progress being made in learning about God's Word.

The camp experience itself, held on the site that has today become Amigo Centre in southern Michigan, was always the highlight of my summer. It involved meeting friends from a three-state area, learning arts and crafts, swimming in the lake, worshiping outside under a big tent. We listened to resident missionaries—the only regular resource people—tell stories from far away lands. We woke up each morning to George Beverly Shea's loudspeaker-projected gospel music. We were taught how to cultivate the rudimentary disciplines of personal and group Bible study. The message communicated clearly to participants in this program was not only that the Bible was to be taken seriously but also that the church, through its active sponsorship of the program, was giving this highest priority for its children and youth.

All of the early exposure I had to Scripture came in the form of seventeenth-century English poetry. There was only one Bible, the King

James Version (KJV), not the fifty translations, paraphrases, and denim-covered hip versions that the church has managed to concoct in the last half-century. The disadvantage of the KJV was, of course, that you didn't always understand what it said, but it *felt* like you did—or at least you were convinced the preachers and deacons did—and, at one level, that may have been all that mattered.

I remember my great fascination with and attraction to the newly emerging "contemporary" versions of the Bible in the 1960s—versions that spoke the language of my generation and connected me in a new way to the ancient story. But even as I look back with appreciation on all the tools and resources that have been created and are now available for more fully understanding the Bible, I am equally convinced that something's been lost.

It was soon after I bought my first other-than-KJV translation that I stopped memorizing Scripture. It got too complicated and somehow didn't seem as important or necessary. Enter also at this time the "translation/paraphrase wars," which resulted in much more energy being spent on discussing what someone did to the text than what relevance the text might actually have to one's daily life. This was the beginning of a growing suspicion among many that anyone can do *anything* to the text and that we don't really know what the text says or means anyway. Consequently, we came to think we needed specialists to help us read and understand the text, but this might not really help much at the end of the day because the specialists themselves didn't agree on what's being said.

In some ways, it is harder to "receive" Scripture today than it was in my childhood—just like it can be more challenging to get news with hundreds of cable channels at our disposal than it was when we only had three network channels. I am quite grateful for contemporary versions of the Bible. They have aided my own study and assisted me in teaching Scripture to students whose minimal educational background would have made it virtually impossible for them to access the KJV—however poetic the "original text" might be. I am also aware, however, that more is not always better and that the recent diffusion of focus has not always served us well in keeping Scripture central to our faith and life as God's people.

Researching the Scripture (1971-1976)

For five years—as an upper level student of Bible, Religion, and Philosophy at Goshen College and in the M. Div. program at Associated Mennonite Biblical Seminary—I gave almost my entire energy to the scholarly disciplines of studying Scripture. It was a wonderfully rich period of my life, getting beneath the text to the original languages and the authors' oral and written sources and behind the text to the socio-politico-cultural and religious contexts in which the biblical story was played out. I found answers to questions I had been asking for many years and discovered questions to answers I had never seriously thought about.

Five principal mentors played significant roles for me as Bible professors during this period. Each contributed out of their own unique personalities, particular interests and areas of expertise to my "journey with Scripture" during this phase of my life. I can only highlight with a few descriptive phrases what some of those invaluable contributions were:

Stanley Shenk—joyful, inductive approach to the Bible as literature;

Millard Lind—comparative Mid-Eastern politico-religious cosmologies as the backdrop to Israel's life with Yahweh as Warrior;

Jacob Enz—prayerful integration of the Old and New Testaments;

Howard Charles—meditative scholarship insisting that any serious preacher of the Word should spend one hour in study and research for every minute preached;

Clarence Bauman—mystical ethicist/ethical mystic; Sermon on the Mount guru.

At the time of my studies, I thought of these five individuals as being quite different from one another in style, approach, and focus. And in many ways, as I indicate above, that was in fact the case. But later, when I moved more fully into the third phase of my life, i.e., the international, cross-cultural years, it became increasingly evident that these early mentors actually held in common far more similarities than differences between them. They were, after all, for the most part—

- older, nearly retired from life-long careers;
- experienced in pastoral ministry before accepting assignments as professors;
- white male;

- Mennonite (although two of them pushed my Mennonite Church "ecumenical" limits by being General Conference Mennonite and Mennonite Brethren);
- in primary dialog with American, British, and German mainline Protestant scholarship;
- "specialists" in particular fields of research (as in "I did most of my study in Old Testament and don't feel well-versed enough in New Testament scholarship to really answer your question");
- text-driven, shaped by the world of books, and trained to train others in treating the Bible as a written document to be dissected by use of literary questions, tools, and methods.

Revisiting the Scripture (1976-1996)

These common characteristics became more obvious in autumn 1976, when my wife Jeanette and I left American shores, first for a two-year language and orientation stint in France, then for Africa, where we lived and worked for most of the next eighteen years. Here we were to discover new lenses for reading, hearing, interpreting, and applying Scripture. Among the most important to shape us were—

- the world of *francophone* and multiple African languages and dialects;
- the many important theological and biblical resources produced by French scholars;
- perspectives on Scripture from our primary dialogue partners within the local Christian family: Roman Catholics, Evangelicals, Pentecostals, and grassroots indigenous church movements;
- the encounter with Islam;
- the African traditional worldview, life, and culture;
- widespread illiteracy;
- the reality of regarding books and paper as fetish and magic;
- the richness of orality in the form of proverbs, fables, songs, and liturgy;
- the role of women in hymn composition, in teaching, praying, and prophesying.

Four short stories, all occurring within the first year of our move to the village of Yocoboue, Ivory Coast, in 1982, perhaps best illustrate the very different reality we were to encounter in this part of God's world:

Story 1: On my third day as a Bible teacher in Yocoboue an elderly gentleman raised his hand and said, "Okay, I have a question for you. There is something I have never understood about the Lord's Supper. Here we live daily with the reality of witches who exist only because they drink the blood and eat the flesh of other family members they wish to destroy. So now we say that Jesus is our best friend. Why is it, then, that we would want to harm or kill this good friend of ours by drinking his blood and eating his flesh?"

Story 2: To introduce the life and ministry of Jesus, I adopted the practice of reading through one of the Gospels with my students. I remember the day we got to Luke 22. Jesus sends out a delegation to prepare for the Passover with these words, "As you go into the city, a man carrying a jar of water. . . ." At that point the students broke into leg-slapping laughter which continued unabated until I finally asked, "So . . . what's so funny about that?"

"Carrying water?" they looked at me incredulously. "That's *women's* work! There must have been only *one* guy in town who'd be doing that. Jesus sure was pretty clever, wasn't he?"

Story 3: The elderly head preacher, N'Guessan Benoit, who first invited us to Yocoboue, had already been preaching for almost three decades when we arrived in 1982. Amazingly, Benoit had no formal schooling and could understand but a small percentage of the nineteenth-century archaic French-language Bible he carried with him each week into the pulpit. Wycliffe Bible translators had just arrived in the village at about the same time we did and had done little more than manage to establish the alphabet in the local Dida language, so the old French *Louis Segond* version was all that Benoit had. How, then, did this preacher manage to prepare sermons all those many years and carry out his ministry of counseling the flock?

At the beginning of each week, Benoit would call into his courtyard a young elementary school lad, hand him his Bible, and tell him to pick a passage. Then Benoit would say, "Now, read it to me." The young lad, himself with only a few years of French-language instruction, would do his best to bumble through. "Now, tell me what it means."

At this point, the young boy would attempt to take what he understood of the text and translate it into the Dida language—the medium Benoit would be using on Sunday morning to transmit God's Word to the faithful.

This was in 1982. Today, twenty years later, Benoit is *still* head preacher in Yocoboue, still preaching as he has for almost half a century.

Story 4: The church we attended in Yocoboue composed all of its own music. It literally sang *nothing* imported from the outside. Most of the hymns, particularly the earliest ones dating back to the early 1900s, were written by women and transmitted orally over the years from one generation to the next. The church possessed no hymnbook; everything was stored away in the head and heart and brought forth when needed during one of the seven weekly worship services.

On our first Easter Sunday in the village, an elderly woman stood up during the service and began to sing. Music in this church is done antiphonally, with the leader lining the song as the congregation repeats what they hear in echo-style response. Most songs during worship are three to five minutes long. But this one went on for twenty minutes before the woman finally finished and sat down.

My curiosity got the best of me, and I asked at the end of the service, "So . . . what was *that* all about?"

"Oh, that was the story of Christ's last week on earth, beginning with the Triumphal Entry and moving through the Last Supper, death, resurrection, and on into the Thomas story where Jesus says, 'Blessed are those who never see yet believe.' The song ends by asking the congregation, "You are among those who have never seen. Do you *believe?*"

I was eventually able to transcribe the full text of this song—along with over 500 other hymns composed by this village congregation. The "Easter Song," Christ's passion set to music, turned out to be the longest one of all, a full 108 lines of text.

One can't have such repeated encounters with Scripture and remain unaffected. Within weeks after my arrival in Yocoboue, I knew I would need to revisit the whole Bible, asking, "What would it mean to be reading this age-old text through *African* eyes? What would I see that I have, up until now, totally overlooked? What questions would I bring to the text? What answers would I be looking for? What parallels would I find between biblical thought and culture and my own? And where would I feel the most challenged and disconnected?"

I learned so much from this discipline that it is difficult to know where to start. I recently went back over the forty-some "American Abroad" columns my wife and I wrote for *Festival Quarterly* during these years, and I was fascinated to discover that at least half grappled with

Scripture-related themes and issues. It would require a paper on each of these topics and more to fully describe all of the ways Africa shaped my journey with Scripture during this twenty-year period of my life:

TITLE	THEME/ISSUE
"On Reading a Gothic Harlot"	Visual images in telling the biblical story
"Tossed Salad from a Distance"	God's people as alternative community
"Jesus Who?"	White-skinned Jesus in black-skinned Africa
"Worthy is the Pig That Was Slain"	Dynamic equivalence in Bible translation
"Don't Tell Me the Old, Old Story"	Bible competing with TV in village context
"The Early (African) Church"	Connections between Africa and the N.T.
"Ahmed and (Big) Ben"	Concept of time in Bible, Africa, West
"On Taking Nothing But a Stick (or Two)"	Missionary lifestyle from Luke 10
"Bark, the Herald Angels Sing"	Christmas story in Africa
"Power to the Paper"	Magical powers of paper in non-literate society
"To Put It In Other Words"	Comparing African and biblical proverbs
"Jacob, Why Did You Do This To Us?"	Death, funeral rituals
"The Resurrection According to Matthew"	Celebrating Easter African-style
"The Church of Your Choice"	Translating "church" in African languages
"On Witches, Laundry Soap and Loving Jesus"	Jesus and the spirits in traditional worldview
"And the Three … Shall Be One"	Christian marriage and polygamy
"Too Much of Not Enough"	Understanding death, funeral practices
"Spiritual Lessons from the Bat's Bottom"	Narrative theology from African fables
"New Light on African-Amish Relations"	Simple lifestyle, appropriate technology
"A Creepy Thanksgiving at St. George's"	Slavery
"Baptism by (Re) Immersion"	Baptism and witchcraft

So . . . What About Phase Four (1996-)?

In summer 1996, we moved back to North America as a family. Since then, we have been trying to get catch up with all that has happened in our absence. Some of my own itinerary during this time has been working to integrate what I've learned about Scripture from each of the three previous chapters of my life:

- *receiving:* simple love of Scripture, heart-felt desire to know and obey more;
- *researching:* digging *beneath* and *behind* the Scripture, asking the hard questions;
- *revisiting:* looking at Scripture through new lenses, widening the hermeneutical circle.

I have been helped in this process by the "cage/helium balloon/kite" analogy some have used to describe the human quest for Truth in its broader dimensions, applied here to my journey with Scripture. Each of the three images has at times applied to my situation:

- *the cage:* Where my understandings were safely secured behind locked doors, with little chance for exposure and change from outside influences.
- *the helium balloon:* When I was tempted to cut ties with all constraints and simply let the wind carry me wherever it wished;
- *the kite:* Where I recognize that the only way I will fly and move freely about in God's world is if I remain "grounded" in this remarkable Book, unlike any other, through which God has chosen to pass along to past generations, and now to me and to my world, the most incredible, life-transforming story of all time.

CHAPTER 17

True Stories

Susan Mark Landis

Beginning

I search my past for memories of the Bible as I begin this reflection. Hard as I try, I can't conjure up that first impression I desire—an idealized Norman Rockwell image of our family gathered around an open Bible having animated conversation. I can't even find a memory of us kids listening to Mom read Bible stories. I know she read to us often from *Coals of Fire* and *Martyr's Mirror* (leading me to assume that if I truly followed Christ, I'd be dead by the age of thirty). But I find no mental snapshots of listening to the Bible as a young child.

Oh, I do remember attempts at family devotions. The only time we all seemed to be together was supper, so my mom would put all the hot, tantalizing food on the table in front of a hungry family, then proceed with the evening's devotions. In a home where serving food at the wrong temperature didn't meet expected high culinary standards, this idea didn't last long. The guilt Mom felt because we didn't have family devotions did last.

My first childhood image that repeatedly comes to mind is putting a star sticker on the Bible school memory sheet. Although my parents didn't support Bible memory camp, this every-year task taught me that memorizing Scripture for future answers in difficult situations mattered considerably to God. One of these important passages I learned from my paternal grandmother—a Methodist and a woman quite different from any covering-wearer in the Mennonite church—spoke to how we kids got along. She didn't visit often, but when we quarreled while she was there, we could guarantee we'd soon hear her exclaiming, "Love one another, love one another! This is the happy way, Love one another!" When we visited our grandmother's church, after the service she'd always ask if we could hear her singing in the choir.

I grew up at Prairie Street Mennonite Church in Elkhart, Indiana. I remember the sermons as far-ranging in content and strict in tone. The Bible had answers to all questions, and clearly God did not allow drinking, dancing, or short skirts. Knowing that many of my peers, my parents, and their friends did these things caused me turmoil and self-righteousness.

Yet amid this I was a deeply devoted Christian who believed strongly in the power of prayer and felt God moving in my life. I did not have the strongly negative finger-wagging feeling for the Bible many of my peers from other congregations had. I read the Bible myself, wrote poems and songs about my relationship to God, and led Mennonite Youth Fellowship (MYF) Bible studies. On the one hand, I thought reading the Bible would tell me exactly what God wanted me to do, if I could just find the proper part to read. On the other, I thought only goodie-goodie types (I most assuredly was not one) spent time reading the Bible. More intellectual types already knew what the Bible said and spent time reading biblical scholarship and critique. Thus my Scripture study was variously motivated by guilt, classroom or Sunday school assignments, and inner stirrings.

Education

I easily recall images of my Sunday and Bible school classes; I learned my lessons well. Simple, hour-long sessions with easy lessons and moral underpinnings sought to keep me out of hell. Oh, I certainly got whiffs of other ways to look at the Bible as I sat at the feet of John Howard Yoder, a member of our congregation, and heard visiting preachers from the seminary, such as J. C. Wenger. From them I learned the wonders of seeing the Bible as an integrated whole, a history of God's love for humans, the story of people stumbling in their search for God.

During my junior year I transferred to Bethany Christian High School in Goshen, Indiana, and had Ray Gingerich as my Bible teacher.

Not only did the Bible become an academic subject, it also became a radical instrument for revolution as I took to heart the shouts for justice of minor prophets of the Old Testament and their modern disciples, the Berrigan brothers. I began to see biblical scholarship as a way to make sense of the injustice of the world and to learn how to live. A new world of discipleship opened.

My love of words and the desire to share that love led me to graduate from Goshen College with a literature major and high school teaching diploma. My critical reading of the tales of the world led me to believe that storytelling is not an accident but carefully planned and rehearsed. Either the storyteller believes the community needs to hear a particular tale told a particular way, or the teller personally feels the need to say something. Stories are carefully crafted with goals in mind. The Bible became the literature of my people, my God, my beliefs.

My thrill with the dance of words and wit led me to want to teach others. My education courses taught me about high schoolers, but the more important understandings were the stages of learning and moral development.

During my seminary education at Associated Mennonite Biblical Seminary, Jake Elias opened the world of biblical scholarship to me as we learned how small pericopes make up our Bible chapters. Although some people were aghast at the idea that God might not have dictated directly to Scripture writers, I was intrigued by this surprising complexity. As I understand it, this method of criticism examines each phrase in a thematic section of verses, tracing its origin historically, ethnically, and so on. Thus we might find that a saying we attribute to Jesus was a common proverb of the day.

This concept delightfully deepened my understanding of the writing of the Bible, making it more human and accessible. I wanted to delve into each writer's mind, wonder why such a line was chosen here and another left out there. The Bible changed from a staid moral story to a carefully crafted gift to a community. Not only did I want to know why a particular writer might have chosen words for the historically intended community, but I also wanted to study how a passage has spoken to people through the ages. What is it about this group of stories and instructions that has stayed persistently inspiring, surprising, and foundational?

After we had carefully dissected one passage and I was brimming with excitement, a fellow student raised questions at lunch. "Jake, if I tell my congregation all this in a sermon, I'll lose them. They don't want to know where the thoughts come from; they just want practical ideas for living."

Hearing Jake's well-rehearsed analogy, I realized this was a common question from future preachers. "When you prepare a meal for guests, you bring carefully adorned dishes to the table. You leave the mess, the garbage, and the dirty dishes in the kitchen. They are all necessary in the creation process, but they don't belong in the final presentation."

I can easily say that God has spoken directly to me, but I only remember that happening once during Bible study. I was on silent retreat for three days with some Catholic women at Camp Luz, the Ohio Conference camp in Kidron, Ohio. As a mother with young children who did volunteer peace education, I came to the experience with my mind going a mile a minute. I spent the first day just calming down so I could listen to the silence. One of our last exercises was to read Scripture as though it were a love letter written to us from God. I was given Isaiah 43:1-7. I read the passage over and over. As I was lulled by the reassuring words, God said, "Take this passage with you when you go on a Christian Peacemaker Team (CPT) trip." Since I had always assumed that sometime years in the future I would go on a short CPT delegation, I tucked this away for far future reference. Two days later members of my congregation called and asked me to go to Haiti in two weeks with CPT as a representative of the congregation. The Bible *is* God's living voice!

Madeleine L'Engle is one of my favorite authors. She stretched my childish imagination and my adult devotional life. One time when she spoke at Goshen College, I took my kids out of school. We drove the five hours to hear her that evening, then went back the next day. The comment I best remembered was her take on the Old Testament. Too often I've found this part of the Bible boring and difficult, but Madeleine delights in retelling these stories. She described them as a "series of white-bearded old men saying to God, 'You want me to do *what?*'" I realized anew what strange, miraculous stories I had come to take for granted.

Crises: When Experience and Bible Just Don't Jibe

People learn best different ways—some by study, some by hearing, some by story; I often learn from experience. When I feel something is right in my gut, I set about to understand it in my mind. Thus, my crises with the Bible came about when I couldn't harmonize what I read with what my gut felt to be right. (Quite likely, of course, my gut has been well-informed by Bible study, sermons, and readings.)

I had two times of crisis in high school. For some reason, my MYF chose to study Corinthians two years in a row; even odder, both years I ended up reading aloud the verses about a woman's long hair being her glory. The second time I looked up from the Bible, laughed as I pointed at my short hair, and said, "Why do I always get stuck with these verses?" My understanding was that this concept was for the historical community Paul wrote to, and not to me at all. But a male friend sitting next to me leaned over and said seriously, "Maybe God wants you to pay attention to these verses." This was 1974, long before I considered a career that included preaching, but it was certainly a harbinger of hurdles to come: the balancing of gut feelings about who I am in God's eyes, and an interpretation of Bible passages that said my gut wasn't God-inspired.

Even as a high schooler, I was too young to understand why the biblically based baptism of the Holy Spirit divided congregations and families. I was horrified, however, when I realized that some friends of mine, whose mother was dying of cancer, told her that if she would just confess her sins, she would be healed. I read the Bible carefully, trying to understand why I didn't have the gift of tongues, whether I could still be a real Christian, and why the Spirit was tearing our churches apart.

My biggest biblical crisis comes when I see the church's biblical interpretation hurting those whose love of God and church are deep by not allowing such people to use their gifts from God. At these times, the biblical sleuthing of understanding how and why passages were written and for whom is no longer intrigue but a despairing cry of *Why?*

The Bible and Me Today

In my adult life, two Bible stories have undergirded me. The first is the story of David. Contrary to my childish beliefs about the goody-two-shoes images of Bible heroes, David is about as fallen a hero as exists. He commits the really big sins—murder, adultery—yet some Bible writers claim he is still the man closest to God's heart. Here I find more grace than I can understand, the surety that no matter how I disappoint, I can remain close to God.

The second is the story of Christ's resurrection. In my work, currently as Peace Advocate, I hear despairing tales daily. I was so frustrated when Israel went to war with Palestine one spring that I went to the woman who cuts my hair and said, "I can't change the Israel/Palestine situation, but I can change my hair. Do something!" Some people wear sackcloth; my hair got shorter. Especially in times like these, I hold tightly to the resurrection story, the wonder of the light shining in the darkness—knowing by gut and by story that the darkness shall never overcome the light. It's good to remember some of the crazy things prophets did as they came to terms with the despairing events of their day and know that I am not alone.

My Work

My job as Peace Advocate is biblically based. A large part of my work is to help our congregations understand that my agenda is not motivated by politics but by my understanding of God, the teachings of Jesus, and the movement of the Holy Spirit.

As I teach and preach God's peace and justice as found in the Bible, I need to discern where people are in their ability to deal with moral dilemmas and unanswerable questions. Most likely, if I approach people far beyond their moral-understanding comfort zone, I will scare them. Their fear will cause them to firmly stand where they are, and I will have lost an opportunity to invite them to go beyond their current understandings of God or the Bible. I sincerely believe that the ability to deepen one's understanding about the Bible has as much to do with one's stage of learning and willingness to risk not getting an easy answer as it does with education and intelligence.

I'm torn about Jake Elias's dinner preparation answer from my seminary days. On the one hand, the analogy is perfect. I've learned to not want to see restaurant kitchens. On the other hand, the members of many of our congregations are intelligent and knowledgeable about many fields beyond their regular jobs. People with no medical training take part in their own health-care; we surf the Internet to find answers to a multitude of questions; we read the best-selling books on psychology to better our relationships. In other words, in many areas of life and learning, we know the dirty dishes of preparation.

But amid this highly educated community, many adults are stuck with a child's Sunday school understanding of the Bible. They want to be told what the Bible says and how they are to live. This eliminates the "aha" moments of learning; it is the difference between dogma and story. Story is full of paradox, of surprises, of gaps, but it gives the assurance of a direction and a hope and encourages us to rely on the Spirit for discernment.

I wonder whether we've been doing a disservice to our people by showing them only the carefully created meal/sermon and not encouraging them to delve into thoughtful biblical scholarship. Why is biblical scholarship ungodly and scary to our people? We've all heard it: "Well, if you have to go back to the Greek, there's something wrong with your interpretation!" Have we been overly protective?

True Stories

I titled these thoughts "True Stories." When I educate for peace and justice, I tell many stories. I figure that when people are faced with a violent situation, they won't remember the three points of my sermon, but they might remember a story I've told. I've discovered that if I tell the stories well, people don't mind too much if the sermon runs a bit long.

I often tell about an experience Lynn Miller, a stewardship educator, had. I preface it by saying, "This is Lynn's story, but he has given me permission to tell it to you. Sometimes Lynn tells it one way, sometimes another, and I tell it yet a third way. That makes what you're going to hear a true story."

I delight in the Bible, the truest of stories, the unlikeliest of tales. May God have the glory.

CHAPTER 18

From Generation to Generation

Cynthia A. Lapp

M y story begins with my family name. I am a Lapp. I am also a Nyce, a Ruth, a Swartzentruber, a Yoder, and a Stutzman. As I read Scripture and interact with the body of Christ, I act out of family that has been Anabaptist since coming from Europe in the eighteenth century. I am firmly rooted as a postmodern Mennonite in the twenty-first century United States.

From my father's family, the Lapps, I gain a strong appreciation for education and for Scripture as an art form. I think especially of my grandfather, Bishop John E. Lapp, who began doing *Fraktur* at age seventy. I have learned to see the Bible as a strong foundation for peace. My grandmother, Edith Nyce Lapp, memorized the Sermon on the Mount for her baptism as a teenager. From the Lapps I know that the voice of the community is where God's voice is found. I have learned one ought not to rock the Mennonite boat lest you get thrown overboard.

I observed the Swartzentrubers, my mother's family, reading Scripture at meals and during long sleepless nights, memorizing Bible verses and sharing them in long handwritten letters. I watched as my grandparents, Ernest and Fannie, found a passage in the Bible for every occasion. I learned that one holds fast to one's understanding of the text even when that might be contrary to what the church teaches.

My mother, Nancy, was a Mennonite feminist maybe before anyone thought there could be such a thing. She instilled in me a healthy dose of skepticism for the way the institutional church sometimes understands Scripture. She inherited the skepticism from her mother Fannie.

Fannie was born Amish but her skeptical family became Mennonite when she was six. My mother, Nancy, saw her mother, Fannie, argue with the church in Virginia in 1940 when it said that whites and African-Americans could not share communion, the holy kiss, or wash feet together. As a child I saw my mother argue with the church in Pennsylvania and Oregon over pianos and other instruments in the church, or about things such as women cutting their hair and removing their head coverings, about divorce and remarriage, and about women preaching or being ordained.

My own interaction with the Bible started at home and at Perkasie Mennonite Church in eastern Pennsylvania. As a fifth grader I proudly recited Psalm 23, without prompting, when I received my Gideon Bible in public school in Albany, Oregon. As a public high school student, I dabbled in a Bible study with fundamentalist students on Wednesday evenings and prayed on campus with them before school in the morning.

As a preacher's daughter and granddaughter, I knew the Bible stories from Sunday school and Bible school. I heard more than my share of sermons. Most are forgotten, though I still remember a snippet from one sermon I heard as a teenager. My father preached on Jeremiah 32. God instructed Jeremiah to buy a field in hope that there would be a future for Israel. This was during the Cold War, and I had my own doubts about the future. I was certain the world would end in nuclear winter before I finished college. God's words to Jeremiah connected with my adolescent faith and the story continues to feed me.

Despite this "preacherly" pedigree, in many ways I was biblically illiterate. I had little understanding of where biblical stories come from or why. I had no understanding of the Hebrew Scriptures as a separate text for the Jewish faith. I had not learned about the historical, cultural, or literary context of different Scripture passages. I knew nothing of the Apocrypha. I'm not sure I even understood that the Bible wasn't first written in the King's English. I did hear talk that there might be discrepancies between the warrior God of the Old Testament and Jesus who blessed the peacemakers.

During my first semester at Eastern Mennonite College, I took a class on the book of Genesis. I was overwhelmed with information about multiple writers with different agenda, two creation stories, and Genesis 1-11 as prehistory. It was kind of the teacher (my father's college roommate) to pass me despite my lack of comprehension.

In my second college Bible class on the Old Testament, I had a crisis of faith (or an epiphany). Perhaps the story of Jonah and the whale is only a metaphor. If I hadn't gotten it in Genesis class, I certainly got it now; the Bible is not the simple story and rulebook I had thought. By the time I got to acting class I was ready to say (while acting of course) that maybe God wasn't like I had always thought either. I toyed with throwing it all out, the Bible and my faith in God. After all, I reasoned, it is better to be genuine and truthful than to hang on only so as not to be left behind. I left college with my personal version of my inherited family skepticism even as I began reframing my understanding of God and the Bible.

In 1992, I began attending Wesley Theological Seminary in Washington, D.C. I supplemented my studies with classes at Associated Mennonite Biblical Seminary, Eastern Mennonite Seminary, Howard Divinity School, and a local Catholic seminary. I was an eager seminary student surprised by my new love for the Bible. Classes with teachers such as Sharon Ringe and Bruce Birch were a gold mine for me. We studied the community out of which the text came as well as the larger historical and cultural context. I was introduced to literary criticism. We read the interpretations of women and men from around the world and their understandings of the biblical text from their own context and experience.

I was excited and challenged by new ways of exploring Scripture. The hermeneutics of suspicion as described by Elisabeth Schüssler Fiorenza rang true for me. The Book of Revelation finally made sense when read from the perspective of a Latin American community under threat from the government. Reading the story of Hagar and Sarah through the eyes of womanist theologian Delores Williams was revolutionary. A Native American classmate told us how she and other First Nation people identify more with the Canaanites than the Israelites in the story of entering the "Promised Land."

As part of my seminary study I had an internship at WATER (Women's Alliance for Theology, Ethics, and Ritual). There I worked with Christian feminist theologians Mary Hunt and Diann Neu, who don't use the Bible all that much. They do their theology working from other "sacred texts"—the sacred lives and stories of women who struggle daily to earn a living wage, raise a family, and seek the Holy where they live.

My seminary training, internship, sermons, and my own sermon preparations have been formational for me. Even more powerful and transforming was when I experienced the biblical story in my own body.

In December 1998, my mother Nancy died after an intense battle with cancer. I spent months watching her waste away and watching my baby, Jamie, grow. May 1999 brought the tragic death of two-year-old Schuyler, the daughter of my teenage cousin. In June 1999, my maternal grandmother died after a long illness. In August 1999, I was devastated to find out I was pregnant. Twelve weeks later, on World Communion Sunday, I had a miscarriage. I lay in bed for a week, finally forced to stop and grieve the litany of losses.

In the recesses of my mind I began to hear the words of Jesus, "This is my body, broken. . . ." I began to feel it in my body. "This is my body broken. . . ." My body, the bodies of the women in my family had been broken, our blood poured out. Through all the broken bodies I had tried to continue living my life as if not much had changed. But I had changed. My ability to trust and love was greatly diminished, while my capacity for anger, doubt, and self-reliance had increased exponentially.

But then that little body that had gestated only twelve weeks, that sent me to the hospital, that took me away from my two children— spoke the words, "This is my body broken, for you." It was not only my body that had been broken, my blood poured out; it was the lifeblood of that little being. That broken body became bread for my soul, as I lay in bed weak from my own loss of blood.

I saw that I could not go it alone. I did need God, in the community and in myself. The bread of the community, women who shared their own stories of miscarriage and loss, fed me. Friends bearing cinnamon rolls, foot lotion, and candles ministered to me. My children were cared for, meals made, the laundry washed, the house cleaned. After months of death, loss, anger, and grief I began learning to trust and love again. Through the brokenness of that little creature I was given a new life, a new calling, a new understanding of the Christian story.

The year of many deaths was a conversion experience. The four spiritual laws had never made sense to me. I cannot point to a time when I asked Jesus into my life. But when my experience collided with the biblical story, with the words of Jesus, I was converted. I have new reason to tell the Jesus story, to share the many stories that the Bible contains.

As a pastor (and a parent) I want to help others see the Bible as a family photo album rather than a prescriptive rulebook. Our ancestors in the faith have given us this book. It is the story of how "our family" has understood God, our relationship with God, and our relationship with God's world.

This is its power. As God's people, the Bible is our story too and we continue to live it. Our task is to find the way into this universal tale in which all of us have a role. When we find our place in the text, our picture in the book, we encounter God who waits for us there. We are given new life.

Now I am a feminist pastor and mother. Like my mother and grandmother before me, I have my arguments with the church (and thus with Scripture). My children hear me talk about inclusive language, numerous interpretations of a single passage of Scripture, reclaiming the body and the senses in the Christian tradition, and the inclusion of all people in the body of Christ.

I know that I have passed on the family skepticism. Already six-year-old Cecilia asks, "Did Jesus really live? He wasn't a real person." But perhaps the living story is being passed on too. Four-year-old Jamie retorts, "Yes, Jesus lived, and he died and he is alive now."

CHAPTER 19

Uncovering Our Faith Assumptions

G. Craig Maven

Beginning the Journey

As I considered my journey with Scripture, I found what I really was considering is my journey of faith. The two are inextricably intertwined. My faith is shaped by Scripture, and my understanding of Scripture is shaped by faith. So in many ways the consideration of my journey with Scripture is an exercise in uncovering the faith assumptions—the foundations, if you will—concerning Scripture. As someone has said, "We all are thrust into the middle of a stream." That stream has carried me through various understandings of Scripture and faith and continues to carry me to the yet unknown end of my journey.

My family was a churched family, but not a religious one. We attended a small Episcopal church in the historic section of Newtown, Bucks County, Pennsylvania. The Bible was somewhat of a mystery to me. I knew it contained something supposed to make my life meaningful, but I was ignorant of what that was.

One of my most vivid memories of Sunday school was memorizing the books of the Bible, Psalm 23, the Ten Commandments, the Sermon on the Mount, the Lord's Prayer, the Apostles' Creed and the Nicene Creed. There was not much difference in my mind between the Bible and Book of Common Prayer, each of which we received after reciting the appropriate memory work. All of these words were somehow sacred—but disconnected from my daily life.

I entered catechism at age eleven and tried to practice the disciplines of the faith: devotional Bible reading and praying the appropriate morning and evening prayers out of the Prayer Book. The ancient forms and King James English never struck home. After the equally impenetrable ritual of confirmation (all that stuck with me was being repulsed at the idea of kissing a man's ring that everyone else had), the daily disciplines were abandoned. My Bible got shoved in a drawer and forgotten.

For me as a young teenager the Bible—really the church—became irrelevant. Faith was completely individual and separate from organized religion. Sunday morning was an excruciating exercise of boredom. Here I developed my distaste for liturgy, finding the words to be someone else's and not a reflection of my faith, my journey, my life. The Bible got lumped in with all the other "church stuff." I saw the Bible as nothing more than a collection of disconnected stories of people I could not relate to, written in outdated and difficult language, and if it had any meaning I would discover that through some other avenue. As far as I was concerned, Scripture was a dead book written by dead men.

On the Way

As a Baby Boomer being raised in the Northeast, I was thoroughly indoctrinated with modernism. I was comfortable with a Kantian world view that neatly separated the noumenal and phenomenal world. I began to recognize that faith was important to one sphere of my life, but the content of that faith was fluid and could even be contradictory. There was enough of cultural Christianity in me to make me respect Jesus, but the church and its documents were unnecessary for faith.

That all changed during six months encompassing the end of my junior year and beginning of my senior year in high school. The change began with friendships. I became friends with a young woman who attended the Baptist church in Newtown and with some peers who were part of the Church of the Good Samaritans (a General Conference Mennonite church) in Holland, Pennsylvania. I was intrigued by the difference I saw in the lives of these people, but leery of church.

Without going into the gory details, I found my life in a crisis of my own making right at the beginning of summer break. My brother had attended a Fellowship of Christian Athletes meeting where he had been given a copy of the Living New Testament, and he had simply placed it on the night stand we shared. I picked it up and began reading, looking for something. For the first time I actually read the words of Jesus—at least that's what it seemed to me. The New Testament, now freed from Elizabethan language (and to my mind the cultural trappings of Medieval Europe) jumped to life. The Sermon on the Mount, which I had dutifully memorized in the King James Version, now made sense; it was as if I was hearing Jesus deliver the words himself. Could it be that the Scriptures really did have something meaningful to say to me? Was there really forgiveness and new life available to me?

I devoured the entire New Testament, then pulled the King James Version out of exile and waded through the Old Testament. It did not make much sense, although the stories of faith and faithfulness impressed me, but the New Testament spoke to me. Romans and Ephesians captivated me. Hebrews with all its references to the law gave me a framework to approach the Old Testament. And Revelation, though confusing with the symbols and images, made me consider for the first time that this world could end. Judgment would be more than an individual accounting. I wondered if any of these things could be happening now.

At the beginning of my senior year of high school, I was dared to attend a Bible study for youth led by an older couple from the Baptist church. They had no children but "adopted" everyone else's children. They were warm and welcoming, and in the tiny living room of their rented home up to twenty-five young people crammed in weekly. Here I heard the phrases "receive Jesus as your personal savior" and "God's plan of salvation." Soon I asked the Lord to forgive my sin and be my savior. This wonderful experience of release and newness was truly a new birth.

Now the Bible became a source of truth and guidance. I found encouragement and instruction in its pages. I enthusiastically shared my newfound faith with other classmates. All the while I was being nurtured by the Wednesday evening Bible studies. I also began to move more and more into the sphere of John Sprunger, the pastor of the Church of the Good Samaritans. His influence shaped much of my early faith.

From Sprunger and the older Baptist couple, I absorbed the concept that the Bible *is* the Word of God. I heard such words as *infallible* and *inerrant*. I was also exposed to dispensational fundamentalism and found myself drawn to its sense of surety and firmness.

As I reflect on my journey with Scripture, I recognize how I used my modernist world view to set the *a priori* through which I understood the Scripture. The Bible was the absolute through which all fields of knowledge are unified in some fashion. The Bible was the source of all knowledge and truth about God. There was a subtle shift in my faith; I had faith in my ability to (rationally) discover all that I needed in the written word apart from a meaningful relationship with the living Word. The *a priori* was rationalism. I was still stuck in a modernist world view, and by faith I chose to accept the construct that the Bible was absolute.

Please understand that I had no conscious or critical understanding of what I was doing. As this was developing I was a music education major at Temple University. I was not studying philosophy or theology.

The first crack in my faith in rational Christianity was made in my sophomore year in college. I was involved with both a rigid fundamentalist group and Inter-Varsity Christian Fellowship. The leader of the fundamentalist group accused me of teaching doctrines of demons when I dared disagree with him on a matter of biblical interpretation. The rift was swift and complete. I was left somewhat stunned that dialogue was not permissible and that reasoned people could not rationally resolve disagreements.

I turned completely to the Inter-Varsity chapter, where the philosophy was training student leaders and encouraging dialogue and debate. The two advisors were students at Westminster Theological Seminary, one of whom was a charismatic Mennonite from Landisville (his last name was Landis!). The authority of Scripture was reinforced, but the necessity of vital spirituality to understand God was laid alongside for a more balanced faith.

After finishing college, I enrolled at Westminster Theological Seminary, where I was exposed to classic Reformed theology, but more importantly, to the apologetics and philosophy of Cornelius Van Til (presuppositionalism) popularized by Francis Schaeffer. It was here that I understood the philosophical role of faith. Everyone has an *a priori*. We start with a reasonable starting point—but no starting point can be reasoned to. Each starting point is chosen by faith. Every argument, then, is circular. You end where you begin, so choose wisely!

It was in this context that Scripture moved from being the source of ahistorical truth to a living document through which God revealed the plan of redemption, the good news of salvation, and the kingdom of

God. What I came to understand was also that my *a priori* had to be the person of God, and that my understanding of God would determine the theology through which I would argue back to that same understanding of God.

I came to understand the hermeneutical circle into which I jumped when interpreting Scripture. Again, the *a priori* determined the ending point. This did not produce profound doubt about the Scripture but rather a dependency on God to guide my faith. Theology did not cease to be important; rather doing theology became the way to test the *a priori* to see if it could hold the weight of reason and reasonableness. The Scriptures became source material for theological constructs, and part of the challenge was to discover the *a priori* of the human authors in their theological constructs and adopt them as my own.

On graduation from seminary and entering the ministry, I soon realized that what people needed were not theological lectures, no matter how tightly woven and exegetically correct, but an encounter with the living God. However, my seminary education did not give me the tools to lead people into this encounter. In classic Reformed style I could properly teach the Word but was ill-prepared to help people encounter the Word. This has been the source of much searching over the years.

Gaining Your Bearings

In the past few years I have been working on a D. Min. degree, having come to feel I needed to retool for the second half of my career. This has given me the opportunity to reengage academics and catch up on what is happening in the broader Christian community. In this context I have read a bit about postmodernity, some developments in literary criticism, and generational demographics and characteristics, while visiting churches seen as on the cutting edge.

As this relates to my journey with Scripture, I find postmodernity both a refreshing break from the hubris of Western modernity and a frightening peek into the abyss of hopelessness and chaos. On the one hand, Scripture can finally be freed from the modernist/fundamentalist debate. As I understand the anti-foundational nature of postmodernity, it demands that our *a priori* be clearly displayed for examination. Postmodernity has laid bare the common foundation of the modernist/fundamentalist debate as rationalism. The sad reality is that neither side needs the presence of the resurrected Christ through the empowerment of the Spirit to be understood. I appreciate Rodney Clapp's insightful critique of this debate in his book *A Peculiar People.*[1]

On the other hand, the anti-foundational nature of the more nihilist forms of postmodern thought reduces anything anyone says about Scripture—and even Scripture itself—to meaninglessness. It is worse than deconstruction, for the goal is less to rebuild than to unmask the emptiness of certainty. And with no metanarratives recognized there is no reign of God to announce, no story of salvation to proclaim which has universal meaning. The church is stripped of a message.

What postmodernity has done is help me to see that my presuppositions about Scripture are my attempts to provide a framework to both understand Scripture and have Scripture impact my life. The concepts of infallibility and inerrancy I feel comfortable with are not absolutely necessary to encounter the risen Christ through Scripture, and are human constructs open to reinterpretation and examination. Again, this does not inject doubt into my thinking about Scripture. Rather, I find this a healthy reminder to constantly examine what really lies at the foundation of my understanding of what Scripture is and how I understand and appropriate Scripture.

My recent exposure to advances in literary criticism has allowed me to hear more clearly the harmony and dissonance of the canonical voices in Scripture. I have gained a greater appreciation for the humanness of the Scripture without losing the sound of the divine voice.

My personality makes me more of a mechanic in my approach to Scripture. I analyze and tinker, pulling from here and there to make something hopefully of use to someone. Perhaps in one sense, my mechanic's approach allows me to shield my life from the penetrating power of the Scripture. It is I who operates on the Scripture, rather than the Scripture that operates on me. Too often I approach Scripture looking only for sermon material or wind up making notes for future sermons.

In thinking of "Scripture as a journeying partner through life," I am engaged in an attempt to recover the wonder of my first reading as a high school student. To have Scripture be life-giving and directive. For the works of God to astound, inspire and awe me. To more than find truth about God in the text, but find the God of truth.

What I am trying to say is that I am still trapped in modernity, and recognize that. I am trying to loosen Scripture from the confines of my abilities to analyze structures, culture, forms, and syntax. The written word comes alive as the Spirit breathes into our hearts. I am not looking for some mysterious hidden meaning in the text; rather I want to smell God's breath as I hear God speak.

Conclusion

Where am I in my journey with Scripture? To get the posturing out of the way, let me say I still am comfortable with the concepts of infallibility and inerrancy. But I recognize that these are faith statements. These are choices I have made that cannot be reasoned to, nor reasoned out of. This does not make me a card-carrying member of the Flat Earth Society or a member of the radical right. I believe that the Bible is the word of God written. The process of inspiration delivered to us what God wanted and the word has been providentially protected in its transmission in a way that makes it trustworthy, even though we do not have the original autographs. The Bible is still the source of truth. And yes, even propositional truth can be constructed from Scripture.

I also recognize and freely accept that Scripture is a human product. It is humans who put writing implement to corresponding medium. Scripture fully reflects the personality, style, and culture of each author. Yet the Bible is more than simply a collection of writings that reflect humanity's attempt to understand God. It is fully human and fully divine.

I also understand, and have attempted to be open about that understanding, that my position is based on foundations that lie outside of Scripture itself. There are philosophical and epistemological presuppositions that predetermine the direction of my thought. When an artist picks up brush and palette, she will not make a wrought iron sculpture. I have an *a priori*; so does everyone else. My hope is that we can help each other more fully investigate and understand our own presuppositions so we can stop talking past each other and truly understand each other. I am not sure what understanding each other will allow us to accomplish. However, nothing constructive will happen if we never attempt to listen.

Note

1. Rodney Clapp, *A Peculiar People: The Church as Culture in a Post-Christian Society* (Downers Grove, Ill.: InterVarsity Press, 1996).

CHAPTER 20

Munching on a Mattering Text

Keith Graber Miller

A decade ago, in a plane bound for Albuquerque, I found myself browsing through the January issue of *American Way* magazine, the airline's promotional publication. There I came across an interview with Robertson Davies, Canada's "champion of letters," widely recognized before his death as Canada's greatest writer. After speaking about everything from David Letterman to whether there is a kind of evangelical mission in his writing to his non-use of computers, Davies turned his attention to the Bible.

In earlier speeches Davies had spoken about the loss of the Bible not only as a religious guide but also as a shared source of literature for our culture. When asked about this by the *American Way* interviewer, Davies said, "Well, it's a source of reference, you see, and it's a very great thing in any culture to have some classical literature to which you can refer with the confidence that most of the people you're talking to share it and know what's in it. That used to be the case with the Bible because it is a classical literature . . . which everybody used to know. But they *don't* know it anymore and that means that a big frame of reference has been lost."

Moments after reading the interview with Davies, I was off the plane and at the Society of Christian Ethics' annual conference. Ironically, the *first* session I attended that day included a paper titled "Does Scripture Matter? Scripture as Ethical Norm in a Time of Ecclesial Crisis."[1] The paper began with a reference to Ezra and Nehemiah's accounts of the return of the Hebrew exiles to Judah. The story is familiar to many: Jerusalem had fallen to the Babylonians in 587 BC, and now, half a century later, the Babylonian king Cyrus had allowed some of the exiles to return and attempt to rebuild the temple and the walls of Jerusalem. When Ezra summoned the people to hear the words of the law of Moses, they gathered together before the Water Gate. He and others read from it from early morning until midday, and the ears of all the people were attentive to the book of the law. And as the readers spoke the holy words from the book, all the people wept as they recognized their own fallibility and God's grace.

Beginning a paper at an academic conference with this story was extraordinarily moving, and adeptly led the listener into the author's argument that Scripture does indeed matter, that it has compelling power, and that it continues to be the source of the church's life.

What was striking to me were the common themes in the lamentations of these two quite distinct voices—ones I heard over the course of a few hours. The novelist and the ethicist, for different reasons, were both disturbed at the diminishing of biblical knowledge and biblical authority in the North American context. Both were calling, either implicitly or explicitly, for a rediscovery of the text, encounters with that Word which has decisively influenced the multiple individuals, communities, and cultures preceding us.

I begin with this account because it so resonated with my own personal and professional journey with Scripture at that stage in my life. In my teaching, I was developing a renewed commitment to deepening students' appreciation for the biblical text and my own relationship with the text and the God behind it.

From here I want to move both forward and back, in something shy of chronological order. And I should offer a disclaimer, too: I teach religion and philosophy at Goshen College, leaving the formal teaching of Bible to my learned colleagues Jo-Ann Brant and Paul Keim. Truthfully, had I not had an excellent biblical education during my years at Associated Mennonite Biblical Seminary (AMBS), I would have left my doctoral program in Ethics and Society at Emory University with a tragically slender knowledge of the text. At AMBS I was fortunate to have courses with Millard Lind, Howard Charles, Marlin Miller, Willard Swartley, and some of the other great biblical and theological church leaders at the time.

It's also impossible for me to think about my own journey with Scripture except in the context of my Goshen College teaching over the last decade and my desires for how my students will view the role of Scripture in their lives. Consequently, I'll make several overtures to that pedagogical context. Because my natural inclination may be to be more critical and skeptical of the biblical text or its application to particular issues, I want to focus more on affirmation rather than critique of the text or its function.

Back when I began teaching in 1993, gone were the days (if ever they existed) that erudite, urbane college professors needed to dismantle their charges' rural, naïve embrace of a flat text. Many or most of our students now come to us with only minimal biblical knowledge, unless they have been to a Mennonite or other denominational secondary school. They don't even know the basic biblical narrative well enough to reject it. And many come convinced that—whatever the Bible might say—it can be made to say anything we want it to.

Or so it has seemed from what they have observed in church fights during their brief lives. In a paper one student wrote for my Religious History in the Americas class recently, she said, "The Bible has become a place where warring factions go for ammunition." Most students have seen the biblical text aggressively launched over issues related to homosexual practice. Earlier, some of them had cut their biblical teeth on arguments about divorce or women in leadership.

The battle I witnessed was over head coverings. As a child growing up in a faithful Mennonite congregation (Howard-Miami Mennonite Church in rural Kokomo, Indiana), I often heard stories of God's holy people in sermons and Sunday school as well as at home during weeks we took time for family devotions. Dark images from my blue softcover Bible were burned into my soul—images of faces turned heavenward when terror struck, when lions gathered, or when Abraham wondered whether to plunge the knife into the terrified Isaac. Other than those images and stories about larger-than-life biblical characters, my first cognitive encounter with the biblical text as a source of authority in the life of the church was in 1970, when my two slightly older sisters joined their peers in refusing to wear the headcovering upon their baptism into the church. I was eleven then, awestruck by the bravery of my sisters.

After congregational leaders preached sermons and discussed the issue at church council and debated about what the Bible said about women covering their heads, they determined that young women would be encouraged to wear the headcovering, but that it would not be obligatory. And slowly, incrementally, the headcoverings vanished, not only from these seventh- and eighth-graders' heads but then even from those in their later teens, then the twenty-somethings, then the mothers of the adolescent girls, then . . . well, most Mennonites alive back then remember how this went. And indelibly etched in my pre-pubescent mind was the recognition of the interpretive possibilities of the biblical text, the way in which the Bible was a humanly constructed and sometimes deconstructed authority.

In an all-or-nothing context—and that's how many of these debates are constructed—change inevitably undermines that which has come before. But it need not be "all" or "nothing"; there are alternatives. As Stanley Hauerwas has written, "Traditions by their nature require change, since there can be no tradition without interpretation. And interpretation is the constant adjustment that is required if the current community is to stay in continuity with tradition."[2] Hauerwas approvingly quotes J.P. Mackey's remark in *Tradition and Change in the Church*[3] that "Tradition means continuity and change, both together and both equally."[4]

On Biblical Significance

Today our Mennonite college students have seen far more acrimonious debates about the biblical text than most of us ever did and partly as a result, many have lost a sense of biblical significance, or what we sometimes call "biblical authority." Nonetheless, I hope I and my students can continue to see—or learn to see—the Bible as a key source for guiding Christians' faith and practice.

A friend who teaches at another denominational school told me recently about an assignment she gave her students. They were to read a section of Nazi Holocaust survivor Elie Wiesel's *Night* as well as the Book of Job. When they came to the following class session, one student said, "I thought Wiesel's book was helpful, but I didn't really like Job." My friend said to her student, "Whether or not you like Job isn't really the issue. It's from the Bible, and it reveals some divine truth about human existence, even if it makes us uncomfortable. We simply need to sort out what that truth is."

When our son Niles was coming into his own, it was delightful to observe him as he developed notions of authority. By age two he knew that Mommy and Daddy were authorities, so he began playing us off of each other, asking one and then going to the other if the first answer was unsatisfactory. One day, as we were preparing for dinner, he asked if he could have a cookie.

I said, "No, honey, we're just getting ready to eat."

His response: "But *God* says it's okay."

Already he had realized that there was an authority higher even than his parents, and he was using that authority to supersede ours.

Even more provocative was another encounter we had a week later, once again over the issue of dessert before a meal. This time when I said, "No, you can't have an ice cream sandwich before dinner," Niles quickly scanned the table in front of him, picked up a piece of paper with some words scribbled on it (likely a grocery list in process), and said, "But it says *right here* that I can have one." What interested me most about that moment was that Niles had intuitively recognized that the written word carried more authority than the spoken word.

My hope is that my students see the biblical word as appropriately authoritative—as significant and essential in guiding their faith and life. Together we try to explore the source and nature of that authority. And just as Niles is trying to sort through the various authorities in his life, we attempt to help students understand the multiple authorities that compete for their commitment and their attention and their loyalties in a postmodern world. Often in my Ethics and Morality and Christian Faith classes, we examine the various sources typically used for guiding life and thought within the Christian tradition. Those sources, often referred to as the Wesleyan quadrilateral or Methodist quadrilateral, include Scripture as well as the larger Christian tradition that has developed around it. Another source is individual and corporate human experience—what truths life and the church have taught us. A final source often drawn on is human reason, which includes philosophical speculation, studies from the natural and social sciences, and basic human reason and logic. I remember an intense discussion I once had with Willard Swartley, whom I respect immensely, about whether the Bible was *a* source for Christian ethical reflection or *the* source for that reflection.

Sometimes these four sources are mutually reinforcing, and that's the hope. Sometimes they conflict with each other; then tough decisions need to be made. All of the sources need to be interpreted, and all need to be critiqued, certainly. In any event, I hope in my teaching I can reaffirm the Bible as a primary source for guiding faith and life.

I remember how grateful I was for Stanley Hauerwas's rendering of the nature of biblical authority when I first came across it in *A Community of Character*, initially published the year I graduated from college. Hauerwas writes,

> By regarding Scripture as an authority Christians mean to indicate that they find there the traditions through which their community most nearly comes to knowing and being faithful to the truth. Scripture is not meant to be a problem solver. It rather describes the process whereby the community we call the church is initiated by certain texts into what Barr has called the "vivid and lively pattern of argument and controversy" characteristic of biblical traditions.[5]

To claim Scripture as authority, then, is not claiming that it is errorless, or that its genres or understandings are unique, or that its images are essential for us to know who we are. "Rather," says Hauerwas,

> to claim the Bible as authority is the testimony of the church that this book provides the resources necessary for the church to be a community sufficiently truthful so that our conversation with one another and God can continue across generations. . . . By trying to live, think, and feel faithful to its witness [we] find [we] are more nearly able to live faithful to the truth.[6]

Interpretive Biases

I also hope students learn to acknowledge their own interpretive biases (and I my own)—the way in which we all read the text through our own distinctive lenses. In a church I once attended, the pastor led a Sunday school class on women in church leadership. He began by saying he wanted everyone to come into the course leaving their baggage at the door—their preconceptions about this issue, their social locations, the fact that they were men or women, their life experiences, their education, ideas which came from their culture, and all other notions which had shaped them. Having left that baggage behind, the pastor said, they would simply look at the Bible, and see what the unadulterated Scripture had to say.

I thought, "What a horrendous deception! It's impossible to leave all of these things at the door." As Walter Brueggemann writes,

> In our best judgments concerning Scripture, we might be aware enough of our propensity to distort in the service of vested interests, anxiety, fear, and hurt that we recognize that our best interpretation might be not only a vehicle for but also a block to and distortion of the crucified truth of the gospel.[7]

When I teach a Sunday school class—or one of my college courses—I want people to bring their baggage in with them. Together we open up that luggage and place it out in front of us on the floor. Over the term we sort through the luggage, unpacking, laundering, repacking, shifting. We throw out some of the muck that's there—some of the soiled underwear and maybe those bellbottom jeans from the 1970s or the 1990s. And we exchange or share some of our finer articles with others. In the end, we try to make everything fit a little better. But we won't get anywhere, with any integrity at least, unless we see how much we are shaped by all of these other factors and to a certain extent accept their impact.

I also hope students can learn to live with the tension of not having one right answer for every question, or realize that several people or churches who take the Bible seriously may come to different conclusions on a given passage or issue. That doesn't mean we stop talking with each other, but that we continue to sort out why there are differences in our perspectives or interpretations.

My hope is that, as professors and congregational leaders, we can model for students and congregants an ability to talk about Scripture humanely, respectfully and, with a spirit that trusts that our conversation partners seek to know God's will just as we do. We all need to learn to call each other to faithfulness. But we need to do so with humility. I need to humbly admit that my interpretations may be out of whack, perhaps hyper-shaped by my desire for the text to consistently speak lovingly and peacefully and inclusively. And we need to be comfortable with some flexibility in understanding and application of the Bible.

Finally, I hope I and my students can learn to read the Bible devotionally. Frankly, I'm horrible at this, and in my weaker moments I've described regular spiritual disciplines as a middle-class, late middle-age luxury few others can embrace. But I want to be better, and not just because I believe reading the text devotionally is a Christian obligation. I'm wishing I could read the Bible more regularly purely for inspiration and edification, to be formed by its truths.

With time I have been able increasingly to feed on Scripture in worship, as I hear lectionary passages read powerfully from the pulpit. Early Benedictine monks, whose spiritual disciplines and scholarship were admirable, essentially memorized large portions of Scripture by hearing and repeating it daily. Sometimes they were known as the "munchers" because they would recite Scripture to themselves as they worked, "munching on the Bible as though chewing the cud." They took seriously the observation of Deuteronomy 30:14: "The word is very near to you; it is in your mouth and in your heart for you to observe."

With my skepticism about and criticism of the text, my growing edge would be to develop a kind of intimacy with the Bible. And I would wish this for my students, too: a form of intimacy which would allow them to enter into fruitful discourse about their faith and would inspire them to faithful living. May God help us teach and learn with a spirit of respect for, love for, and trust in the Scripture, where God is revealed to us and where we meet the one we call Christ.

Notes

1. Society of Christian Ethics Annual Meeting (January 1996).

2. Stanley Hauerwas, *A Community of Character* (Notre Dame, Ind.: University of Notre Dame Press, 1991), 61.

3. J.P. Mackey, *Tradition and Change in the Church* (Dayton, Oh.: Pflaum Press, 1968), 42-43.

4. Hauerwas, 61.

5. Ibid., 63.

6. Ibid., 63-64.

7. Walter Brueggemann, "Biblical Authority: A Personal Reflection," *Christian Century* (January 3-10, 2001): 18.

CHAPTER 21

The Mystery
of the Living Word

Lee Snyder

I was startled recently to discover an image from Ralph Waldo Emerson referenced by Margaret Wheatley in her work, *Leadership and the New Science*. Emerson writes about "life as an ongoing encounter with the unknown," notes Wheatley, and created this image: "We wake and find ourselves on a stair; there are stairs below us which we seem to have ascended, there are stairs above us which go out of sight."[1] I had worked through the essays of Ralph Waldo Emerson during graduate school but had not remembered this passage.

I can scarcely describe the effect of stumbling on that image. Why? Because, at the time I was reading Wheatley, a magazine had crossed my desk—the full-color sketch a striking rendition of the Emerson image of awakening on a stairway. This magazine cover showed a figure ascending a floating flight of steps—a great staircase arising out of blue depths and ascending into the obscured heights. The magazine artist, I realized, also had captured something of the power of a dream I had had. This dream was of a curved highway, stretching up and out into space—then disappearing into the ether. The dream had evoked both a sense of heightened exhilaration but also a terrifying sense of the unknown. I am not given to introspection about dreams and in fact remember few of them. I am skittish about even talking about dreams. After all, respectable academics do not do this. But the convergence of images in my chance readings—readings that served to heighten the impact of a similar dream—caught my attention.

I can tell you that picking up Wheatley and rediscovering Emerson at the very same time that this magazine cover showed up in my mail was at the very least astonishing. But not, in my experience, all that unusual. The writer Robertson Davies said once, "By an agency that is not coincidence . . . we find, and are found by, the books we need to enlarge and complete us."[2] This is simply the recognition that there is mystery in the intersections and convergences that make up our experiences, in this case words and images.

The Word of God, I have come to understand, is likewise mediated through relationships and encounters—including encounters with Scripture. I am humbled and awed by the way that God speaks to us in myriad ways. I simply have had to come round to pay attention to the way God speaks through a particular Scripture which, with sometimes uncanny circumstance, is brought to my attention at the precise time when I need just those words. Dare we confess this, since we rarely talk about it?

A belief in the revelation of the Scripture through the Holy Spirit has always seemed, on the one hand, a scary and dangerous proposition. On the other hand, I have come to rest in the mystery and absolute inscrutability of God entering our lives—of experiencing what I can only conclude is the Holy Spirit as a force in the life of the church and in our personal lives as well. Perhaps that is how I most often experience what biblical scholar Walter Brueggemann calls the "inherency" of Scripture. As Brueggemann suggests, Scripture as a guide in ordinary circumstances and in the necessities of the mundane truly reveals itself as "endlessly 'strange and new.'"[3]

Shaping Influences: Meeting God

But I am getting ahead of the story. My first remembered encounter with Scripture was a literal one. It was also private and personal, though it grew out of a child's unmitigated belief, absorbed from the life of the faith community, that the Scriptures were true and that God meant what he said. I was probably five or six years old. My most prized possession was a maroon Gideon New Testament. When I lost it one day, I was devastated. When it did not turn up after much searching, I began praying that God would give it back. My prayers were pleading and demanding. I knew that God so choosing could simply open up the heavens, reach down, and return the New Testament. It was as simple as that. My prayers continued for a number of days, with a fierce insistence and an unshakeable belief that God would intervene and honor his promise, "Ask and you shall receive."

I have no idea if my parents knew about this desperate drama going on between their oldest child and God. What would Heaven do with a six-year-old who believed literally that God was going to give back the Gideon Testament?

God gave it back. One day a car pulled up into the driveway. A man got out and knocked on the door. From way on the other side of town, Mr. Edwards showed up with the New Testament in hand. The Edwards, it turned out, had found the Bible sometime after our family had stopped in to see their new house. My parents were planning to build, to replace our four-room farmhouse, and were interested in seeing the Edwards' floor plan. When we had stopped at their new house, apparently I had taken along the Gideon Testament and left it behind.

While that experience appears to an adult as embarrassingly naïve, I have no doubt that God answered my prayer—it was as though the heavens had opened and God had handed back my book. A child's experience of God and of Scripture can be a profound and shaping influence—for that I am thankful.

The Scriptures also became a living Book to me—still a child—in the context of the faith community, the Harrisburg Mennonite Church. Bishop John Yoder had a special gift, nurturing a love of story. His sermons provided the foundation that would give me an understanding of the grand story from Genesis to Revelation. In contrast to much of the pinched-mouth religion associated with a rigid and nonconformist Mennonite community, John Yoder's vision was loving and lovely.

In our congregation, communion was a frightening time of calling to account. Preparation for communion was taken seriously: adults fasting on Good Friday, the ritual of "counsel meetings" where each examined her or himself to be able to declare truthfully, "I have peace with God and my fellow man." Twice a year communion involved at times the discipline of a member. It involved private examination of some members in the anteroom of the church house. In this context, it was John Yoder's love of narrative that redeemed the Scriptures. His view of God was expansive and large; I *felt*, more than understood in any rational way, the love of God through John Yoder's rendering of the biblical story. Even his wife's whiskery holy kiss for the girls at baptism could not taint the regard I felt for Bishop John.

I am still pondering how love of story through the Scripture has shaped me and how, I sometimes think, being captivated by story has saved me from the blight of anger and rebellion. Growing up in a setting where men were the keepers of women's souls, accepting a "woman's place" with the symbolic head covering and distinctive dress meant silence and unquestioning obedience. However, nothing could extinguish imagination and a love of learning. And here, no doubt about it, Scripture was a primary source.

The Widening Path: A Lived Theology

My journey with Scripture must include another strand, also rooted in the faith community that met every Sunday morning and evening and Wednesday night among the rye grass fields of Oregon's Willamette Valley. This was a widening path from the church house at the corner of Powerline Road and Diamond Hill Road to the university years later. The Scripture teachings I received growing up were largely from ministers chosen by lot to take on the responsibility of diviner and divider of the Word. These were men, mostly farmers, whose calling to the ministry was in addition to whatever they did to make their living.

In our congregation there would be three or four ministers who took their turn preaching each Sunday. Without theological training, these simple men of God nevertheless took up their responsibilities with humility and an earnestness that taught me even as a small child to revere the Scriptures as God's revealed Word. After each Sunday sermon, the supporting cast of ministers who were not preaching that morning would solemnly rise one by one to offer their "yea and amen" to the message. It became a ritual, but not a meaningless formality. It was a way of reminding all, as I understand now looking back, that in the believers church tradition interpreting Scripture was no one individual's prerogative.

Furthermore, I now recognize that whatever might have been lacking in sophisticated theological teaching was to some extent made up through a lived theology—the Anabaptist call to discipleship, believer's baptism, the witness to peace and nonviolence, nonconformity to the world. There was a reality to the lived faith I observed that was powerful. The cost of taking a peace position in that community became clear in the accounts we heard from my grandfather. When these Mennonites would not buy war bonds, antagonism ran high around Harrisburg. A yellow streak was painted around the church building, the church doors were chained and padlocked, and a crude sign was nailed over the door that said, "This church is closed for the duration of the war."

At one point, my grandfather himself was threatened with tar and feathering. As he tells the story, the town rowdies determined "to show" these Mennonites, to make an example of them. The rowdies stopped at a couple of homes before ending up at my grandfather's. But after only a few words, the fellows got back in their Model T, turned around and left, not having touched him. Only many years later, did my grandfather learn the rest of the story. One of these men confessed that he was sorry that he had been a part of the gang. At each of the three places they had stopped, he told my grandfather, there had been a protector, a figure who stood between the attackers and their intended victims.

Yet another example of a "lived theology," of a commitment to discipleship and service, was the decision by my father and mother to respond to a call to ministry on skid row. My parents rented out the farm, moved to Sacramento with their four children, and with three other families supported themselves for a number of years in this mission. This proved to be a transforming introduction to a larger ecumenical community. But underlying this whole venture was the shaping experience of seeing my parents and their mission colleagues taking God's call seriously, of being willing to risk something, not assured of either success or results in this work. This is what I have come to understand as a model of "holy recklessness," taking literally Christ's call to follow Him.

Making Peace with Ambiguity

Much later at university, the power and the problem of Scripture became a part of my experience in a different way. By the time I got to the University of Oregon, I had chosen literature as my field. In World Literature, taught by a brilliant scholar from India, I was confronted for the first time by a direct challenge to the views of my church community. Our readings included selections from the New Testament. As was her pattern, the instructor provided historical background to the text, with the matter-of-fact explanation that actually the authors of the Gospels could not have been Jesus' disciples of those names, Matthew, Mark,

Luke, and John. I was astounded. How could the church's understanding of Scripture be brought together with those of scholars? It was one of those moments, one of many I have learned, in which the questions must be honored.

One of the most faith-building experiences I had at the university came later in Professor Stanley Maveety's class in Literature of the Bible. Here was an academic in a secular setting who loved the Scripture. He introduced me for the first time to the richness of examining the Word in all its complexity, ambiguity, beauty, and context. Never shall I forget the sense of a new light dawning when Professor Maveety set the historical context and laid alongside each other the story of Ezra, of the foreign wives and children being cast out of the community, and the story of Ruth—a foreigner being accepted into the community, a woman who would become the foremother of Jesus the Messiah. This was for me a startling and liberating insight into biblical interpretation.

The Text as Endlessly Strange and New

Where am I now? In what "odd and intimate ways," as Brueggemann puts it, does this "endlessly strange and new" text shape our lives? I have been blessed by wonderful teachers; by the witness and writing of poets, prophets, and plain people. Word with a capital "W" and word with a small "w" sustains me. My teachers have been and still are Wendell Berry, T. S. Eliot, Cardinal Newman, Donald Hall, Kathleen Norris, Parker Palmer, Rainer Maria Rilke, Madeleine L'Engle, Anne Lamott, Robert Greenleaf, and Henri Nouwen.

I got to formal Anabaptist history and theology late. Professor Ray Gingerich allowed me, as the academic dean at Eastern Mennonite University, to audit his college class in which we read J. Denny Weaver's book, *Becoming Anabaptist: The Origin and Significance of Sixteenth Century Anabaptism*. We studied the thought of Mennonite scholars like H. S. Bender and John Howard Yoder. But my first teacher was John Yoder, there in the little white frame meetinghouse in Oregon, who taught me the power of story.

The biblical record is the story of God in relationship with us, his human creation. The Scriptures themselves, in their variety, in their paradoxical simplicity and complexity, give us permission to live the questions, to rest in the knowledge that we do not have to settle everything.

We are allowed to leave some things up to God. In fact, I have wondered sometimes if we, in needing finally to determine things, to arrive at clear answers, do not come close to yielding to the serpent's temptation in the Garden—the temptation of the Tree of Knowledge of Good and Evil—aspiring to be like God, all-knowing?

When my mother-in-law—a saint if I ever knew one—would read through the Scriptures again and again, she sometimes would protest out loud at certain accounts included in the canon. Reading those Old Testament X-rated stories, rereading the narratives of deceit and debauchery, of faithlessness in gory detail, of violence and intrigue, she could only ask, "*Why? Why* are these stories included in the Bible?"

I am glad they are included. The biblical characters and narratives give me hope, because they are reminders that we also are persons God has invited to participate in the unfolding drama of salvation. We too may become a part of the life-giving narrative. These days, I am still discovering the Scripture as a living force.

I continue to discover something about the power of the Holy Spirit as a significant force in the church. We are called to bear witness, and so in that spirit I am still pondering two experiences in the more recent transformation of Mennonite Church USA. I offer these, I must confess, with some tentativeness, because I do not fully understand them. In spring 1998, before the joint assembly at St. Louis, Jonathan Larson preached a conference sermon at Eastern District Conference. This was a time of great unrest and trepidation as the General Conference Mennonite Church looked forward to the upcoming joint assembly with the Mennonite Church. There were wide polarities in Eastern District itself—some leaders were not willing to accept the new Confession of Faith because of particular language that was omitted—or perhaps included. Divisive issues facing both denominations coming together at St. Louis were on everybody's minds.

As President of Bluffton University, I attended Eastern District Conference, one of our constituency groups. I went with a great personal burden, struggling with the request that I allow my name to be submitted to the July Assembly as the first moderator of Mennonite Church USA and chair of the new Executive Board to be appointed in St. Louis. I was overwhelmed with fear and the enormity of the task.

That morning, Jonathan Larson rose to speak, selecting as his text a passage from Colossians 3: "Let the peace of Christ rule in your hearts."

His message was one of encouragement, challenging the conference to *let the peace of God* enter their hearts—to let some things up to God. He reminded us all of how hard it is to *let God* do the work. That proved to be a message that God used for the gathered representatives that day. It was also a message I desperately needed. Paul's words as selected by Larson and (I am convinced) by the Holy Spirit, *"Let the peace of God. . . . "* became my comfort and sustenance over the months to follow. I would recite them in the night when I could not sleep. In the early morning before the day's schedule overtook me, those words became living words of faith and hope. Imagine how startled I was months later to learn that the Nashville worship planning committee had selected for the 2002 Assembly a passage from Colossians 3 as the conference theme, including those words from Jonathan Larson's sermon to Eastern District Conference.

Many of the transformation leaders throughout the church were living on the edge in those days. The twenty-four months between the national assemblies at St. Louis and Nashville included countless consultations and anguished attempts at discerning membership guidelines which rested on varied and heartfelt interpretations of Scripture. The newly formed Constituency Leaders Council (CLC) met regularly to enable representatives from across the church to meet face-to-face, to develop relationships for furthering understanding, for building trust across and above political alliances.

The work was hard; the path convoluted. The church press reported the outcome of a particularly critical meeting. The CLC representatives, struggling with the final formation of the membership guidelines, ultimately could not agree. The media focused on the "not agreeing."

The real story, I would argue, was nearly missed. At that defining meeting, the assembled representative leaders, coming together praying for God's Spirit to lead, praying for proper discernment, decided to put aside their differences on issues upon which they could not agree. More important than their differences, they concluded, was the larger call to unity. The prayers of many across the church were heard; the Spirit was faithful. That CLC meeting marked a turning point in preparation for the work ahead at Nashville.

I am still learning what it means to yield to the ineffable mystery of the living Word. God's promise, through Moses, to the people of Israel in Deuteronomy 30 is one to which I return again and again. I believe it has something to say not only to me but to the church as well:

Now what I am commanding you to do today is not too difficult for you or beyond your reach. It is not up in heaven, so that you have to ask, "Who will ascend into heaven to get it and proclaim it to us so we may obey it?" Nor is it beyond the sea, so that you have to ask, "Who will cross the sea to get it and proclaim it to us so we may obey it?" No, the word is very near you; it is in your mouth and in your heart so you may obey it. (Deut. 30:11-14)

Notes

1. Margaret Wheatley, *Leadership and the New Science* (San Francisco: Berrett-Koehler Publishers, 1994), 150. Wheatley actually is quoting from Loren Eiseley who quotes Emerson in *The Star Thrower* (San Diego: Harvest/Harcourt Brace and Jovanich, 1978), 214. Ralph Waldo Emerson's original quote appears in "Experience," *Selected Writings of Ralph Waldo Emerson* (New York: New American Library, 1965), 327.

2. Robertson Davies, *The Merry Heart: Reflections on Reading, Writing, and the World of Books* (New York: Penguin Books, 1998), 26.

3. Walter Brueggemann, "Biblical Authority: A Personal Reflection," *Christian Century* (January 3-10, 2001), 14.

CHAPTER 22

Reading the Bible Again for the First Time

Dorothy Jean Weaver

Beginning the Journey:
How Did They Write That Story?

I had a simple childish curiosity, nothing more. A curiosity that led to a not-so-simple question: How was the story of creation written, if no one was around to witness it? My thinking was neither rebellious nor revolutionary. Far from it. My family was an "orthodox" Mennonite family. It was a family well to the center of the Mennonite community in theological terms, located spatially right on the edge of the Eastern Mennonite College (EMC) campus, a family whose very life revolved around the academic and social worlds of EMC in the 1950s. It was a family headed by my grandfather, Chester K. Lehman, longtime professor of Bible and theology at EMC and academic dean of the college during my early years. "Brother Chester," as he was widely known, was the epitome of Mennonite theological orthodoxy (questions of "dispensationalism" aside, on which he had rather more sober and less fanciful perspectives than some of his contemporaries, especially at EMC). If it is possible to come from an orthodox family, I surely qualified for that distinction.

But the question of the history of creation was still there. What intrigues me most about that question from my childhood is not that I had it in the first place, but rather that it never once occurred to me to ask anyone for an answer. Instead, I just "pondered these things in my heart" and said nothing to anyone. Perhaps this was the beginning of a lifetime journey of critical reflection on the biblical text. For the most part, though, I lived simply and uncritically with the Scriptures.

I had a concept—I would never have called it "magical"—of the Scriptures as "inspired," but exactly what that meant and how it was defined, I could not have spelled out in any clear terms. What it seemed to mean to me was that there was a unique and unquestioned authority about these writings that simply "was."

I recall that Bible reading was a significant element of my childhood approach to the Scriptures—the little blue four-page Bible-reading schedules, with tiny boxes to fill in for each chapter of the Bible. I'm not sure if I ever once checked off all those little tiny boxes. I did do Bible memory work, though, lots of it. In our Sunday school gathering time one year my aunt, Esther Lehman, had us all memorize Psalm 148; I think I still have much of it in my long-term memory. In summer Bible school we learned to recite the books of the Bible—New Testament books one year and Old Testament books the next year—a simple endeavor that has over time proved more useful and practical on a daily level than most things I have done.

Bible teachers who came to Park School month by month had a program of Bible memorization by which one could earn little prizes, from small tokens of whatever kind (I no longer remember what they were) to Testaments to Bibles to a week at Children's Bible Mission camp in the Blue Ridge Mountains to the east of the Shenandoah Valley. I loved earning prizes. So of course I went for it. I memorized all the verses for the lesser prizes. Then I memorized all the verses for the week at summer camp. Little did I know, however, what I was getting into. The Children's Bible Mission was in fact a thoroughgoing "child evangelism" organization, one that operated on understandings far different from those reflected in my orthodox and yet very Anabaptist community.

Here, as a very young Christian, age thirteen, I was assaulted by a straightforward theology of child evangelism which was new to me. This theology considered virtually no child too young to be in need of "salvation," and the practitioners of this theology exerted group pressure on the collected children evening by evening in the form of regular campfire invitations and sometimes even hellfire and brimstone sermons. As young and theologically unschooled as I was, I knew that this sort of theology and practice was not for me. One year, on coming home troubled from camp, I was given a book by Gideon Yoder to read, *The Nurture and Evangelism of Children*, a beautiful treatment of an Anabaptist approach to the faith development of children. But I deeply respected the Christian faith and commitment of the camp directors and counselors; I in turn was deeply nurtured by the love and acceptance that I found in this circle of people. I returned, happily and on my own volition, for the following three summers as well.

My high school years at Eastern Mennonite High School (1963-1968) and my college years at EMC (1968-1971) did nothing significant to dislodge the simple, unencumbered view of the Scriptures I had inherited from my childhood faith. To be sure, I was growing in my awareness of the Scriptures and in my appreciation for them as a genuine resource for a daily life of faith. But my basic understandings (or rather, lack of understandings) about the origins of the Scriptures and the significance of their "inspiration" remained fundamentally untouched. I received a beautiful, leather-bound RSV Bible from my mother as a high school graduation present, a token of her estimation of what was important in life and a gift I received with equal gratitude.

Bible was far from my major in college. Not that I was turning my back on the Scriptures. But the idea of a Bible major, let alone the idea of seminary studies, simply never entered my thinking. One semester I took a course that included a significant dose of Ancient Near Eastern history. I recall being completely bored—whether by the course material or by the professor I will never rightly know. And as I walked past the corner of the EMC library where the seminary students gathered to study, I recall only a sense of distance from and disdain for the likes of the "seminary nerds." Had someone told me back then that I would not only go to seminary one day but would actually live out my working life as a seminary professor, I would have been amazed.

But biblical studies did have a draw, as it turns out. At Philipps University in Marburg, Germany, during my senior year abroad, I decided to "visit a lecture" (the German idiom for taking a course) on the Psalms. But when I walked into the first class session and found the professor writing Hebrew on the board, I knew I was out of my league. I walked out and never came back. So much for that attempt at biblical studies!

Following my year abroad in Marburg, I returned home to the U.S. Through a strange and totally unexpected turn of events, I found myself heading to New York City and ending up with a job, my first ever full-time job, as periodicals librarian at the American Bible Society, 61st and Broadway. Here I worked with Bibles every day. I gave people tours of our rare book library of thousands of printed Bibles. I answered the "Old Bible letters," providing people with information from our catalog cards and other resource tools when they wrote asking about the Bible they "found in Great Aunt Sally's attic." I learned the fine art of using a concordance to answer queries: "Can you tell me who Lot's uncle is?" or "I am thinking of this verse and it goes something like this. . . . Can you find it for me?" These were all fascinating activities; they all put me in touch with the Scriptures in one way or another.

But the staff meetings stand out in my mind most powerfully. Once a week, or perhaps it was once a month, we had chapels in which we heard stories from Bible Society workers who had come back from their assignments in places all around the world. What all those stories indelibly imprinted on me was the power of the Scriptures, power to reach not only the minds but also the hearts of persons who read them for the first time ever, power to change the lives of those readers in ways that even they could neither understand nor explain. Listening to such stories week by week and month by month, I found myself increasingly in awe of these Scriptures and of the God who chose to speak to human beings and to change human lives through the reading of these words. I still had no idea that my own life was soon to be caught up, captivated, and impelled beyond all questioning by the study of these Scriptures. God has a very interesting sense of timing.

On the Way: The Book I Never Finished.

Then my life took a sudden and unexpected turn. I thought I was on the road to teaching German. I had been a Modern Languages major, with German and French as my two languages, in that order. I had just completed a year in Germany and was interested in going back. I tried every means I knew how to get myself back to Germany: a Rotary scholarship, a voluntary service assignment, enrollment at Middlebury College in Vermont with a year abroad attached to it. Nothing worked. Every street was a dead end.

While I was making all these applications and working on all these dead-end plans, I was doing something else as well. I had borrowed from my mother a copy of my grandfather's book on Old Testament theology, one of a set of two books, the other on New Testament theology, which he wrote and published out of his long years of lectures in the classroom at Eastern Mennonite Seminary (EMS). I am no longer sure why I borrowed the book. But I remember with great clarity what happened when I began to read that book. I never got farther than the first few pages. All of a sudden, I found myself drawn by a fascination I had never before encountered and thinking thoughts I had never thought before: *You know, you could go to seminary for a year or so and study Bible; you would really enjoy that.* It was a brand new idea. No one had ever suggested it to me. There was no forewarning. As far as I was aware then, the idea came straight out of the blue sky. But from my present vantage point I know it came from well beyond the blue sky.

I was a young Mennonite woman who had grown up in the heart of the Mennonite community. The year was 1974. I had no aspirations to be a pastor. That never once came into my thinking. All I knew was that seminary was a place I could study the Scriptures. Suddenly studying the Scriptures was something that I very much wanted to do.

I pondered my options. All I ever considered were Mennonite seminaries; it never occurred to me to look beyond the Mennonite world. There were two Mennonite seminaries I knew of, EMS and Associated Mennonite Biblical Seminary (AMBS). I wrote for catalogs. When the catalogs arrived, my decision was perfectly clear: AMBS was the school. As I sent in my application, I took note of the fact that an Elementary Greek course was taught in the summer term before the fall semester. I figured if this were a prerequisite for any other courses, I wouldn't want to miss them by not taking Greek. So I signed up for the summer Greek course. God not only has an amazing sense of timing but a great sense of humor as well!

Here, with the Elementary Greek class and all that followed it, began the "revolution" in my life, a revolution that I had never once counted on, the total refocusing of my energies and my passions, the emerging of a strong, clear, undeniable sense of call to the teaching of Scripture. I had always loved languages but I was unprepared for the major excitement that I would find in studying Koine Greek. On the one hand it was fun, just like languages are fun! But well beyond my de-

light at the language itself there was a profound excitement about studying Greek, because now, for the first time ever, I could read the New Testament in the language in which it had been written. One thing led to
another. Beyond the language courses lay Bible courses.

Step by step I found myself being drawn, as if by a powerful magnet,
toward the study of the Scriptures. In my first semester I was signed up
for fieldwork under Willard Roth, writing articles for the Mennonite
Board of Missions. I did in fact write one or two that were published in
Purpose magazine. I had thought that I wanted to "marry" my writing
skills with my biblical studies, then go on to become a "religious journalist." But even while writing those few little articles for Willard, I
found myself thinking, *I can't be bothered with this! I want to be studying
the Bible.* And I knew that I wanted all the courses AMBS could offer
me. So at the first opportunity I switched from the two-year M.A.R.
program in which I had originally enrolled into the three-year M.Div.
program.

The next three years were some of the richest of my life. They were
also some of the most challenging. Day by day, semester by semester, I
began to come alive to the study of the Scriptures, as beautiful and as
challenging as that was. I recall my initial deep struggles with historical
criticism, something I had somehow never come face to face with in any
of my college Bible classes. My undefined-yet-quasi-"magical" childhood views about the character of the Scriptures came under intense
scrutiny and eventually had to be discarded altogether as I struggled to
find my way from where I had been to where I was now headed.

But at the same time I was beginning to find a new and ultimately
much firmer piece of ground to stand on. I began to discover the dynamic character of the inspiration of the Scriptures, and I began to view
that inspiration in a fundamentally new way as the presence of God in
the very human processes of life, faith, and reflection within the biblical
community. These learnings were hard-won for me. But when they
came, they were for that very reason all the more valuable. What I
brought with me out of my seminary education was a view of the Scriptures no less high but far more sturdy than the house of cards with which
I had entered seminary.

That was not all. What I brought with me out of my seminary education along with my new perspectives on the Scriptures was a profound
sense of calling to the task of teaching the New Testament. There was no

questioning this calling, there was no denying it. It was there, vividly, insistently. It was as if God were saying to me, "Here is your life! You just never knew it until now." I recall sitting in Howard Charles' classes and thinking to myself, *Yes! This is what I want to do with my life, to open the Scriptures to others as Howard is opening them to us.* I had privately chuckled at what I deemed the over-enthusiastic dreams of Gertrude Roten, when she had told me toward the end of the summer Greek course that she saw me someday becoming a Greek teacher. I knew that I was not interested in teaching *Greek!* But by the end of my seminary career I knew I was headed toward a life of seminary teaching and that a graduate program in New Testament lay not so far down the road.

I felt the need for some new academic challenges. But if I was ready to sit on my laurels, God had other plans for me. From seminary I headed straight into what I have since dubbed my "Jonah experience," a job teaching Bible and German at Christopher Dock Mennonite High School in Lansdale, Pennsylvania. I never really wanted the job. I tried as hard as I could to run away from it. But as hard as I tried, I could not escape it. This job came running after me until I finally realized that I was being chased by "the hound of heaven," and I said "Okay, God, you win."

When I did, I had much to learn about the grace of God. Partway through my first year there, I fell flat on my face, as flat as anyone ever might without resigning a job outright. My subsequent experience of the grace of God in standing me back up on my feet, sending me back into my classroom, and teaching me how to love myself even in the face of failure was an experience more profound and more empowering than anything I had ever encountered. It was in those days of vulnerability and grace that I found myself adopting as my own the stories of Peter walking on the water and the lame man rising up and walking on legs that he knew wouldn't carry him.

God knew that I could never make it through life, and certainly not through graduate school, on the intolerable "success ethic" with which I emerged from seminary. So God saw to it that I wouldn't have to try. I emerged from that two-year crucible experience with an even deeper conviction that God had a task for me to do. I knew that it wasn't high school teaching. I still believed it was seminary teaching.

So it was that I enrolled at Union Theological Seminary in Virginia. Although I had been accepted at Princeton and at Candler School of

Theology, I chose Union. It was a good choice, though initially terrifying. All throughout my first semester and up through our final exams I kept wondering, *When are they going to weed me out?* On the last day of exams I sat outside the dean's office, waiting to receive the fateful envelope which would contain our questions for the day, and thinking to myself, *I can't even think of a question they could ask which I could answer.* Somehow the grace of God was sufficient to the day. I survived, but just barely. I was on academic probation for the exegesis seminar in the spring semester. There I finally achieved the "honors" I needed to achieve. God is truly gracious.

Beyond the terror there was gift, significant gift, in my tenure at Union. I stood at the feet of a gifted, committed, and highly exacting Matthean scholar, Jack Dean Kingsbury, and learned from him what it means to engage in rigorous and disciplined encounter with the biblical text. Here it was as well that I discovered the immensely freeing and empowering character of literary-critical study of the Gospels. I had cut my exegetical eye-teeth on historical-critical study of the Scriptures, a methodology which, while immensely informative in every way, for the most part simply does not "preach." Now I found myself drawn to, and liberated by the approach to "Gospel as story." This was an approach which could always preach, an approach everyone sitting in the pews could understand, since everyone knows how to listen to stories. My exegetical instincts have been profoundly shaped by the schooling I received as I worked with Kingsbury and absorbed by example and osmosis a keen respect for the literary character of the Gospels. I am grateful to him for the gift he gave me in teaching me how to bring the Gospels, whole and unsliced, back into the classroom and the congregation in a form which the readers and listeners can both understand and actively engage.

This was a gift I needed. I was headed back into the classroom and the church. From Richmond my road led me back to Harrisonburg, the place of my beginnings, and back into the classroom, this time a seminary classroom. I was not yet finished with my dissertation but had run out of all means to put a roof over my head and bread on the table. So I sought out a teaching job at Eastern Mennonite Seminary (EMS).

It was autumn 1984. I was the first full-time faculty woman at EMS. Everyone around me seemed impressed by that fact. They all seemed to need me to respond to their amazement and delight. But for me there was no surprise or amazement, only gratitude. It had been ten full years since I had started down the road toward this destination. I had known for ten years that I would end up in a seminary classroom, teaching Bible. It was simply the next step down the long road I had been traveling. And it was altogether natural and non-amazing.

Where My Path Has Led: Reading the Bible Again for the First Time.

The rest is history—the enormously rich, energizing, challenging history—of the past nearly two decadess in the classroom teaching Bible in Harrisonburg, Virginia; in Elkhart, Indiana; in Beirut, Lebanon; in Bethlehem, Palestine; and in Cairo, Egypt. That deep, strong, magnetic pull toward the study of the Scriptures has never abated. And there is enormous delight for me in the energetic push-and-pull of dialogue around the Scriptures which happens regularly in my classroom. It is a push-and-pull I will never outlive.

Early in my teaching career at EMS I encountered a series of television commercials which have ever since given name and focus to what I seek to do in the seminary classroom as I teach the Scriptures. The commercials showed unwary passersby being invited to taste-test unmarked bowls full of Kellogg's Corn Flakes. When the uninterested taste-testers eventually perked up, recognizing the unanticipated culinary delights of this ordinary-looking bowl of flakes, they asked, conveniently enough, what they were eating. The answer came back from the magisterial "voice of God," offscreen and unseen: "Kellogg's Corn Flakes! Taste them again for the first time!" This is the passion which energizes me, as I open the Scriptures, to call my students—nudge them, cajole them, challenge them, if at all possible inspire them by example—to read the Bible "again for the first time." It is a passion and a calling worthy of a lifetime.

CHAPTER 23

From Nonresistance to Engaged Nonviolence

J. Denny Weaver

Introduction

My journey with the Scripture began in the Argentine Mennonite Church in Kansas City, Kansas. It was a congregation of perhaps 120 members, comprised of some ethnic Mennonites and a few persons who had been "converted" in the years before I was born, when Argentine was still called a mission congregation. That congregation constituted my church home until I went away to college. My parents eventually left Argentine, and I have had no contact with that congregation since college.

From Argentine Mennonite Church I learned several things: (1) that the faithful church is a small minority in a world that does not follow Jesus; (2) that the Bible is true, in all its parts; (3) that questions of theology, religion, and the Bible have right answers, *if* we can find them; (4) that the Mennonite church has the best chance of finding those answers; (5) and that an inviolable and inseparable part of the church is belief in nonresistance.

I am still oriented by and working out of those learnings from my first church home. My journey with Scripture has been an ongoing search for answers to questions—some questions about the Bible, some about the world—that grow out of my early conviction that the Bible is true, that there are some right answers, that Mennonites have many of those answers, and that nonresistance is an intrinsic and inseparable part of whatever church is. At the same time, I have made major adjustments in both the form and content of all those learnings, so much so that for some people the continuity might seem invisible until I point it out.

My family reinforced those teachings, particularly the point about nonresistance. And my family added one additional teaching—about racism. From my family I learned that I was supposed to see black people as equals, even as I was also formed by the intrinsically American idea that skin color is the first and most important thing to notice in a person. In very different ways, those two issues of nonresistance and confronting racism have been driving forces in my developing understanding of the Bible and in the teaching and writing that has been my calling. At one point, I would have considered these separate, independent issues. Today I am still surprised how they have intertwined themselves and become integral pieces of my journey with Scripture and my understanding of what it means to be a disciple of Jesus.

For the most part, the changes, adaptations, and revisions I have made in those early learnings were not provoked by crises. While I had the routine bumps and doubts of many young people, I went through no period of profound doubt or distancing myself from Scripture or from the church. My learnings—even the profound ones that required major reorientation of my views—came through encounters in normal life experiences, and I negotiated the process of changing my mind without going through major crises of faith.

Further, a number of my ongoing learnings developed gradually, sometimes over very extended periods of time. I find that I returned several times to issues that had seemed settled and discovered that some views that themselves had already been revisions now no longer worked, and I had to pursue further. In describing my pilgrimage with the Bible, I will discuss my journey with respect to several of these particular themes, which will provide insight into how I see the Bible as a whole.

Nonresistance

The first theme is nonresistance. In a broad sense, I can say that my entire lifelong journey with the Scripture consists of an effort to understand the fullness of what nonresistance means for me and for the church that we belong to.

Growing up, I always knew that "church boys" were supposed to be nonresistant. This nonresistance had two concrete components: if anyone hit me at school, I was not to resist, I was to do nothing; and it meant that when I was old enough, I would not go into the army. In both situations, nonresistance meant to stay away from any activity that involved fighting or violence of any kind. This nonresistance was passive. And its foundation was Jesus' teaching in the Sermon on the Mount about not resisting evil, turning the other cheek if hit, giving the coat as well as the cloak if sued, and going the second mile by doing more than my share of any work I was involved in. In other words, nonresistance stood squarely on the Bible.

My understanding of Jesus' teaching and of what it means to be "nonresistant" has changed markedly from this view that I carried from Argentine into college. Several factors challenged and redirected my commitment to that facet of what it meant to be the church.

The civil rights movement first posed a challenge to this understanding of nonresistance that I believed was biblical and a *sine qua non* of Mennonite and Christian faith. In the late 1950s, when I was in high school, civil rights protests were just beginning to creep into my awareness. At that time, I thought that protests, marches, bus boycotts, lunch counter sit-ins violated the principle of nonresistance; they were acts of force, forcing white people to do things against their will. And that force was wrong. But along with that thought, I also knew that African-Americans were discriminated against.

That discrimination did pose a dilemma for me. I realized that by asking black people to be nonresistant, I was telling them not to resist the discrimination against them. That did not seem fair to me, but I assumed that it was part of being faithful to Jesus. And it did seem strange that African-Americans should be better off for rejecting rather than accepting the Mennonite faith that I, as well as many other Mennonites, advocated at that epoch. Although I did not recognize it as such at the time, the idea that it might be unfair to tell African-Americans to not resist racial discrimination constituted the faint and feeble beginning of change in my view of the Bible and what it taught about nonresistance, nonviolence, and the rejection of violence.

A second nudge toward change occurred in my junior year at Goshen College. In a college Sunday school class, I heard Norman Kraus describe his participation in civil rights activity during his time in graduate school. At the time, I was scandalized that Norman was abandoning the sacred idea of nonresistance and supporting violence. A similar nudge came from the stories Guy F. Hershberger told about traveling in the segregated South and asking for extra plates to share food with a black companion in a restaurant when the owner of the restaurant allowed the African-American to be seated but then refused to serve him. I remember telling my roommate that "old Guy went too far."

A few years latter, as the Vietnam War grew heated, my wife and I found ourselves in Algeria with the Teachers Abroad Program of the Mennonite Central Committee (MCC). After a year of French study, I taught English as a foreign language in a public high school in Algeria. We arrived in 1966 to an Algeria still flushed with the thrill of victory in their war of liberation from France. To a person, the Algerians all believed that their freedom was the fruit of that war. I went to Algeria with MCC because I was a conscientious objector to war and wanted nothing to do with killing people in Vietnam. But the joy and satisfaction expressed by the Algerians about their war impressed me. And I really wondered what I had to say to them out of my understanding of Christian nonresistance. The Algerians were Muslims. If they had become Christians and had become nonresistant Mennonite Christians like myself, it seemed they would still be a French colony. What kind of a gospel was that, I wondered, when they would be better off staying Muslim than becoming Christians? I really did not have an answer for them.

Those questions compelled an answer. I had gone to Algeria after completing two years of seminary. By the time I returned to study at Associated Mennonite Biblical Seminary in the fall of 1969, after four years abroad and with the protests of the Vietnam War cascading all around, I was waiting to learn about nonviolent resistance as a biblical motif. In Millard Lind's courses on Jeremiah and Ezekiel I learned about the protests and the resistance activity of the prophets.

I will skip quickly over the stages of my learning how the people of God are called to make a witness to the reign of God in the world and how that witness is and often should be a confrontational witness—like that of the biblical prophets who sometimes did strange and offbeat things to show the way of God in contrast to the rule of evil. It also became obvious to me that acts of Jesus fit that prophetic mode—deliberately healing the withered hand on the Sabbath when he could have done the healing the next day without getting anyone upset; disregarding conventional expectations about interaction with women, with Samaritans, and with other people considered ritually unclean; and the so-called temple cleansing that provoked the authorities to seek his death.

More recently Walter Wink has demonstrated that the texts of turning the other cheek, giving coat with undergarment, and going the second mile, which we had long believed were statements of passive nonresistance, were actually suggestions regarding how an oppressed person without power might turn the tables and nonviolently resist the oppressor.[1] Wink's argument became for me the current step in a long transition from nonresistance to nonviolent activism that had begun with my first vague question about the fairness of nonresistance in the civil rights movement.

I want to underscore and emphasize that this transition from nonresistance to nonviolent activism is a *biblical* argument, and a discussion about how to understand the Bible as the book that guides our life and thought. A series of questions I encountered at college and in Algeria brought me to understand that the Bible was not a book of passive nonresistance. Instead it showed that if the people of God were faithful in witnessing to the reign of God on earth, they engaged in specific actions and in a way of life composed of nonviolent activities that confronted those powers of evil unwilling to acknowledge the reign of God.

I still believe fervently that Jesus refused to use violence and that the reign of God is characterized by the refusal to use violence. But I have come to understand that refusing to use violence does not mean passively accepting and acquiescing in the evil and injustice that abounds. When we see the character of God's people, from the prophets in the Old Testament through the life and teaching of Jesus, we see that the biblical people of God engage actively in witnessing to the presence of the reign of God and in exposing the injustice that opposes the reign of God.[2] If we are not involved in this liberation agenda, we are not being faithful to the Bible, to Jesus, or to the reign of God. Today, I am grateful for the challenge to nonresistance I received from Norman Kraus and Guy Hershberger, and I would have something to say to the Algerians about nonviolent resistance.

How the Bible is True

A given in my home congregation was that the Bible is true. I still have no doubt that the Bible is true. What has changed greatly over the years is my understanding of *how* the Bible is true. This includes my understanding of biblical inspiration.

I still have a very nice King James Bible in Morocco leather with thin paper and gilded edges that my parents gave me in high school. I remember looking up 2 Timothy 3:16 in that Bible and reading, "All Scripture is given by inspiration of God, and is profitable for doctrine, for reproof, for correction, for instruction in righteousness." And I recall working through a logical progression: "inspiration" guaranteed the truth of every word of Scripture because it was illogical to think that God would give us a guidebook with errors in it.

In my early years, there were several verses that I checked pretty regularly with that logic in mind. These verses included the following: 1 Peter 3:3 "Whose adorning let it not be that outward adorning of plaiting the hair, and of wearing of gold," which was why my mother did not have a wedding ring and why it would have been sinful for me to buy a high school class ring; or Deuteronomy 22:5, "The woman shall not wear that which pertaineth unto a man, neither shall a man put on a woman's garment; for all that do so are abomination unto the Lord they God," which was why I would not let my girl friend wear pedal-pushers in the summertime; or the first 16 verses of 1 Corinthians 11, which explained why my mother and all the women in our congregation had to wear that "little white cap," and why it would have been sinful for them ever to cut their hair, even to trim up the ends so that it would hang straight. I really did not want any of those three texts to be there, but they were—and if the Bible was true, then we had to "obey" those verses.

These verses were singled out as things that had to be obeyed if one were to be obedient to the Scripture. It gradually dawned on me that even if the Bible was true, that straightforward approach to biblical obedience had a problem attached. These items were singled out from many other things that we did *not* obey—beginning with the command *not* to plait, that is, braid hair in 1 Peter 3:3, when all the women at church did braid their hair. And then there was a long list of other stuff that included things like not mixing milk with meat (Exod. 23:19; 34:26; Deut. 14:21), which would disallow cheeseburgers, or stoning the rebellious son (Deut. 21:18-21). Figuring out how to deal with such commands, when the Bible was true, was a task I had to negotiate. The answer appears below, in the discussion of change over time.

Evolution was another item I had to deal with under the category of truth of the biblical witness. When I arrived at college, I assumed that Genesis 1 stated a factual, scientific account of creation of the earth in six days of twenty-four hours each. After all, when I read the text it talked about "day" and I certainly knew that the Bible was inspired and therefore true. I recall a conversation with Mr. Hoover, the Argentine high school biology teacher when I was in tenth grade. Mr. Hoover asked me if evolution bothered my religious faith, and I said that it did. He replied, "It doesn't bother mine." I was proud of myself for having "witnessed" to Mr. Hoover about the truth of the biblical record.

The challenge came at Goshen College in Norman Kraus's course in Protestant Christianity. Norman neither taught nor advocated evolution in that course. He did present the historical context for the development of the idea of evolution and how one could understand the Bible in relation to it. I went back to Shoup House dorm and talked to two seminary students about how upset I was that Norman appeared not to believe the Genesis story of creation and was opening the door to evolution.

For the two seminary students, that conversation with me no doubt has been long forgotten—they were just explaining what they already knew. I remember it, however, as the beginning of a different—and much more fruitful—way of understanding the Bible. I learned that Genesis 1 and 2 were true—still true—when I could see that they were theological statements about God and the meaning of creation rather than attempts to provide a scientific explanation for creation. And even more importantly, I saw that these creation accounts actually had more—rather than less—meaning when I saw them as theological rather than as scientific statements. It took only a couple days to work through that set of issues in Genesis 1 and 2, and I was ready for biblical studies in seminary a couple years later.

Bible as History

Another part of my journey with Scripture was learning that it is a history book. French President Charles de Gaulle is one of the people who helped me see the Bible as a history book.

When I lived in Algeria from 1966-68, I listened to European news, particularly French news, on the radio nearly every day, and I read the French newspaper *Le Monde*. The news from France contained a lot of tumult. The list of items I remember includes France expelling NATO from Paris, France vetoing Great Britain's entry into the Common Market, France attacking the American dollar, France boycotting Israel after the Six-Days War, month-long student riots in Paris provoked by de Gaulle's university reforms, France's refusal to sign a nuclear test ban treaty, and de Gaulle's visit to Canada when he bypassed Ottawa on his way to Quebec and then made a speech that appeared to support Quebec separatism. The elderly president Charles de Gaulle was at the heart of all this tumult that angered and perplexed both Europeans and Americans. And I certainly did not understand why de Gaulle would be acting in such contrary fashion.

Jacques, my best French friend in Algeria, just happened to be the son of a member of the Gaullist party in the French senate. I often asked him, "What's de Gaulle doing?" And he would tell me, "You have to understand," followed by a longish history lesson. Finally, probably weary of my constant questions, he gave me a set of books to read, saying that everything I needed to know was in those books. The books were a profusely illustrated, three-volume, embossed-leather, guilt-edged edition, with a Bible-like ribbon to mark one's place, of Charles de Gaulle's *Mémoires de Guerres*. In my hands I was holding a special limited edition of de Gaulle's memoirs of World War I and World War II, given by Charles as a gift to the Gaullist members of the Senate. My friend Jacques had his father's copy, and I got to read it.

I was thoroughly captivated by these volumes. De Gaulle wrote like a gifted novelist, telling a fantastic, larger-than-life tale of good versus evil, with Charles himself leading the forces of good, which consisted mainly of France, against the forces of evil, comprised of virtually everyone who was not French. It was fascinating reading, and I learned many things about both world wars that did not make it into United States history books.

And Jacques was right—what I needed to know to understand what de Gaulle was doing in 1968 was contained in these three volumes written some twenty years earlier. His policies in 1968 were a continuation of his antagonisms, battles, and policies from the war years. Seeing how a document from the past illuminated the present showed me the importance of history. And in the space of the perhaps three weeks that it took to read those volumes, I decided that when I returned to the United States and entered graduate school, I would study church history rather than the Bible. In graduate school, then, I did study church history, in particular Anabaptist history, which is still an important part of my academic career.

In one way, switching from the biblical studies of my first stint in seminary to church history was an apparent step away from the Bible. But, in the long term, this had a major impact on how I would understand the Bible. The continuing thread that ties the Bible together is a story, a historical narrative—the narrative of God's people that began with God's call of Abraham and continued through the story of Israel and onward to Jesus, into the early church whose account appears in Acts, then Revelation. It just seemed obvious that if historical context was important for understanding current events, then it is equally important to understand the historical context of the Bible's narratives. What I learned from reading de Gaulle's war memoirs directed me into historical study, but eventually it also helped me to understand the significance of history for understanding the Bible and the importance of seeing the historical context to understand the Bible.

And more than that, thinking about history in this way made the Bible personally meaningful to me. I learned to see history as important, starting with the contemporary church. We ask where we came from, and history tells us that. We trace our history back through history in North America—like John Ruth's monumental history of Lancaster Conference[3]—back to history in Europe and the Reformation. We keep on going through the medieval period to the early church. And where do we read about the origin of the early church? In the book of Acts! That history goes back through Jesus, through the history of Israel until we reach Abraham, whom God called to be the father of a people in whom all the peoples of the world shall bless themselves.

And that is where we see that as history the Bible is still personal to us. It is a history of my and our origins as Christians. As Christians, we are living in and continuing the narrative that began with Abraham. The Bible really is my book and our book. If I am a Christian, I must take it seriously as the book that locates me and the people of God in history.

The narrative of the people of God from Abraham to the church in Revelation provides the Bible's unity. Other kinds of literature in the

Bible take their meaning from that history. For example, Psalms contains the people's worship music; Proverbs contains its wisdom. The books of the prophets contain their commentary and critique on the people's acts, their life, as God's people. Like the prophets of the Old Testament, Paul's letters provide critique and commentary on the efforts of the early church to be God's people.

The Hermeneutical Community

Interpreting this history book is vitally important. In 1970, I posed a question in a seminary class. That question is still with me, and it focuses the question of biblical interpretation for Mennonites. In a course in sixteenth-century Anabaptist theology I asked, "How do Mennonites always know how to make the Bible come out right on issues like adult baptism and nonresistance when the exegetical method we are learning down the hall with Clarence Bauman differs so markedly from that of Menno Simons that we are seeing in this course?" I meant it as a zinger, a question that would put the professor on the spot. I do not remember the answer, but I do recall thinking that the answer was not very good. Now I suspect that the answer was better than I thought.

Even though I do not remember the answer given in that class, the question has stuck with me. Today I could give at least a partial answer. The answer involves terms like *hermeneutical community*. The fact that over the decades there is some continuity of issues, such as adult baptism and nonviolence, means there is something superior to the particular methodology in use at a particular moment. That which provides continuity is commitment to be a disciple of Jesus. Disciples who genuinely pattern themselves on the narrative of Jesus will be nonviolent, since that was how Jesus confronted the world. And that commitment takes precedence over—that is, it guides—the methodology that we all use.

Violence in the Old Testament

As I hinted earlier, the Old Testament contains much violence. If the Bible is our book and if we are shaped by Jesus' rejection of violence, then violence in the Old Testament poses a problem. It is particularly a problem when we talk about the Bible as our book and see the Bible as the story that we live in and that still shapes our lives today.

My journey with the Scripture has passed through two stages concerning violence in the Old Testament. Developing these stages sets up answers to other questions.

When I was young, the basic idea I learned was that the New Testament superseded the Old. Between the two Testaments came a change in God's rules for God's people—violence was allowed or commanded in the Old Testament but was then banned with Jesus in the New Testament. That answer took seriously the teaching and example of Jesus. But it also entails problems. It renders the Old Testament virtually meaningless as a book for us. It implies that the nature and methodology of God's work in the world changes—God shifts from one who countenances violence to a God who does not countenance violence. It also seems to imply that God has abandoned the children of Israel as God's people—God shifted loyalty from the Jews to Christians. I have abandoned this view.

The violence in the Old Testament is real—that is undeniable. This violence comes from the record of God's people trying to understand how to live as God's people. The question for us is how to understand the violence in the Bible.

Frequently missed in the discussion of violence in the Old Testament is the fact that alongside the stories of violence in Israel's efforts to understand who they were as God's people, the Old Testament also contains examples of nonviolent resistance. One of my favorite examples is the story of Gideon and the 300 men who defeated the Midianites through a ruse with torches, pitchers and trumpets, with virtually no killing (Judg. 7). Or one can site the example of Isaac, who kept digging new wells rather than fighting (Gen. 26:12-22). Or the story of Elisha who prayed that the marauding Arameans be struck with blindness, then led them into Samaria, where the king was prepared to kill them. But Elisha said no. Instead, he told the king to "Set food and water before them so that they may eat and drink; and let them go to their master." And thus the king prepared a "great feast; after they ate and drank, he sent them on their way, and they went to their master. And the Arameans no longer came raiding into the land of Israel" (2 Kings 6:22-23).

After seeing these nonviolent accounts, the question becomes, "Is it the violent actions or the nonviolent actions that best reflect the will of God for Israel?" If we take the life and teaching of Jesus as the embodiment of the rule and the will of God, then there is a right answer to that question. It must be the nonviolent actions that best reflect the will of God. If we take Jesus seriously, we should not be citing examples of violence in the Old Testament to justify violence today.

There is still another way that violence is limited in the Old Testament. In discussing capital punishment, John Howard Yoder pointed out something that is usually missed concerning the well-known text of an "eye for an eye" or a "tooth for a tooth." This statement originally appeared in a context where the prevailing pattern was to wipe out an entire family or tribe in retaliation. In that case, an appeal for only compensatory damage was actually a limitation on violence rather than its authorization. That limitation indicates a change in the direction of lessening of violence. Jesus' teaching then continues the direction of that change.[4]

These two observations—that the Old Testament contains examples of nonviolence, and that it has a trajectory moving in the direction of lessening violence that culminates in Jesus—shows that the Bible as a whole teaches nonviolence.

Direction of Change

The previous section used the idea of a change in an identifiable direction. The specific instance was development from violence to nonviolence as the will of God. Identifying a change of attitude regarding a specific theme is a direct implication of seeing the Bible as a history book. Seeing change over time reflects its historical character. And with the idea of change in mind, it is much more important to know the *direction* of change than it is to know the stance at any particular location along the trajectory. The movement in the direction of less violence is ignored, for example, if the "eye for an eye" text is lifted out as a legitimation of the violence of capital punishment, or if an example of assassination or war from the Old Testament is used to justify war today. In essence, to lift out a particular point from the trajectory as the answer to a contemporary problem is to freeze the development at the particular moment chosen.

Here is the place to return briefly to the previously mentioned items of biblical obedience Mennonites have largely abandoned as a church—prohibition of all jewelry, and proscribed hair style, head gear, and clothing for women. When we have clearly in mind that the Bible is a historical book, recounting the history of the efforts of God's people to understand what it meant to be God's people, we can more easily see that not all their efforts were in line with God's will, and we can see that some things which once were significant no longer apply to our context, or would be understood much differently in our context. When that is the case, it becomes clear how our cultural practices can change without thereby becoming disobedient to the Bible.

Conclusion

The Bible contains the story of God's people from Abraham to the early church. This story provides the Bible's unity. Since we are living farther along in that same story, the Bible is very much *our* book. It takes much faith to live in the Bible's story as though it reveals God's will for the world.

It takes faith to read the Old Testament and our own history through the lens of Jesus who reveals the will of God. It takes faith because it gives priority to the rejection of violence, a stance that makes little sense in our society, which has such profound faith in redemptive violence.

It also takes courage to read the Bible this way. It takes courage because it puts us in tension with the way the majority of Christians read the Bible. Reading the Bible in a way that makes clear the nonviolent rule of God will challenge much of Christendom rather than blend the peace church into it. Do we have the faith and courage to read the Bible to discover whether our lives are aligned with God's nonviolent agenda for the world?

Notes

1. Walter Wink, *Engaging the Powers: Discernment and Resistance in a World of Domination*, The Powers, vol. 3 (Minneapolis: Fortress Press, 1992), 175-84.

2. For a statement of nonviolent resistance built on Old Testament prophets, see J. Denny Weaver, "Making Yahweh's Rule Visible," in *Peace and Justice Shall Embrace: Power and Theopolitics in the Bible: Essays in Honor of Millard Lind*, ed. Ted Grimsrud and Loren Johns (Telford, Pa.: Pandora Press U.S., 1999), 34-48. This essay was later reprinted as a stand-alone pamphlet and distributed by Christian Peacemaker Teams as a statement of their biblical mandate. Nonviolent resistance for disciples of Jesus is

the clear implication of the understanding of Jesus' work in my *The Nonviolent Atonement* (Grand Rapids: William B. Eerdmans Publishing Co., 2001).

3. John Landis Ruth, *The Earth Is the Lord's: A Narrative History of the Lancaster Mennonite Conference*, Studies in Anabaptist and Mennonite History, vol. 39 (Scottdale, Pa.: Herald Press, 2001).

4. John Howard Yoder, *The Christian and Capital Punishment*, Institute of Mennonite Studies Series, vol. 1 (Newton, Kan.: Faith and Life Press, 1961), 6-7.

CHAPTER 24

Between Text and Life

Earl Zimmerman

One of my earliest memories is of sitting in church beside my dad listening to Grandpa Sensenig preach. Growing up in an Old Order Mennonite community in Pennsylvania, I experienced our church services as austere. Adults dressed in severe plain clothes. Men sat on one side of the meeting house. Women sat on the other side. In the center was a table and long bench where the preachers sat. Pulpits were *verboten* (forbidden) because they represented a worldly Protestant influence that was resisted.

I loved listening to Grandpa preach because he spoke in English and told stories. Most of the other preachers spoke in German using a tired sing-song voice. When I got older I sat with the other boys in the boy's section. The wooden benches were hard and my feet didn't touch the floor. They would fall asleep no matter how much I wiggled and squirmed. I was allowed one trip to the outdoor privy in the middle of the long church service. To help me endure the service, I always calculated that trip carefully. When I was outside I spent as much time as I dared watching the birds in the trees or anything else that caught my attention before slowly returning to my seat.

Grandpa's sermons and the children's Bible story book in our home were my first introductions to Scripture. In a home without radio or TV, I became a voracious reader and practically memorized that Bible story book. I also listened carefully to what Grandpa had to say. Several things he said stayed with me and became my bridges as I grew older and did my own wrestling with Scripture in very different worlds. Grandpa was a self-educated preacher but told me he could distinguish between the different biblical authors because they had different styles of writing. He told me that he liked to compare his German Bible with his English Bible.

These observations served me well when I first encountered the challenges of biblical literary criticism. Such criticism helped me understand that the Bible did not come directly from God. I was beginning to see that, however we understand biblical inspiration, we need to recognize that people wrote the Bible. Even Grandpa Sensenig knew that.

Grandpa also complained about young preachers who love to speculate about the book of Revelation but don't even understand Jesus' teaching in the Sermon on the Mount. This favoring of a text within the text later helped me as I encountered other questions of biblical authority and interpretation. What we know of God in the life and teaching of Jesus is our key to how we understand the rest of the Bible.

But I didn't only read the Bible. I read everything else I could get my hands on, including the local newspaper and the *National Geographic* magazines in Grandma Zimmerman's house. Once a month, Mother took me to the bookmobile when it visited our town. I would stock up on all kinds of books and always had one with me wherever I went. When there was a break between chores, I got out my book. I now find it surprising that my parents didn't more strictly monitor the things I read. I am also very grateful.

A Collision of Worlds

My two worlds were on a collision course. As a young boy I never dreamed of leaving my Old Order home. I loved my people and our farm community. But when I entered my teenage years things came to a head. Dad insisted that I drop out of school to help on the farm after my first year of high school because he was afraid I was being pulled into a world outside our Old Order community. I loved school and being forced to drop out felt like a kind of death to me. This alienated me from Dad. More and more, it alienated me from our Old Order community. And it alienated me from the Bible.

I sensed that the Bible was at the root of my problems. I now refused to read it because I could not deal with the way it was understood in our Old Order world. Instead, to my parents' chagrin, I hung out with a rebellious group of teenagers. This was the 1960s. We were discovering fast cars, wild parties, rock-and-roll music, and weekends at the beach. The slowly escalating war in Vietnam was a storm cloud that hovered on the horizon of my teenage years.

That war eventually created another personal crisis for me. I, like many other young people of my generation, hated it with a passion. Every day in the newspaper, I read the body counts of soldiers who were killed. A former classmate was killed in action. Stories of American military atrocities began leaking out in the press, making me and my generation cynical and distrustful of anything our government told us. Official lies to the public just became another part of the game. Then I received a notice to report to our local draft board. As a religious conscientious objector, I had to find an alternative service assignment in several months.

I knew I didn't want to go to Vietnam. What did a farm boy from Pennsylvania have against the North Vietnamese? But I felt like a hypocrite when I applied for alternative service as a religious conscientious objector. My religious beliefs were in a muddle, to say the least. Was refusing to fight simply another Old Order taboo? These questions plagued me as I moved to Elkhart, Indiana, to begin my conscientious objector assignment as an orderly in the psychiatric ward of a local hospital.

I was now far away from friends and had plenty of time to think. I knew I had to find some kind of resolution to the contradictions in my life. I was angry about so many things and that vicious, senseless war was on the top of my list. My anger about the war and my alienation from the Old Order community was exacerbated by an Old Order preacher who, upon hearing about the rock festival at Woodstock, said they ought to move the army in there and clean the place out. I retorted that he should be thankful we live in a country where they don't do things like that. Such a reckless and violent condemnation of Woodstock— coming from a supposedly pacifist Mennonite—only escalated my anger and frustration with the Old Order community and pushed me to search for answers elsewhere.

Reading the Bible Again

Picking up my Bible again, I found it wooden and lifeless. Then one day I gathered up enough courage to walk into the Mennonite mission board office in Elkhart. I asked a receptionist if she could recommend some literature on the morality of war. After conferring with someone in another room, she returned with the title of a book. It was *War, Peace, and Nonresistance* by Guy Hershberger.[1] I went to a local Christian bookstore, which the receptionist had directed me to, and bought the book.

Over the next several years I kept returning to that store to buy other books. I read Hershberger's *The Way of the Cross in Human Relationships*.[2] At some point I picked up *The Politics of Jesus*, by John Howard Yoder.[3] I read *The Cost of Discipleship*, by Dietrich Bonhoeffer.[4] I owe my life to these books. They gave me a whole new vision of the church and what it means to follow Christ. What I found in them was different from the Old Order separatism I had rejected. Yet they also challenged the American social status quo. Jesus had something to say about the Vietnam War and other social ills that I found so troubling.

With this new perspective and the help of a modern English translation, the Bible came alive. My study of the Bible focused on the Gospels and the epistles of Paul. I later picked up a little booklet on studying the Bible called *The Joy of Discovery* by Oletta Wald.[5] This was a helpful little tool for reading biblical texts. It taught me to be observant to the content and structure of a text. It taught me to consider the original context including the author, the social situation, and the implied readers. This became pivotal in helping me negotiate the distance between the biblical text and my world.

However, I still didn't understand the ways that my own world shaped my reading. I didn't know the extent to which we humans create a world that then confronts us as a given reality. My later cross-cultural experiences and my studies in sociology of knowledge would help me see this with more clarity.[6]

When I returned from my conscientious objector assignment, my fiancée Ruth Hoover and I left our Old Order world and became members of Kralls Mennonite Church, a small Lancaster Conference congregation near my home. We were married a year later. This was my first cross-cultural journey. Ruth and I left one religious world and entered another. Here we were introduced to a more pietistic form of Christian faith. We were also introduced to a form of Mennonite fundamentalism that was strange to us. Copies of the Mennonite-related fundamentalist periodical, *The Sword and Trumpet*, were regularly placed in our church mailboxes, introducing me to polemics against liberalism. Fears about losing the authority of the Bible swirled through our churches.

I was not interested in such reactionary fears but I became more and more at home in evangelical and charismatic circles. I was interested in a kind of Christian faith that was relevant to the world outside our religious cultural enclave. This included getting involved in a prison and inner-city ministry in the nearby city of Lebanon, Pennsylvania. My mother cried when Ruth and I, along with our small children, moved to the city. She instinctively knew that we had become part of yet another strange and fearful world.

During this time, I read my Bible through a lens combining Anabaptist, evangelical, and charismatic influences. We knew that the people we were relating to in Lebanon would never fit into the traditional Mennonite congregations in our area, so we started holding church services in a former rescue mission on the poor side of town. We learned to know people in our neighborhood. We became deeply involved in the charismatic movement. It felt like the new wave of God's Spirit. We were excited about exploring spiritual gifts.

Then one Sunday evening Sam Smucker, the charismatic pastor of the Worship Center, came to speak at our church. He and his wife were dressed like slick TV evangelists; they were an ex-Mennonite version of Jim and Tammy Baker. He spoke about how God wants us to prosper because we are children of the King. We could "name and claim" things in prayer. God had blessed him with a splashy new maroon Cadillac as an answer to such prayer.

At the same time, I was reading Art Gish's little book *Beyond the Rat Race*.[7] This biblical perspective on simple living and economic justice told me that Sam Smucker was full of himself. He was peddling a religious version of American consumerism. But others in our church were persuaded and eventually left for more "alive" charismatic congregations unshackled from such moralism.

Many of the other searching young people I related to during that time ended up leaving the Mennonite world for evangelical and charismatic congregations. I owe the different trajectory in my life to the influence of people like Guy Hershberger and John Howard Yoder. They convinced me that Jesus' way of peace was central to the gospel. I also owe it to Grandpa Sensenig's insistence that we begin our study of the Bible with the Sermon on the Mount.

During this time I spent one school year at the Rosedale Bible Institute in Ohio. I studied there because of pressure from church leaders in our conservative church district who thought our Mennonite schools were too liberal in their interpretation of the Bible. One year at Rosedale, however, was enough for me. Even though there was much that was positive, I was turned off by the wooden biblical literalism and cultural isolation.

One example is the Old Testament teacher who was struggling to figure out how the children of Israel could have multiplied so rapidly during the generations they were in Egypt. When I suggested that there might be gaps in the recorded genealogy, he accused me of being a liberal. He further accused me of falling into the trap of the documentary hypothesis on Old Testament studies. I had no idea what that was, but I immediately decided that I'd find out. Something had to give. His kind of biblical interpretation didn't make sense.

The Philippines and Different Kinds of Education

About a year later, Ruth and I made the huge decision to pack up our family and take a mission assignment in the Philippines. We were committed to Christian ministry and wanted to expand our horizons. We sold our house. We gave away or stored all our earthly belongings that did not fit into our suitcases. We made arrangements to study at Eastern Mennonite University (EMU) when our first term of service was completed. This turned our world upside down for a second time.

In the Philippines we encountered grassroots Filipino Christians, a dictator named Marcos, leftist revolutionaries, and radicalized Mennonite Central Committee volunteers. We saw the raw edge of U.S. military and economic policies. Here, for the first time, I encountered the twisted face of real poverty and hunger. I saw the limits to which human brutality and violence could go. I learned to know real, existential fear. And I saw how global inequalities skew all relationships, including those in the church.

This experience drove into my consciousness an awareness of the intimate relationship between our world and the biblical text. Hearing Mary's Song (Luke 1:46-55) read during a Christmas service in Manila was an epiphany. In this place it became a revolutionary document. Where we are and the things we experience enable us to hear things in

the biblical text that we missed or couldn't comprehend before. The social realities of poverty, exploitation, imperialism, and revolution in the
Philippines have striking similarities to the first-century Palestinian realities Mary was responding to.[8]

When I finally got to EMU, I had all kinds of questions. I was
thirty-three, finishing my college degree while Ruth supported our family as a nurse. For the second time in my life I was plagued with radical
doubts. My faith no longer fit easily into the boxes of my religious community. Feeling this tension, I plunged into my studies with a passion,
finishing my college degree in two years and spending another two years
completing a master's degree at the seminary. Along with biblical studies
and theology, I studied economics, sociology, missiology, and peace and
justice. I found teachers who became confidants and were not alarmed
by my anger and my doubts. They gave me the courage to explore new
worlds.

I loved biblical studies. I studied the original languages and gained
new critical tools. I finally learned about the Old Testament documentary hypothesis. I wrote my master's thesis on Matthew's Gospel. It was
centered on the Salt and Light pericope in the Sermon on the Mount. I
was trying to figure out what it means to be a people of God in relation
to the kind of world I had experienced in the Philippines. Even more, I
was trying to figure out how this fit with what I now knew about my
identity as an American in relation to global American military and economic domination.

Back to the Philippines

As soon as I completed my thesis, we returned to Manila. In the
meantime, Marcos had been overthrown and Cory Aquino took power
in a nonviolent People's Power Revolution. The following years were full
of tumultuous change as the new political order struggled to survive and
the old one refused to die. We learned the meaning of perseverance as we
lived through electrical blackouts, water shortages, and repeated coup
attempts from reactionary military forces. We also learned about the
deep love, faith, and commitment of our Filipino friends as they coura-
geously fought for a more just and equitable society.

Here my journey with Scripture took another turn. I had a deep respect for our Mennonite biblicism but became increasingly disturbed by

our penchant to think we could somehow read the Bible straight. We think we can approach it as dispassionate exegetes in the comfort of our classrooms and middle-class churches. We think of the Bible as a deep well containing truth which we haul to the surface and apply to our lives. We don't know that, when we peer into the well, part of what we see is our own reflection. José DeMesa, a Filipino Catholic theologian, taught me about a correlational theological method in which Scripture and tradition are placed in conversation with contemporary human experience.[9] Becoming aware of how our lives shape what we hear helps us become more faithful readers.

One example is that my pastoral work in Damka, an urban poor community in Manila, slowly taught me to read the Bible from the perspective of the poor. Simple things such as prayers for food took on new meaning as I walked in their streets, sat in their homes, and, confronted their daily struggle to survive. The hospitality and faith of these Christians has profoundly shaped and enriched my life in unexpected ways. I realize that I can never completely enter their world but, in my mind's eye, I still find myself sitting in their company as I read my Bible. I think of our many conversations and allow their lives and their faith to help shape my understanding.

Pastoral ministry, Teaching, and Doctoral Studies

When we left the Philippines six years later, we moved back to Harrisonburg, Virginia. Ruth began working as an administrator for the newly created Center for Justice and Peacebuilding at EMU. I took a part-time pastoral assignment with Shalom Mennonite Congregation, a small group that was meeting on the EMU campus, and began doctoral studies at Catholic University in Washington, D.C.

My pastoral role has given me a new appreciation for the way Scripture shapes our lives as a people of God. We structure our worship and teaching around the lectionary and its three-year cycle of Scripture readings. I develop my sermons as a conversation between our experience and Scripture. We are experimenting with ways to more intentionally relate central biblical signs or sacraments such as baptism and communion to our life together.[10] For example, we try to explicitly connect our communion rituals with our fellowship meals and even our work at a local food pantry.

We sometimes jokingly refer to ourselves as the church of the "last door" and the "first door" because we tend to attract people who have almost given up on the church as well as people who are finding the church for the first time. This is no accident. We intentionally focus our ministry around people who do not naturally fit into more established congregations in our community. We are passionate about the gospel of peace. We get involved in various kinds of social action and are deeply concerned about global issues. We believe we cannot really understand Scripture apart from this application in our lives.

In my doctoral studies I gained new insights into biblical interpretation as a conversation with Scripture and tradition involving intriguing layers of complexity. Scripture is a "classic" authority that continues to be heard through the centuries.[11] Our reading of this authority, however, needs to engage the scientific and historical consciousness of the contemporary world; we cannot return to a pre-critical world. At the same time, the emerging postmodern world now calls into question the hegemony of the modern world and its categories. This offers the promise of honoring various and multivalent voices.

More recently I am beginning to understand that Scripture is a religious phenomenon much broader than the Bible. My world religions professor at Catholic University introduced me to the work of Wilfred Cantwell Smith, who has done comparative studies of the way Scripture functions in various religious traditions. According to him, Scripture is more than a written text. It involves a richly textured web of relationships between a text and a community of people through time. It symbolizes and mediates the transcendent in the relationship between self, community, and world. In this way we recognize it as sacred.[12] Such insights become especially important as we learn how to relate to other religions in our increasingly diverse local communities.

A Conversation with Scripture

All this has helped me understand that if we truly honor the authority of Scripture we will not see it as a one-way conversation. Indeed, we can and must talk back to Scripture. We interpret it in light of our experience. This gives us freedom to respect its authority while interpreting it in ways that are life-giving as we confront new challenges. This is especially important in controversial issues such as the current debate about homosexuality that tears at the fabric of our religious communities.

Our ability to encounter and listen to the "stranger" and the "other" in our midst is an indication of our ability to hear Scripture because Scripture itself confronts us as "strange" and "other." Scripture connects us to many voices from eras and cultures radically different from our own. If we look hard enough, Scripture can help us recognize the other in ourselves. Such recognition enables us to reach out to all people with the love of God as demonstrated in the life of Jesus.

It has been quite a journey. It began when I was a young boy listening to Grandpa Sensenig's simple but insightful understanding of Scripture. My subsequent travels have led me through other strange worlds where I met different and sometimes confusing voices. I needed to appropriate the truth they spoke while steering around the dead end alleys down which some of them would lead me. It was not always easy. Sometimes it was frightening and excruciatingly painful. It occasionally took all the courage and insight I had. Sometimes I failed. Even so, I'm thankful because it has helped me realize that the person or faith community that will not take risks has not really lived. To live is to struggle and this always includes some degree of failure. This recognition comes as a sign of grace. I meet God in this struggle—this interplay between text and life.

Notes

1. Guy Hershberger, *War, Peace and Nonresistance,* 3rd. rev. ed. (Scottdale, Pa.: Herald Press, 1969).

2. Guy Hershberger, *The Way of the Cross in Human Relationships* (Scottdale, Pa.: Herald Press, 1958).

3. John Howard Yoder, *The Politics of Jesus* (Grand Rapids: Eerdmans, 1972).

4. Dietrich Bonhoeffer, *The Cost of Discipleship* (New York: Macmillan, 1959).

5. Oletta Wald, *The Joy of Discovery: In Bible Study, In Bible Teaching* (Minneapolis: Bible Banner Press, 1956).

6. I have been especially indebted to Peter Berger, *The Sacred Canopy: Elements of a Sociological Theory of Religion* (New York: Anchor Books, 1969).

7. Art Gish, *Beyond the Rat Race* (Scottdale, Pa.: Herald Press, 1973).

8. A biblical scholar who has worked at the connection between the biblical text and contemporary political meaning is Richard A. Horsley, *Jesus and Empire: The Kingdom of God and the New World Disorder* (Minneapolis: Fortress Press, 2003).

9. José was a personal friend and teacher but I'm also indebted to the little book, written from a liberation perspective, which he co-authored. See José De Mesa and

Lode Wostyn, *Doing Theology: Basic Realities and Processes* (Quezon City, Philippines: Claretian Publications, 1990).

10. For a helpful guide to structuring community life around these signs read John Howard Yoder, *Body Politics: Five Practices of the Christian Community before the Watching World* (Scottdale, Pa.: Herald Press, 1992).

11. David Tracy, *The Analogical Imagination: Christian Theology and the Culture of Pluralism* (New York: Crossroad, 1991).

12. Wilfred Cantwell Smith, *What is Scripture? A Comparative Approach* (Minneapolis: Fortress Press, 1993), 221-231.

Part Three

Presuppositions and Theological Grids

CHAPTER 25

Presuppositions for Interpreting Scripture

The Nature of Presuppositions in Our Interpretation of Scripture

One reason we have differing understandings of Scripture is because we bring differing assumptions and expectations to the Scriptures. What we *presuppose* is often left unexamined—sometimes because it appears so "obvious" it doesn't demand examination, sometimes because to examine and seriously to ask questions would seem almost sacrilegious.

Presuppositions are those beliefs and understandings that we hold but seldom stop to carefully identify. Presuppositions may be derived from the Scriptures or they may be based on *prima facie* cultural values which we, and likely those who taught us the Bible, read into the text as we study the Scriptures. Whether from the Bible or from a system of values and a way of life more closely at hand, our presuppositions play a major role in our understandings of Scripture—both in the questions we ask and the answers we receive. For example, when we told our stories, we shared some understandings of how the Scriptures came to be. It became clear that we had a variety of differing answers (and differing journeys) because we brought differing philosophical and theological presuppositions to the task.

One reason our church has so much difficulty understanding *itself*—understanding between generations, between gender groups, and increasingly between vocational groups—and understanding the Bible is that we have so little awareness of what is prepackaged deeply inside us and what, as a consequence, we bring with us when we read the Bible. Without awareness of our *inherited* prepackaged "biblical goods," differences between us tend quickly to become personal and dialogue becomes threatening. Given our endemic penchant toward conflict avoidance, there is little incentive to dialogue about our differences and to test our assumptions.

For some the Bible, even in cases where we share a common Anabaptist heritage, is an all-inspired book equally authoritative from cover to cover. For others the focus may be the Gospels and a few snippets from Paul. For some the meaning is immediate; for others the real meaning can only be found behind the Greek or the Hebrew. Some freely hear Jesus speak when we read the Bible; others walking beside us struggle with the fact that the Bible is a hand-me-down in a process of nearly two thousand years from a premodern, preindustrial, prescientific culture in many ways more akin to African tribal religion than to any contemporary Western mode of thought.

We assume a word is a word, all the more so if it is a word from the Bible. "Any old fool, and particularly if we allow ourselves to be fools for God, knows what that means!" Quickly, degrees of spirituality and moral rectitude are attached to scriptural understanding. So it is not surprising that even within our small group of twenty-three persons, all dedicated Christians and all members of a single religious denominational heritage, our *differences*, had we begun with those as our focus, might well have become frightening and divisive.

How these Sets of Presuppositions Emerged in the Context of "Our Journeys with Scripture"

How were we to creatively, and if possible non-threateningly, explore the differences in our understandings? As the next step beyond telling our stories and trying to locate the meta-themes, we began to unpack the "self-evident"—though often elusive—differences. We began not by debating them but by simply identifying them more clearly—by openly stating our heretofore non-verbalized starting points, our presuppositions that we bring to our understandings of the Scriptures.

Why is reading the Bible and having an encounter with God practically a daily affair for some of us while for others such a devotional experience is quite alien, almost magical? Are some more spiritual? Are others more intellectual? Or does all this merely reflect personality types? Are such responses not cultural and theological presuppositions which need to be identified before they can be creatively discussed?

Circumstances, both preparation and sharing time, did not allow all of us to share our presuppositions. So the planning team tapped the shoulders of four persons to share the presuppositions they bring with them when interpreting the Scriptures. In selecting these persons we attempted, as much as possible, to span the theological and gender spectrum of the group. When we arrived at this third stage of our journeying with Scripture (stage one: sharing our individual stories; stage two: finding the common themes), this seemed an obvious next step.

All the authors of the following sets of presuppositions share a common christocentric confessional stance and work from within the Anabaptist theological tradition. Beyond that, as becomes evident in their articulation of the presuppositions that inform their reading of Scripture, they are also shaped by different theological orientations, life experiences, fields of study, and vocations, among other things.

Nancy Heisey, the author of the first set of presuppositions, comes from a Brethren in Christ background, where she learned to "get the steps right." Her childhood years in a Navajo community and her later service in Africa shape her understanding of the Bible being rooted in the experience of a particular people. Her graduate studies in the New Testament and early Christianity have taught her to carefully consider the various components of a faithful reading of Scripture. Her responsibilities in church leadership and her vocation as a New Testament professor add to the distinct gifts she brings to this task.

Craig Maven, author of the second set of presuppositions, could not connect with his childhood Episcopal religious heritage and became immersed in a modern worldview before reading the Bible again as if for the first time. Subsequent studies at Westminster Theological Seminary underscored the challenge of defending the Bible from the nihilistic tendencies of modern and postmodern intellectual constructs. He also brings the challenges of his vocation as the pastor of a large and theologically diverse congregation to his presuppositions for reading Scripture.

Dorothy Jean Weaver, author of the third set of presuppositions, grew up in a secure, "orthodox" Mennonite family headed by maternal grandfather, Chester K. Lehman, a longtime professor of Bible and theology. As a young adult, she found herself drawn to the formal study of the Bible, almost despite herself. She now brings her passion for biblical languages and the Palestinian people to her vocation as a seminary New Testament professor. The christocentric center of her faith informs her presuppositions for interpreting Scripture.

J. Denny Weaver, author of the fourth set of presuppositions, learned from his childhood congregation that the church is a faithful minority in a world that does not follow Jesus. Two areas in particular in which the church stood against the world were in matters of violence and racism. As a seminary student, he wrestled with the historical and literary tools in our interpretation of Scripture. The Vietnam War and a teaching assignment in Algeria shaped his theological journey from nonresistance to engaged nonviolence. His vocation as a professor of religion at a Christian liberal arts college also informs the presuppositions that guide his reading of Scripture.

Set 1: Some of My Presuppositions in Biblical Interpretation
Nancy R. Heisey

First, the Bible is, for me, the word of God. When I say that, I speak metaphorically, and I understand that the image carries me over from a world where the printed marks on a page are God's Word to one where God's voice is heard through the printed page—but also through the voices of others, the realities of nature, and through particular nonverbal experiences of God's presence. Any human expression about God is limited by our humanness, and we need to be careful not to make an idol of a human view of how God speaks and reveals God's self to human beings.

Second, I understand the Bible as a book rooted in a particular story of a people. Learning as much as possible about the historical, social, religious, and economic setting for the story helps me to hear more clearly what the Bible says. Because the Bible is a historical book which developed over many centuries, I understand God's Spirit to be working through the entire process of telling, writing down, collecting, editing, choosing, and translating the texts. At the same time, I believe that the Bible always offers a "surplus" of meaning, that some people may read it without considering all the context described above and still come to true and useful understandings in their reading. I also have experienced that coming back to a biblical text again and again opens new, different, or enriched meanings with each encounter.

Third, I believe that biblical interpretation is "multiple"—being built first by the dialogue among the scriptural writers themselves (for example as Deuteronomy interprets Exodus or Paul interprets the prophets) and later by the hearings and readings of all who have come to Scripture down through the centuries, from varied backgrounds, experiences, and training. Some of this diverse mix is involved, whether we realize it or not, whenever a contemporary group meets for worship or Bible study. In our world, it is also beginning to take place as people from very different geographical and cultural contexts learn from each other's readings. Within that multiplicity, I accept as primary the readings of members of the faith community and more specifically those who share presuppositions shaped by the heritage of the Anabaptists.

Fourth, central to the Anabaptist heritage is an approach to interpretation called "christocentric." This term encompasses several important understandings. First, it recognizes that Scripture never speaks of itself ("writing") as the word of God but rather describes Jesus Christ as the Word of God. Second, reading the Bible christocentrically means recognizing that Christians should not only read the Old Testament as looking toward the New but also read Jesus and the New Testament writers as looking back to their own Scripture to explain who God is, how God works, what God wants of God's people, and what God intended through Jesus. Third, it acknowledges that the whole Bible should be read through the lenses of Jesus' life and teachings and his death and resurrection. When conflicts seem to appear in the text, the history of the Christian use of the Bible calls for digging deeper to find the underlying unity of meaning, and at times choosing Jesus Christ's way above that called for by other voices of Scripture.

Set 2: Presuppositions in Interpreting the Scriptures
G. Craig Maven

Let me begin with my definition of presupposition. Presuppositions are those principles or measures that exist *a priori* to any discussion or inquiry. Thus, my presuppositions about Scripture are a priori to any hermeneutic, exegesis, or theology. Why? I believe that ultimately all reasoning is circular. We wind up where we begin. If we begin a priori that all truth is accessible through empirical means, then we are bound to determine that the Bible is the work of ancient peoples who sought to give meaning to their lives. It is no more authoritative than any other ancient religious text. At best it becomes our book of myths and teachings and takes its place beside other ancient texts for academic study. Since the starting point determines the ending point presuppositions must be examined and clearly revealed. What, then, are my presuppositions?

First, I believe that the Bible is God's Word. I believe the Bible contains exactly what God wants it to contain and is the infallible, inerrant guide for faith and life. Therefore, when I approach the task of interpreting the Bible, I begin with the idea that God has spoken in the Word, and that there is a correct and incorrect interpretation.

Second, because the Bible is God's Word, I believe the Holy Spirit leads us into correct interpretation. Therefore biblical interpretation is as much a spiritual as an academic discipline. Believing the Bible is God's Word and that the Holy Spirit is the guide who aids in interpretation in no way relieves us of the hard task of exegesis and interpretation—of personally engaging in a hermeneutical task.

Third, there is a hermeneutical circle into which I enter. I break into the circle with the presupposition that God has spoken and what God has said is available to me. Since it is a circle there is no set beginning or end; rather we break into the circle. The hermeneutical circle consists of exegesis, interpretation, and theology. Each affects the other and is dependent on the other. How a text is exegeted affects the interpretation and theology. My theology will affect how I exegete and interpret a text. My interpretation will affect the way I exegete and the theology I develop.

Fourth, the Bible has human authors who wrote from a very human perspective. The infallibility, inerrancy, or perspicuity of Scripture does not mean that the Bible is some book dropped out of heaven with no historical contexts. The Bible is a rich banquet of different tastes from different cultures and different times. Only a few very select portions of Scripture were dictated to the human author.

Fifth, the Bible comes to us through the inspiration of the Holy Spirit. This does not mean all the human authors held one common understanding of redemptive history or theology. There is an *intercanonical dialogue* that enables us to more fully grasp the wonder of redemption's story. For example: John's gospel is different from the Synoptics. The differences go beyond chronology. There are theological differences between the accepted gospel accounts. Paul and James did not see eye to eye (James 2:12ff, Eph. 2:8-10). Peter references Paul's writings as hard to understand (2 Pet. 3:15,16). These dialogues are nothing when compared to the Old and New Testament dialogue. Yet this does not mean authors contradict or invalidate each other. Rather the tensions serve as the harmony to the melodies of the meta-narrative of God redeeming creation.

Sixth, the Bible is the authority in daily life that guides and answers questions. There are three perspectives—normative, situational, and existential—that I use when applying Scripture. First, what norms are present that I need to take into account? Commandments are norms that are easily applied. "A new command I give you: Love one another. As I have loved you, so you must love one another" (John 13:34). Love is normative for all of the Christian life. There is also the situational. How do I show love in this situation? Confrontation may not seem loving, but Paul's confronting Peter (Gal. 2:11-21) proved not to damage but strengthen their relationship and further unified the early church's teaching on grace and the law. The existential reality of how God's love has already changed me in Jesus provides the motivation for paying attention to this passage. For I know that when I love other followers of Jesus then "all will know you are my disciples. . . " (John 13:35).

Without the presuppositions that the Bible is God's Word, that it is authoritative, and that it is the infallible trustworthy guide, I am left to wonder what value this text really has. If it is simply the product of the spiritual musings of ancients, then my own insights can be as valid, if not more so. There soon is no faith that can be clearly identified as Christian, no identifiable community of faith can exist, and we are plunged into the hopelessness of individualism. I understand that I find in the Bible the authoritative Word of God because I start with the presupposition that it is exactly that. However, with the Bible as authoritative guide, a genuine faith community can be built. It may not always, if ever, be neat and tidy, but it will be the church of Jesus Christ.

Set 3: Hermeneutical
Presuppositions Concerning the Scriptures
Dorothy Jean Weaver

First, the canon is closed. I accept the confession of the early Christian church that it is through these writings of the recognized

Christian canon that God has uniquely spoken and still today continues to speak.

Second, the Scriptures are inspired. I acknowledge the inspiration
of the Scriptures as an extended and dynamic process in which God has
been present and active from its beginnings—in the events recorded in
the Scriptures, in the oral transmission of these stories, in their transfer
into written documents, in their collection into larger anthologies of
"Scripture," in their translation from language to language, in their
reading and reception by countless Christians from the earliest days onward.

Third, the Scriptures are christocentric. I hold a christocentric view
of the Scriptures in which all things move toward, through, and out of
the Christ-event. Stated conversely, the Christ-event is the ultimate lens
through which all other writings and teachings within the Scriptures are
to be viewed, interpreted, and evaluated.

Fourth, Scripture comprises a unity. I believe that the Scriptures, as
a collection of writings gathered by the Hebrew community and the
early church, create and communicate a single, overarching story of redemption—the story of God and God's people. They are not simply so
many disparate and disconnected tidbits of history, poetry, wisdom, and
prophecy.

Fifth, Scripture forms a trajectory. I believe that the Scriptures, as
individual texts brought into a broad, overarching unity, reflect movement in a direction, both in terms of a single trajectory (the "big story")
and in terms of multiple trajectories (the individual elements of that big
story). The story reflected by the Scriptures is going somewhere; and it is
always of the essence to ask where the Scriptures are headed on any given
question.

Sixth, the Scriptures are a resource for ethical decision-making. I believe that the Scriptures are a primary resource for the ethical decision-
making of the church. But I believe that to use the Scriptures as such a
resource is not to find discrete proof texts but rather to search all parts of
the canon and all levels of the text with regard to the question at hand
and to ask above all for the trajectory of this evidence.

Seventh, Scriptures constitute a privileged authority. I grant the
Scriptures a privileged position vis-à-vis other sources of authority (tradition, science, sociology, etc.) which likewise offer resources for engaging in ethical decision-making.

Set 4: Assumptions in Biblical Interpretation
J. Denny Weaver

First, I assume that the Bible is true—not infallible nor inerrant, but true.

Second, the Bible's interpretation will generally make sense in terms of the world in which we live. Two examples of what I mean by "making sense in terms of the world in which we live": (1) The debate about a young earth (6,000-10,000 years) versus a very ancient earth. Scientific data overwhelmingly tells us that the earth is ancient. I believe it and understand Genesis 1 and 2 accordingly. (2) Is Revelation a book that predicts the future or is it involved in the first century? Are its symbols from our world or the first-century world? There are a host of intellectual complications that arise if Revelation is speaking about things 2,000 years in advance—starting with the fact that it would be impossible to understand and totally irrelevant for first century readers. I go with the explanation that makes sense—read Revelation with its symbols coming from the first century, and interpret it accordingly.

The one specific exception to making sense in terms of the world in which we live is the resurrection of Jesus. The resurrection of Jesus does not fit into the categories of knowing and testing in our known world, but the Bible speaks about resurrection, and it is the basis of our faith. I believe in the resurrection.

Third, the Bible is a *historical* book: (1) It contains the story, the history, of Israel and the early church. The historical material supplies the outline or the backbone or the story-line that supplies the Bible's unity. It also contains the commentary on and the prophetic literature of that story, as well as the poetry, music, and wisdom from that story. (2) Because it is a history, with commentary on that history, to be read truthfully, the Bible must be read in that historical context. (3) Since the Bible must be read in terms of that historical context and as a historical book, it speaks to us *indirectly*. We learn of God via the written attempts of God's people to understand God and who they were as God's people.

Fourth, since the Bible is history, we need to interpret it with the view that there is development and change of views within it. For these views, it is more important to identify the direction of change or the kind of change taking place, than to fix on where things stand at any one point. Important themes would be violence—is there increasing or decreasing violence? Slavery—does the Bible's support for slavery tend to increase or diminish? Role of women—does the Bible tend to increase or decrease the status of women? Keeping in mind the possibility of movement or change is why it is out of order to try to solve contemporary problems by proof texts.

Fifth, the idea of movement/change also indicates why a christocentric reading for Christians is important. The direction of change is not always clear, and there can be change in several directions at once. Those changes that most clearly reflect the will of God are those changes that can be shown to pass through Jesus.

Sixth, the fact that the Bible is a history book indicates why we do not continually add to the canon. When we write history and talk about how we understand the reign of God in relation to that history, we are doing what biblical writers did. When we comment on the course of our history, we are doing what the biblical prophets did. There is no functional difference between ourselves and the biblical writers. The difference is in proximity to the origins of God's people. Christians accept as normative those materials that come from the origin rather than from some later point in the story.

Seventh, the impact of my personal story on my interpretation is key: I came from a small church located on the edge of a big city. There were only three Mennonites in my high school. Thus I have always known that the church, the followers of Jesus who continue to witness to the presence of the rule of God in the world, are a small minority. It is normal for me to think of the peace church as a small minority among Christians in the world.

Thus, reading John Howard Yoder's analysis of the Constantinian shift and the articulation of a smaller motif alongside of and in contrast to the dominant, society-encompassing church of Christendom seemed normal. Jumping over many steps, understanding that the church that witnesses to Jesus is a minority in a dominant world is expressed in my book, *The Nonviolent Atonement*. And I am still perplexed why so many Mennonites seem reluctant to affirm that the church that follows Jesus' way of nonviolent justice-seeking may be a small, witnessing minority, and seem so insistent on linking Mennonites to some version of American Protestantism that ignores the peace and justice dimensions of Jesus.

CHAPTER 26

Theological Grids

The Role of Theological Grids
in Our Interpretation of Scripture

Our theological grids reflect vocational, gender, sexual, and economic orientations. Like presuppositions, they may be held quite consciously and deliberately. Or, as is more likely, our grids subconsciously shape the way we read Scripture. Our grids, or refracting lenses, influence the selectivity with which we all read the Scriptures and the authority we grant certain Scriptures over others. We select which passages get read most frequently and which ones seldom if ever get read; we also "choose" how those Scriptures will be interpreted.

All of us read Scripture selectively; even those among us who might claim otherwise. Anabaptists of the sixteenth century (some more so than others) granted greater authority to those writings most closely associated to the teachings and example of Jesus. In doing so they were implicitly saying, Jesus grants Scripture authority. Explicitly the Anabaptists were saying that followers of Jesus must grant some Scriptures greater authority in our lives than others. Although Jesus is revealed through Scripture, for the Anabaptists Jesus nevertheless stood above Scripture.[1]

If our presuppositions reflect our ideological and theological biases, our grids reflect our most fundamental values and our life commitments. They are a measure of who we are. Consciously or subconsciously, they reflect what we are doing with our lives. Because of this it might be equally appropriate to call these grids our "value meters."[2]

246 ⬜ *TELLING OUR STORIES*

Whatever we may choose to call this phenomenon, it is important to note its impact on our understanding of Scripture—that is, the nature and message of the Scriptures is affected, sometimes in major ways, by who we are and what we bring to the Scriptures.

Women, for example, tend to be more alert than men to those accounts where Jesus engages women and dignifies their role in society. These women need not see themselves as feminists; simply the fact that they are female is sufficient to open them up to a more feminist selection and understanding of Scripture. All of us have likely encountered parents who, upon discovering that their son or daughter is gay or lesbian, have come to a new understanding of the Scriptures, sometimes even referring to it as a conversion experience. Others, less sympathetic to this cause, see the shift as allowing experience to have greater authority than Scripture, or as evidence of encroaching liberalism. To take one further example: We had no persons in our Laurelville group whose life vocation was to make money (however nobly and legitimately that may be conceptualized). Where that is the case, as we are experiencing in an ever more affluent church community, biblical teachings on wealth are receiving new interpretations. As we become more pluralistic and diverse, discerning together our value meters, our theological grids, becomes an ever more important task.[3]

How these Grids Emerged in the Context of "Our Journeys with Scripture"

After our discussion of how our presuppositions shape our reading of Scripture, those of us gathered at Laurelville, probed deeper into the extent to which each of us also have life orientations—here called theological commitments—that shape our reading of Scripture. We noted that our presuppositions and theological commitments have a certain overlapping function. Nevertheless we found them sufficiently distinct in their foci to warrant separate consideration. After the colloquium, we asked four of the participants to write a summary statement of the theological grid that informs their reading of Scripture.

Each of the four authors who articulated a personal theological grid works from deeply held Anabaptist and free-church theological convictions. Nevertheless, fundamental differences are readily evident; these reflect their personal journeys and communities of identity. Their task as it was assigned is simply descriptive, not normative. But we hope that by beginning with the question *Who am I?* the larger ongoing task of discerning *Who ought we to become?*—to be discussed between individuals and groups with Scripture in our midst—will be made easier.

James Krabill, the author of the first grid, for ten years served on a mission assignment in Africa, where he related to African Independent Churches. He now serves as an executive for global ministries at a North American mission agency. It is hardly surprising that a core theological construct that shapes his reading of Scripture is the recognition of God as a missionary God. The emphasis that he places on Christ's atoning work and on the church as followers of Jesus who receive and share God's grace reflects evangelical theological sensitivities. Yet his core emphasis on God's plan to restore shalom to the universe (including transformed human communities) indicates that he is refracting his evangelicalism through an Anabaptist theological prism.

Malinda Berry, the author of the second grid, writes as a young African-American woman who is a doctoral student in theology. Accordingly, she identifies the believer's exercise of reading the Bible as a process of freeing us from the forces in our culture that colonize our minds. This post-colonial reading calls into question the reigning political and intellectual paradigms that shape our world. It is aware of how oppressive these paradigms are for subject peoples. Such a post-colonial reading correlates with a radical Anabaptist reading of Scripture which also calls those reigning paradigms into question.

Earl Zimmerman, author of the third grid, served on a mission assignment in the Philippines. Now a pastor and professor, he teaches university courses in religion and social justice. His emphasis on Jesus' liberating message of God's reign reflects his journey with the Filipino people and their struggle for liberation from poverty and colonial oppression. Furthermore, the years he spent in Asia shape his concern for how we relate to other cultures and religions. These concerns are also refracted through the prism of an Anabaptist theological tradition as seen in his emphasis on the way of Jesus and on the church as a called out missional people of God.

Ray Gingerich, author of the fourth grid, became convinced that our gospel is too preoccupied with minutiae and our God too small when he was a college student. His later mission assignment in Europe exacerbated this tension for him as he saw various Christian groups come up with different kinds of non-answers in response to the radical questions of that era. It was as a seminary student studying under John Howard Yoder that he first encountered the radical phenomenon of a nonviolent political reformer named Jesus. These insights were expanded and deepened in his doctoral research on Anabaptist mission. As a longtime college professor who took various trips to Latin America, he began to more fully understand that God is nonviolent and that the authority of Scripture is determined by its life-giving function in society.

Set 1: God's Plan to Restore Shalom to the Universe
James R. Krabill

The Scripture is for me the story of God's loving, comprehensive plan to restore shalom to the universe.

I believe the God we encounter in the Scripture is above all a missionary God. From the earliest pages of human history when men and women turned their backs on God's love, it was God who took the initiative to pursue them, coming into their world to seek, woo, call, and restore them.

Even before the world was created, God put in motion a comprehensive, long-range plan to "bring everything together in Christ" *everything* in deepest heaven, *everything* on Planet Earth.

Jesus is and always has been at the very heart of God's plan to make things right with the world. It is in Jesus, Scripture tells us, that "all creation will be set free from its slavery to decay" and "brought back to God." Past sins will be forgiven and forever forgotten. The walls of anger and hostility between countries, clans, and classes will break down. Races living in conflict will form one new people and enter into God's presence "by Christ's atoning death on the cross."

That is why Jesus' earthly life and ministry, ending with his death, resurrection, and exaltation, together constitute the single most important event of all time—the event by which all history is divided and all other events are defined and understood.

Furthermore, God has chosen the church—those believing followers of this Jesus, who were and forever will be the undeserving recipients of God's grace and peace in their own broken lives—to be the primary instruments through which that same grace and peace is extended to others.

This calling of the church to be God's collaborators and key carriers of the peace plan goes back to God's promise to Abraham and Sarah: "By you all the families of the earth shall bless themselves." From this point onward in the biblical drama, the Scripture emphasizes repeatedly that the principal means by which God is reaching out to the world is through the people of God. It is through this people-in-mission that God's love is to be most visibly demonstrated and most clearly made known to those who have not yet seen and heard.

Given this "grid," I can do no other than to read the Scripture through a missional lens, inquiring of any given text questions such as these:

- How does this portion of the Scripture contribute to my understanding of God's peace plan for the universe?
- In what ways were God's people faithful—or unfaithful—in this historical context to their calling as participants in and messengers of God's reconciling plan?
- What is the message here for God's people-in-mission today in twenty-first century North America? Africa? Asia? Latin America? Europe?

Set 2: Believing Readers
Reading the Bible and Calling It Scripture
Malinda Elizabeth Berry

The motif of biblical shalom, *which is central to who Jesus Christ is, informs my reading of the Bible as a believing reader who stands against the forces in our culture that colonize our minds and harden our hearts, preventing us from seeing one another as whole people and interconnected communities.*

Believing readers

Before the biblical text becomes sacred Scripture, there is a process of understanding, interpretation, appropriation, ownership, and deep reverence for the text we as believing readers go through that leads to our being able to call the Bible our Scripture. This movement is a kind of journey, as seen in the illustrations that follow. Being a believing reader is simply one way to signify our personal commitments to Christian community and the affirmations that our particular communities make about God as Creator, Redeemer, and Sustainer known through Scripture.

In this movement from text to Scripture, a believing reader's social location shapes the experiences she or he has on the journey. What is an obstacle for one reader because of economic status is nothing to another reader. What is comforting to one reader creates fear and trepidation for another. These realities explain why, when we arrive at Scripture, the text looks different in different communities.

A post-colonial reading of Scripture

In my reading of Scripture, I seek to counter the harmful and even dangerous parts of culture that cause us to look the other way rather than stand up as advocates of God's justice. As a believing reader, my journey of understanding, interpretation, appropriation, ownership, and reverence of our sacred text has been shaped by a number of social and intellectual movements that have impacted Christianity, biblical scholarship, Christian theology, and Christian ethics in the late twentieth century:

- the genocide wrought by Western European and colonial American imperialism and colonization;
- the Abolitionist and Women's Rights movements of the nineteenth century;
- the Jewish Holocaust of the mid-twentieth century;
- the Civil Rights movement of the mid-twentieth century;
- the Women's Liberation movement of the late twentieth century.

These events have been significant for my journey because the people behind such movements all found ways to justify their actions based on their reading of the Bible, whether they saw themselves acting on behalf of the oppressed, out of love of neighbor, or in their own self-interest. To be a believing reader is to reckon with these historical facts and these readings of our sacred text.

Biblical stories of encountering God

Because I believe Scripture is about our God wanting to be known—that is, not always to remain a mystery—I affirm the multifaceted character of the stories we find in the Bible. They offer us many rich models for how we as contemporary believing readers can encounter the Triune God we worship. Among these characters are the following:

- Jacob who wrestles with God's messenger;
- Queen Vashti who resists male domination;
- Job who encounters evil and suffering and argues with God;
- Mary who listens with an open heart and mind to Jesus' teaching.

The motif of biblical shalom

As incarnation, Jesus Christ is the catalyst for us as our communities discern how we transform our particular journeys into a common ethic that gives life and does not take it away. Central to who Jesus Christ is are the motif of biblical shalom[4] and the metaphor of advocate.

- Shalom is about being in relationship, being safe and sound and not experiencing or issuing threats to those around us. It means the presence of justice among everything and everyone from close friends to entire nations. This biblical justice is evidenced by our concern for the oppressed and what they need rather than what we think they deserve. Furthermore, shalom means being a person of integrity, a trait expressed when something or someone acts and we respond to preserve relationships, liberate, and speak on behalf of the oppressed.

- These aspects of shalom are the marks of the reign of God that Jesus proclaimed. They are also central to the common ethic described above and the basis for social movements seeking to give life through liberation; they therefore challenge systems designed to take life away.

- We often think of Jesus Christ as Savior, Messiah, Redeemer, Son of God, and so on. I will add to this list of metaphors that of Advocate. As he proclaims the in-breaking of God's Reign, Jesus is advocating a love of neighbor that we can understand, own, and finally live only if we have encountered the God of Scripture.

Set 3: The Liberating Good News of Jesus
Earl Zimmerman

The theological guide for my interpretation of Scripture is Jesus' liberating message of God's reign. This good news is situated in the biblical story of God's gracious yet demanding and universal yet preferential love.

The story begins with the call of Abraham and Sarah and the children of Israel as God's people. Faithfulness to this call is characterized by

trust in God, hospitality to strangers, and concern for the poor and oppressed. It includes Israel's prophets, who kept calling God's people back
to this covenant relationship. God's liberating love has been most definitively revealed in the way of Jesus Christ as expressed through his life
and passion.

Jesus' message is made concrete by his call to his disciples to follow
him. After his death and resurrection and the Spirit's empowerment at
Pentecost, the band of disciples was formed into the church which em-
bodies his life. Here is a fellowship formed around suffering love, servant
leadership, equality, economic sharing, mutual accountability, peacebuilding, concern for the least, and an invitation to all. In this way the
church is a witness to Jesus and a sign of God's new world coming.

Jesus' message presupposes that God, as known in Jesus Christ, is
the creator of the world and that all creation is good. It also presupposes
that the world, as we know it, includes the presence of evil. As such, it is
dominated by spiritual, political, and economic powers that, even
though created good, have in various respects become oppressive. This
involves us in a personal and corporate struggle with these evil powers.
In this struggle we follow Christ's nonviolent example of engaged and
suffering love.

Finally, we live in the confidence that Christ has overcome these
powers through his death and resurrection. Consequently, we look forward to the consummation of all things in the reign of God. With this
hope we share the good news, form churches that embody healing and
hope, and enter the struggle for peace, justice, and the integrity of creation. This theological grid informs the following premises:

- the conviction that all human cultures, societies, and religious
  traditions, though tainted by evil, reflect God's good creation and
  can be vehicles of God's truth;
- the recognition that God has a special concern for the poor and
  that our salvation involves our commitment to the struggle for
  human dignity and freedom;
- the understanding that truth is formed by right action as well as
  right belief and that we grow in maturity though a process of pur-
  poseful action and reflection;
- the belief that, as a missional people conveying God's love, we are
  witnesses to Jesus Christ and the good news as he lived and
  preached it;

- the conviction that for us the local and global church is the primary carrier of God's purposes in history, not a national government or any other social entity;
- the commitment to join with all people of goodwill in the struggle to create humane communities reflecting God's purpose.

Set 4: The God-Movement Toward Just-Peace
Ray Gingerich

Justice through nonviolence as taught, lived, and embodied by Jesus frames the dynamic theological grid through which I read the Bible—both the Old and the New Testaments.

Justice pursued nonviolently builds peace—wholeness, prosperity, well-being. The pursuit of nonviolent justice characterized the transformative person and work of Jesus and the revolutionary movement associated with his work, which he called the kingdom of God—later called the church. The church eventually dropped nonviolence from its agenda, reneged on justice, and defaulted on peace. After that, it was neither transformative nor revolutionary. But it claimed the mandate of telling us, its members, how to read the Scriptures—in mostly holy, sacralized, dominating, violence-legitimating ways.

Justice[5] that is not nonviolent is neither just nor peacebuilding. Peace that is not just is neither peaceful nor nonviolent. Nonviolence (earlier in my tradition called nonresistance) that is not actively engaged in resisting evil and bringing about justice is neither peaceable (life-giving) nor nonviolent. Nonviolent justice—as I have come to read the Bible and to understand Jesus—runs with the grain of the universe.[6] So intertwined are these concepts—justice, peace, nonviolence—that I cannot speak of one without implying the others.[7] At times I simply refer to them as "the way of Jesus" or as "the coming reign of God." But those terms are too frequently understood ahistorically, apolitically, and metaphysically. So, most straight-forwardly, this is a grid to discern what is life-giving, personally and structurally.

The authority of Scripture (as read through this theological grid) is determined by its life-giving function in society. That which is life-giving is of God. That which is death-dealing is not of God. Because justice-through-nonviolence constitutes the way of the God of Jesus (i.e., the way of the universe), those Scriptures that provide a normative direction in life—that are authoritative—reveal this same God of Jesus. Those Scriptures that embrace models of love, of justice, and of peace conform to the revelation of God in Jesus and therefore hold authority in my life. Those Scriptures that legitimate death, assert domination, and command violence are reflections of the "fallen" cultures out of which they emerged. They are useful for instruction and for correction (as negative examples) but cannot and should not be forced to fit into the larger pattern of the Jesus Way.

From these two components of my theological grid—call it the warp and the woof[8]—several additional multicolored fibers can be added to make the grid more visible and functional in my understanding of Scripture and in everyday life:

- Scripture is the repository of writings over more than a millennium by multiple peoples at various stages in their search for God. They reflect a variety of cultures and value systems. To make them all speak with one voice is to do violence to the diversity of communities from which they emerged. Let us be wary of harmonizing the Scriptures to make them all fit within one theological grid.

- To experience salvation is to carry on in our day what Jesus began in his, to be in our day as Jesus was in his. Jesus asks us to follow him. Nothing more. Nothing less. Let us be wary of claims to salvation that fall outside of the "justice-peace-nonviolence" theology grid.

- Metaphysical constructs—whether expressed as doctrines or as Scripture (the Word of God)—that supersede the ethical teachings and example of Jesus' nonviolent way of life serve as false gods. The Sacred is the friendliest form of seduction and idolatry. Let us be wary of sacred and sacramental components that get added to the simple "justice-peace-nonviolence" grid.

- Prophetic Scriptures reflect a preferential option for the poor. The God whom Jesus revealed is on the side of the marginalized. To see the God of Jesus, I must stand in my sociopolitical context where Jesus stood in his. Let us be wary of a church that proclaims a gospel of wealth, and of administrators and teachers who gain status because they stand with the powerful of this world.

- If nonviolence is central to the wholeness and well-being of the Christian, then it is central to all humanity. Let us be wary of those who claim nonviolence and pacifism as Christians (for themselves or for their church) but reject the adequacy of a justice-nonviolence theology grid because they defend the necessity of war for the state.

Notes

1. Hans Denck, for example, reflected a *discipleship* grid when he proclaimed, "No one can know Christ unless she or he follow him daily in life (trans. Ray Gingerich). See also *Anabaptism in Outline: Selected Primary Sources,* ed. Walter Klaassen (Scottdale Pa.: Herald Press, 1981), 87.

2. Other metaphors that we have used to capture this phenomenon are: "the theological guide" and "the refracting prism."

3. A singularly significant work exploring this topic, although using different nomenclature, is *Through the Eyes of Another: Intercultural Reading of the Bible,* ed. Hans de Wit, et al., (Amsterdam: Institute of Mennonite Studies, Vrije Universiteit, 2004). Even the chapter titles stir the imagination, pointing to the immense significance that "grids" play—e.g., "Is God's will the same for Groningen and Nicaragua?" and "Jesus' surprising offer of living cocaine."

4. For a further discussion of this point of view, see Perry B. Yoder, *Shalom: The Bible's Word for Salvation, Justice, and Peace* (Nappanee, Ind.: Evangel Publishing House, 1987).

5. Biblical prophetic justice includes the following dimensions: sufficiency for all; dignity individually and collectively; participation in one's own destiny; solidarity/accompaniment with the poor and oppressed.

6. My colleague and friend of Colombia, Ricardo Esquívia, calls this movement of God *justapaz* or just-peace. If my assumptions are correct that this dynamic is embedded in the very nature of the universe, then eventually we should find this word in all our dictionaries.

7. Yet each of these words—justice, peace, nonviolence—is freighted with multiple meanings and calls for further clarification that unfortunately cannot be explored here.

8. The "justice-peace-nonviolence" triad rooted in the Christian Scriptures and the "life-giving versus death-dealing" polarities, found within all religions, have virtually universal application.

CONCLUSION

Jesus is said to have quipped to some of his senior religious compatriots, "You search the Scriptures for in them you think you have eternal life; and it is they that testify on my behalf. Yet you refuse to come to me to have life. . . . I know that you do not have the love of God in you."
—John 5:39-42

The Journey Thus Far

Our journeys with Scripture constitute a renewed search of the Scriptures as well as a call to search ourselves. We pursue this journey not presuming it to be an end in itself—not believing as did the Pharisees that in the Scriptures we have eternal life. We search the Scriptures for it is they—as we have discovered again and again—that testify of Jesus.

We have told our stories. And of equal importance, we have listened to each other's stories. We have searched and found certain mega-themes emerging from the Scriptures and running through all of our stories. Our story is not unique in all its parts. How very beautiful and empowering to realize that we belong to a community of journeyers that forms an ongoing cloud of witnesses.

We worked together and have begun to unveil some of the presuppositions that we bring to the reading of the Scriptures. Following the sharing of "presuppositions" we proceeded to develop a sampler of "theological grids." Inasmuch as these former earlier stages were storytelling, they were relatively non-threatening. Each story was after all my story—and that it remains, not something for which one needs approval or critique. But the presuppositions and the grids went well beyond autobiographical storytelling. Nevertheless they remained relatively non-threatening, for they too were stated in descriptive and personal terms while listening to those who differed from us.

We have also experienced that on this journey, done within a community of fellow believers, our reading of Scripture is not necessarily within our control. In this sense, it has become a dangerous process. We read Scripture, then Scripture in turn reads us and becomes a means of our being convicted by God. We may see ourselves in a strange new light that brings both freedom and responsibility. This is particularly what began to happen in the closing worship service at Laurelville. In this back-and-forth process of encountering others and "the other," our lives are given new meaning and purpose. We become aware of a new horizon or what has more properly been recognized as a fusion of the horizon of the reader with the horizon of the text.[1] Such is the nature of the journey thus far.

Where Will Our Journeys Take Us?

Where then, do we go from here? Storytelling appeals to us at all levels in all vocations and in interdisciplinary situations. But storytelling is not the whole task. In fact we might see it as only the beginning of the task—the fun part. Our story is not normative and faithful just because it is our story or my story. What makes biblical storytelling normative is if, after testing in the community of faith, it corresponds with our Lord's story, with the story of Jesus.[2]

We recognize that to find "correspondence" with the way of Jesus in our pluralistic society with its many voices claiming truth is neither simple nor easy. It calls for continued discernment within community and perhaps at times even confrontation—something we at Laurelville tried hard to avoid for the sake of simply beginning a long-neglected dialogue and building a community of trust.

The issues of militarization and homosexuality, which served as catalysts for the experiment in telling our stories, remain with us. To follow Jesus, to be a social embodiment of Christ, is in the final analysis always political and frequently painful. Telling our stories is not, we hope, a way to delay entering the journey nor a detour to avoid tough terrain. It is, rather, an essential part of the journeying discipline, part of working at the necessary cutting-edge issues, whatever these may be, in every particular stage of the church's pilgrimage. Telling our stories provides us with new relational and critical resources.

And what makes it authentic and faithful is if it leads to action for it is in the doing—in the "breaking of bread" and in "taking up our cross"—that our eyes are further opened and we come to know Jesus. The imagery of sacrifice that the Jesus of the New Testament uses, implies the costliness of the way.

None of us knows where our journey will take us. So in conclusion we offer a simple note of encouragement recognizing that—

- to become aware where we have come from in our journeys with Scripture is an important step in continuing our journeys;
- to share our stories with others opens the door to further testing and discernment, for it helps us to understand and to trust—ourselves and our sisters and brothers;
- to struggle together in discernment is better than not to discern or to discern only within myself. True discernment of the way of Jesus may call for confrontation—of ourselves and of others;
- to heed the call of Jesus is to invite others, both believers and "nonbelievers," to join us on a similar journey—not merely to the "Scriptures that testify about Jesus," but to following Jesus by being a social embodiment of Christ in our day.

If Jesus were speaking to us today, might it be possible that he would say, "You search the Scriptures because they testify on my behalf. And you come to me to have life, for I know that you have the love of God in you"? That is the question we keep asking.

Notes

1. For a helpful outline of things that need to be considered in the task of interpretation see Richard Palmer's "Thirty Theses on Interpretation" in his book, *Hermeneutics: Interpretation Theory in Schleiermacher, Dilthey, Heidegger, and Gadamer* (Evanston, Ill.: Northwestern University Press, 1969), 242-246.

2. The Anabaptist theological tradition especially emphasizes (1) the role of the Bible as the primary authority for faith and practice, (2) the guidance of God's Spirit in the gathered congregation, (3) following Christ in life, (4) an ethic of love and nonviolence, (5) the congregation as a voluntary assembly signified by adult baptism, (6) economic sharing, and (7) the mutual responsibility of each church member to give and receive council. See John Howard Yoder, "A Summary of the Anabaptist Vision," in *An Introduction to Mennonite History*, 2nd. ed., ed. Cornelius J. Dyck (Scottdale, Pa.: Herald Press, 1981), 136-145.

Biblical Authority: A Personal Reflection

Walter Brueggemann

The authority of the Bible is a perennial and urgent issue for those of us who stake our lives on its testimony. This issue, however, is bound to remain unsettled and therefore perpetually disputatious. It cannot be otherwise, since the biblical text is endlessly "strange and new." It always and inescapably outdistances our categories of understanding and explanation, of interpretation and control. Because the Bible is "the live word of the living God," it will not compliantly submit to the accounts we prefer to give of it. There is something intrinsically unfamiliar about the book; and when we seek to override that unfamiliarity, we are on the hazardous ground of idolatry. Rather than proclaiming loud, dogmatic slogans about the Bible, we might do better to consider the odd and intimate ways in which we have each been led to where we are in our relationship with the Scriptures.

At my confirmation, the pastor (in my case, my father) selected a verse for each confirmand, a verse to mark one's life. It was read while hands were laid on one's head in confirmation, read at one's funeral and many times in between. My father read over me Psalm 119:105: "Your word is a lamp to my feet! and a light to my path." Providentially, he marked my life by this book that would be lamp and light, to illumine a way to obedience and mark a path to fullness, joy and well-being.

Before that moment of confirmation, through baptismal vows and through my nurture in the faith, my church prepared me to attend to the Bible in a certain way. I am a child of the Prussian Union, a church body created in 1817 on the 300th anniversary of the year Luther posted his 39 theses on the door of the Würtemberg church. The Prussian king, weary of the arguments about the Eucharist going on between Calvinists and Lutherans, decreed an ecumenical church that was to be open to diversity and based on a broad consensus of evangelical faith that intended to protect liberty of conscience. This church body brought to the U.S. a slogan now taken over and claimed by many others: "In essentials unity; in nonessentials liberty; in all things charity."

"In all things charity" became the interpretive principle that produced a fundamentally irenic church. The ambiance of that climate for Bible reading may be indicated in two ways. First, the quarrels over the historical-critical reading of the Bible, faced by every church sooner or later, were firmly settled in my church in 1870, when one seminary teacher was forced out of teaching but quickly restored to a pastoral position of esteem. Second, our only seminary, Eden Seminary, had no systematic theologian on its faculty until 1946, and things were managed in a mood of trustful piety that produced not hard-nosed certitude, but irenic charity.

My first and best teacher was my father, who taught me the artistry as well as the authority of Scripture. After my confirmation came a series of others who further shaped me in faith. In seminary I had an astonishing gift of excellent Bible teachers, none of whom published, as perhaps the best teachers do not. Allen Wehrli, who had studied under Hermann Gunkel in Halle, taught us the vast density of the Bible's artistry, with attention to the form of the text. His pedagogy was imaginative storytelling—long before the work of C. Ernest Wright or Fred Craddock, Wehrli understood that the Bible is narrative. Lionel Whiston introduced us to Gerhard von Rad, who was just then becoming known to English readers. I have ever since devoured Von Rad, who showed us that the practice of biblical faith is first of all recital. I learned from Wehrli and Whiston that the Bible is essentially an open, imaginative narrative of God's staggering care for the world, a narrative that feeds and nurtures us into an obedience that builds community precisely through respect for the liberty of individual Christians.

After seminary, purely by accident, I stumbled onto James Muilenburg at Union Seminary in New York, arguably the most compelling Old Testament teacher of his generation. He taught us that the Bible will have its authoritative, noncoercive way with us if we but attend with educated alertness to the cadences and sounds of the text in all its detail.

Since graduate school, I have been blessed by a host of insistent teachers—seminarians who would not settle for easy answers, church people who asked new and probing questions, even other Bible teachers. But mostly my continuing education has come through the writing and witness of people who are empowered by the text to live lives of courage, suffering and sacrifice, people who have found this book a source and energy for the fullness of true life lived unafraid.

This succession of teachers has let me see how broad, deep, demanding and generous is this text, how utterly beyond me in its richness. "A lamp to my feet and a light to my path. . . ."

How each of us reads the Bible is partly the result of family, neighbors, and friends (a socialization process), and partly the God-given accident of long-term development in faith. Consequently, the real issues of biblical authority and interpretation are not likely to be settled by cognitive formulations or by appeals to classic confessions. These issues live in often unrecognized, uncriticized, and deeply powerful ways—especially if they are rooted (as they may be for most of us) in hurt, anger or anxiety.

Decisions about biblical meanings are not made on the spot, but result from the growth of habits and convictions. And if that is so, then the disputes over meaning require not frontal arguments but long-term pastoral attentiveness to one another in good faith.

A church in dispute will require great self-knowing candor and a generous openness among its members. Such attentiveness may lead us to recognize that the story of someone else's nurture in the faith could be a transformative gift that allows us to read the text in a new way. My own story leads me to identify six facets of biblical interpretation that I believe are likely to be operative among us all.

Inherency

The Bible is inherently the live word of God, revealing the character and will of God and empowering us for an alternative life in the world. While I believe in the indeterminacy of the text to some large extent, I know that finally the Bible is forceful and consistent in its main theological claim. It expresses the conviction that the God who created the world in love redeems the world in suffering and will consummate the world in joyous well-being. That flow of conviction about God's self-disclosure in the Bible is surely the main claim of the apostolic faith, a claim upon which the church fundamentally agrees. That fundamental agreement is, of course, the beginning of the conversation and not its conclusion; but it is a deep and important starting point. From that inherent claim certain things follow:

First, all of us in the church are bound together by this foundation of apostolic faith. As my tradition affirms, "in essentials unity." It also means, moreover, that in disputes about biblical authority nobody has the high ground morally or hermeneutically. Our common commitment to the truth of the book makes us equal before the book, as it does around the table.

Second, since the inherency of evangelical truth in the book is focused on its main claims, it follows that there is much in the text that is "lesser," not a main claim, but probes and attempts over the generations to carry the main claims to specificity. These attempts are characteristically informed by particular circumstance and are open to variation, nuance and even contradiction. It is a primal Reformation principle that our faith is evangelical, linked to the good news and not to biblicism. The potential distinction between good news and lesser claims can lead to much dispute.

Third, the inherent word of God in the biblical text is refracted through many authors who were not disembodied voices of revealed truth but circumstance-situated men and women of faith (as are we all) who said what their circumstances permitted and required them to say of that which is truly inherent. It is this human refraction that makes the hard work of critical study inescapable, so that every text is given a suspicious scrutiny whereby we may consider the ways in which bodied humanness has succeeded or not succeeded in bearing truthful and faithful witness.

Fourth, given both inherency and circumstance-situated human refraction, the Bible is so endlessly a surprise beyond us that Karl Barth famously and rightly termed it "strange and new." The Bible is not a fixed, frozen, readily exhausted read; it is, rather, a "script," always reread, through which the Spirit makes all things new. When the church adjudicates between the inherent and the circumstance-situated, it is sorely tempted to settle, close and idolize. Therefore, inherency of an evangelical kind demands a constant resistance to familiarity. Nobody's reading is final or inerrant, precisely because the key Character in the book who creates, redeems and consummates is always beyond us in holy hiddenness. When we push boldly through the hiddenness, wanting to know more clearly, what we thought was holy ground turns out to be a playground for idolatry. Our reading, then, is inescapably provisional. It is rightly done with the modesty of those who are always to be surprised again by what is "strange and new."

Interpretation

Recognizing the claim of biblical authority is not difficult as it pertains to the main affirmations of apostolic faith. But from that base line, the hard, disputatious work of interpretation needs to be recognized precisely for what it is: nothing more than interpretation. As our mothers and fathers have always known, the Bible is not self-evident and self-interpreting, and the Reformers did not mean to say that it was so when they escaped the church's magisterium. Rather the Bible requires and insists upon human interpretation, which is inescapably subjective, necessarily provisional and inevitably disputatious. I propose as an interpretive rule that all of our interpretations need to be regarded, at the most, as having only tentative authority. This will enable us to make our best, most insistent claims, but then regularly relinquish our pet interpretations and, together with our partners in dispute, fall back in joy into the inherent apostolic claims that outdistance all of our too familiar and too partisan interpretations. We may learn from the rabbis the marvelous rhythm of deep interpretive dispute and profound common yielding in joy and affectionate well-being. The characteristic and sometimes demonic mode of Reformed interpretation is not tentativeness and relinquishment, but tentativeness hardening into absoluteness. It often becomes a sleight-of-hand act, substituting our interpretive preference for the inherency of apostolic claims.

The process of interpretation which precludes final settlement on almost all questions is evident in the Bible itself. A stunning case in point is the Mosaic teaching in Deuteronomy 23:1-8 that bans from the community all those with distorted sexuality and all those who are foreigners. In Isaiah 56:3-8 this Mosaic teaching is overturned in the Bible itself, offering what Herbert Donner terms an intentional "abrogation" of

Mosaic law through new teaching. The old, no doubt circumstance-driven exclusion is answered by a circumstance-driven inclusiveness.

In Deuteronomy 24:1, moreover, Moses teaches that marriages broken in infidelity cannot be restored, even if both parties want to get back together. But in Jeremiah 3, in a shocking reversal given in a pathos-filled poem, God's own voice indicates a readiness to violate that Torah teaching for the sake of restored marriage to Israel. The old teaching is seen to be problematic even for God. The latter text shows God prepared to move beyond the old prohibition of Torah in order that the inherent evangelical claims of God's graciousness may be fully available even to a recalcitrant Israel. In embarrassment and perhaps even in humiliation, the God of Jeremiah's poem willfully overrides the old text. It becomes clear that the interpretive project that constitutes the final form of the text is itself profoundly polyvalent, yielding no single exegetical outcome, but allowing layers and layers of fresh reading in which God's own life and character are deeply engaged and put at risk.

Imagination

Responsible interpretation requires imagination. I understand that imagination makes serious Calvinists nervous because it smacks of the subjective freedom to carry the text in undeveloped directions and to engage in fantasy. But I would insist that imagination is in any case inevitable in any interpretive process that is more than simple reiteration, and that faithful imagination is characteristically not autonomous fantasy but good-faith extrapolation. I understand imagination, no doubt a complex epistemological process, to be the capacity to entertain images of meaning and reality that are beyond the givens of observable experience. That is, imagination is the hosting of "otherwise," and I submit that every serious teacher or preacher invites people to an "otherwise" beyond the evident. Without that we have nothing to say. We must take risks and act daringly to push beyond what is known to that which is hoped for and trusted but not yet in hand.

Interpretation is not the reiteration of the text but, rather, the movement of the text beyond itself in fresh, often formerly unuttered ways. Jesus' parables are a prime example. They open the listening community to possible futures. Beyond parabolic teaching, however, there was in ancient Israel and in the early church an observant wonder. As eyewitnesses created texts out of observed and remembered miracles, texted miracles in turn become materials for imagination that pushed well beyond what was given or intended even in the text. This is an inescapable process for those of us who insist that the Bible is a contemporary word to us. We transport ourselves out of the twenty-first century back to the ancient world of the text or, conversely, we transpose ancient voices into contemporary voices of authority.

Those of us who think critically do not believe that the Old Testament was talking about Jesus, and yet we make the linkages. Surely Paul was not thinking of time crisis over sixteenth-century indulgences when he wrote about "faith alone." Surely Isaiah was not thinking of Martin Luther King's dream of a new earth. Yet we make such leaps all the time. What a huge leap to imagine that the primal commission to "till and keep the earth" (Gen. 2:15) is really about environmental issues and the chemicals used by Iowa farmers. Yet we make it. What a huge leap to imagine that the ancient provision for Jubilee in Leviticus 25 has anything to do with the cancellation of Third World debt or with an implied critique of global capitalism. Yet we make it. What a huge leap to imagine that an ancient purity code in Leviticus 18 bears upon consenting gays and lesbians in the twenty-first century and has anything to do with ordination. Yet we make it.

We are all committed to the high practice of subjective extrapolations because we have figured out that a cold, reiterative objectivity has no missional energy or moral force. We do it, and will not stop doing it. It is, however, surely healing and humbling for us to have enough self-knowledge to concede that what we are doing will not carry the freight of absoluteness.

Imagination can indeed be a gift of the Spirit, but it is a gift used with immense subjective freedom. Therefore, after our imaginative interpretations are made with vigor in dispute with others in the church, we must regularly, gracefully, and with modesty fall back from our best extrapolations to the sure apostolic claims that lie behind our extremities of imagination, liberal or conservative.

Ideology

A consideration of ideology is difficult for us because we American churchpeople are largely innocent about our own interpretive work. We are seldom aware of or honest about the ways in which our work is shot through with distorting vested interests. But it is so, whether we know it or not. There is no interpretation of Scripture (nor of anything else) that is unaffected by the passions, convictions and perceptions of the interpreter. Ideology is the self-deceiving practice of taking a part for the whole, of taking "my truth" for the truth, of palming off the particular as a universal. It is so already in the text of Scripture itself as current scholarship makes clear, because the spirit-given text is given us by and through human authors. It is so because spirit-filled interpretation is given us by and through bodied authors who must make their way in the world—and in making our way, we humans do not see so clearly or love so dearly or follow so nearly as we might imagine.

There are endless examples of ideology at work in interpretation. Historical criticism is no innocent practice, for it intends to fend off church authority and protect the freedom of the autonomous interpreter. Canonical criticism is no innocent practice, for it intends to maintain old coherences against the perceived threat of more recent fragmentation. High moralism is no innocent practice, even if it sounds disciplined and noble, for much of it grows out of fear and is a strategy to fend off anxiety. Communitarian inclusiveness is no innocent practice, because it reflects a reaction against exclusivism and so is readily given to a kind of reactive carelessness. There is enough truth in every such interpretive posture and strategy—and a hundred others we might name—to make it credible and to gather a constituency for it. But it is not ideologically innocent, and therefore has no absolute claim.

In a disputatious church, a healthy practice might be to reflect upon the ideological passion not of others, but of one's self and one's cohorts. I believe that such reflection would invariably indicate that every passionate interpretive voice is shot through with vested interest, sometimes barely hidden. It is completely predictable that interpreters who are restrictive about gays and lesbians will characteristically advocate high capitalism and a strong national defense. Conversely, those who are "open and affirming" will characteristically maintain a critique of consumer capitalism and consensus on a whole cluster of other issues. One can argue that such a package only indicates a theological-ethical coherence. Perhaps, but in no case is the package innocent, since we incline to make our decisions without any critical reflection, but only to sustain the package.

Every passionate vested interest has working in it a high measure of anxiety about deep threats, perhaps perceived, perhaps imagined. And anxiety has a force that permits us to deal in wholesale categories without the nuance of the particular. A judgment grounded in anxiety, anywhere on the theological spectrum, does not want to be disturbed or informed by facts on the ground. Every vested interest shaped by anxiety has near its source old fears that are deep and hidden, but for all of that authoritative. Every one has at its very bottom hurt—old hurt, new hurt, hurt for ourselves, for those we remember, for those we love. The lingering, unhealed pain becomes a hermeneutical principle out of which we will not be talked.

Every ideological passion, liberal or conservative, may be encased in Scripture itself or enshrined in longstanding interpretation until it is regarded as absolute and trusted as decisive authority. And where an ideology becomes loud and destructive in the interpretive community, we may be sure that the doses of anxiety, fear and hurt within it are huge and finally irrepressible.

I do not for an instant suggest that no distinctions can be made, nor that it is so dark that all cats are gray. And certainly, given our ideological passions, we must go on and interpret in any case. But I do say that in our best judgments concerning Scripture, we might be aware enough of our propensity to distort in the service of vested interests, anxiety, fear and hurt that we recognize that our best interpretation might be not only a vehicle for but also a block to and distortion of the crucified truth of the gospel.

I have come belatedly to see, in my own case, that my hermeneutical passion is largely propelled by the fact that my father was a pastor who was economically abused by the church he served, abused as a means of control. I cannot measure the ways in which that felt awareness determines how I work, how I interpret, who I read, whom I trust as a reliable voice. The wound is deep enough to pervade everything; I suspect, moreover, that I am not the only one for whom this is true. It could be that we turn our anxieties, fears and hurts to good advantage as vehicles for obedience. But even in so doing, we are put on notice. We cannot escape from such passions; but we can submit them to brothers and sisters whose own history of distortion is very different from ours and as powerful in its defining force.

Inspiration

It is traditional to speak of Scripture as "inspired." There is a long history of unhelpful formulations of what that notion might mean. Without appealing to classical formulations that characteristically have more to do with "testing" the spirit (1 John 4:1) than with "not quenching" the spirit (1 Thess. 5:19), we may affirm that the force of God's purpose, will and capacity for liberation, reconciliation and new life is everywhere in the biblical text. In such an affirmation, of course, we say more than we can understand, for the claim is precisely an acknowledgment that in and through this text, God's wind blows through and past all our critical and confessional categories of reading and understanding. That powerful and enlivening force, moreover, pertains not simply to the ordaining of the text but to its transmission and interpretation among us.

The spirit will not be regimented, and therefore none of our reading is guaranteed to be inspired. But it does happen on occasion. It does happen that in and through the text we are blown beyond ourselves. It does happen that the spirit teaches, guides and heals through the text, so that the text yields something other than an echo of ourselves. It does happen that in prayer and study believers are led to what is "strange and new." It does happen that preachers are led to utterances beyond what they set out to make. It does happen that churches, in councils, sessions and other courts, are led beyond themselves, powered beyond prejudice, liberated beyond convention, overwhelmed by the capacity for new risks.

Importance

Biblical interpretation, done with imagination willing to risk ideological distortion, open to the inspiring spirit, is important. But it is important not because it might allow some to seize control of the church, but because it gives the world access to the good truth of the God who creates, redeems and consummates. That missional intention is urgent in every circumstance and season. The church at its most faithful has always understood that we read Scripture for the sake of the church's missional testimony.

But the reading of the Bible is now especially urgent because our society is sore tempted to reduce the human project to commodity. In its devotion to the making of money it reduces persons to objects and thins human communications to electronic icons. Technique in all its military modes and derivatively in every other mode threatens us, Technique is aimed at control, the fencing out of death, the fencing out of gift and, eventually, the fencing out of humanness.

Nonetheless, we in the church dare affirm that the lively word of Scripture is the primal antidote to technique, the primal news that fends off trivialization. Thinning to control and trivializing to evade ambiguity are the major goals of our culture. The church in its disputatious anxiety is tempted to join the move to technique, to thin the Bible and make it one-dimensional, deeply tempted to trivialize the Bible by acting as though it is important because it may solve some disruptive social inconvenience. The dispute tends to reduce what is rich and dangerous in the book to knowable technique, and what is urgent and immense to exhaustible trivia.

The Bible is too important to be reduced in this way because the dangers of the world are too great and the expectations of God are too large. What if liberals and conservatives in the church, for all their disagreement, would together put their energies to upholding the main truth against the main threat? The issues before God's creation (of which we are stewards) are immense; those issues shame us when our energy is deployed only to settle our anxieties. The biblical script insists that the world is not without God, not without the holy gift of life rooted in love. And yet we twitter! The Bible is a lamp and light to fend off the darkness. The darkness is real, and the light is for walking boldly, faithfully in a darkness we do not and cannot control. In this crisis, the church must consider what is entrusted peculiarly to us in this book.

Recently an Israeli journalist in Jerusalem commented on the fracturing dispute in Israel over who constitutes a real Jew, orthodox, conservative or reform. And he said about the dispute, "If any Jew wins, all Jews lose." Think about it: "If anyone wins, everyone loses."

—*Walter Brueggemann is professor emeritus of Old Testament, Columbia Theological Seminary in Decatur, Georgia. His book* Theology of the Old Testament *is a foundational work in the field. Among his other books are* Finally Comes the Poet: Daring Speech for Proclamation *and* The Prophetic Imagination.

Conceptual Background to Guidelines for Writing about Our Journeys with Scripture

1: Rationale and Focus for a Colloquy on Our Journeys with Scripture

Several of us (beginning with persons in the Bible and Religion Department at Eastern Mennonite University then expanding to Goshen College including Keith Graber Miller; to Malinda Berry, with MBM and now in graduate school; to Jane Hoober Peifer, pastor and leader in the Mennonite church merger; and to Denny Weaver from Bluffton University), have been having conversations on the idea of a gathering in which a group of us would share our understandings of Scripture. Our goal is to structure this in a way that builds constructive relationships among us by being inclusive and to further the work of the church by cutting through the ethnic and theological divisions within the church. Here is the concept that we began with:

(1) We would share "Journeys with Scripture," giving our personal stories. These would be confessional narratives, not theological apologies. There would be time for questions and discussion following each story.

(2) The group would come together by invitation and would consist of about twenty-five Mennonite persons of considerable diversity (age, gender, ethnic background, geographic and institutional location, and theological position). Persons would all fall under the rubric of church leaders: administrators, pastors, and academics. This would be a deliber-

ate effort to strengthen the complex web of intramural bonds, and especially the ties between academia and the church leaders.

(3) We would meet at Laurelville for a weekend—Friday evening to Sunday noon. We would likely divide into two groups to share our pilgrimages but would gather as one group for certain other activities. We would hope to have at least one, perhaps two, consulting facilitators guiding us through the process. (All presentations would be taped and/or placed on video so that if there are coterminous groups, participants could at least hear all of the other presentations.) Some "fun" should be included as well as a simple worship service on Sunday morning.

(4) We would approach this meeting and prepare for it committed to making ourselves vulnerable, and to share in a spirit of trust and a deep commitment to listen to the other. When not sharing, the entire focus would be to listen, to seek to hear each other, to discern, and to ask where the Spirit of Christ is leading us.

Among the factors shaping the colloquy are the events of this past September 11, 2001. The question that reverberates throughout the Mennonite church in the U.S. is this: What is the meaning of nonviolence and our peace tradition after September 11 and October 7 (the U.S. War on Afghanistan)? We believe the issue of nonviolence is one that has received too little attention during a half century of the Cold War, ending with the Mennonites of the U.S. quietly and affluently participating as citizens in the world's single superpower, enjoying decades during which Mennonites paid little heed to the violence needed to maintain American power and the American way of life. A second factor affecting our understandings of Scripture, and one that has dominated the conversation in the merger/transformation of the Mennonite Church and the General Conference Mennonite Church, is homosexuality. Other issues will soon face us, perhaps even before we meet.

While some of us believe the severe threat these two issues pose to the church to be unfortunate, we also recognize this time of trial to pose unprecedented opportunities to re-examine and bring to a new level of appreciation, substantive components of our Anabaptist heritage—opportunities that have previously been slipping past us. Yet we fear the narrow focus of much of the current conversation on both of these issues will be counterproductive and schismatic. We therefore seek a broader framework in which to carry on the conversation. If the long-range goal of our church is to be transformative, we should pay heed to the enduring, underlying issues facing the church. This colloquy offers us the opportunity to focus on one of these enduring, foundational, potentially broadening issues: our understandings of Scripture.

The Scriptures, we believe, are a significant and an abiding phenomenon in our Christian and Anabaptist heritage. Our understandings of Scripture lie beneath the current discussions on both nonviolence and homosexuality and will play a vital role in how we as a church continue to struggle with these issues. In floating this concept among colleagues and friends, we received unanimous affirmation that the Scriptures belong to the Anabaptist-Mennonite matrix that shapes our ethical understandings and identity—and consequently, how we practice our faith. Our understandings of Scripture will impact all other major issues the church will face in this new era. We believe that as a church we are long overdue an open and confessional conversation, sharing our struggles with Scriptures and our commitment to them.

A catalyst for telling our personal stories as the model for sharing our understandings of Scripture comes from Walter Brueggemann's essay, entitled "A Personal Reflection: Biblical Authority," in the January 3-10, 2001 issue of *Christian Century*. We encourage all participants to read this essay in anticipation of the colloquy.

2: Guidelines for Writing our Journeys

You are writing up *your* story, the story of your *journey*, your journey *with Scripture*. As long as it's honest, and as long as it offers you and your readers/listeners insight into your experiences, it's right; it's good. But your story is interwoven with that of many other people and events, so it's not always easy to know where to begin, what to include and where to end. The questions below are given in an attempt to make writing that story easier. You may not wish to respond to each item, and you will likely have things to add that are not included here. But this should offer some direction and will provide at least a bit of uniformity to our stories as we share them.

Beginning the journey

Where and with whom did your story begin? We all are thrust into the middle of a stream—a family, a clan. What was the particular stream that carried you on that early journey with the Scriptures?

What was your particular community like? What was the place of the Scriptures in that community?

On the Way

What crises did you encounter? Did you experience frightening moments, incredible surprises, or just gradual changes and growth? How did they affect your journey with Scripture?

What issues, or out-of-the-ordinary events, did the community struggle with that shaped your journey with Scripture (e.g., head coverings, divorce and remarriage, sexual infidelity, racism, war, homosexuality)?

Who has over the years kept "looking over your shoulders" (parent, pastor, or teacher)? How significant has that influence been?

Gaining your bearings—
checking outer directions and inner disposition

How have you integrated your evolving relationship with Scripture over the years? How have you taken stock (e.g., through retreats, educational training, conversation partners) of where you've come from and where you are going?

How does your inner disposition and personal makeup shape how you experience life and faith? And how does this influence your journey with Scripture? Are you more oriented toward critical study, devotional reflections, or entering scriptural stories through identification with characters?

If you think of Scripture as a journeying partner through life, what have been those occasions, looking back, on which you renewed your vows and dealt with conflicting loyalties?

Conclusion

Where are you now? For some persons this part of the story will be almost spontaneous. For others this may be the most difficult. Either way, sharing your present stance will help us to understand each other, to fellowship, and to be supportive in the next phase of our journey together.

Index of Names

Subject Index

The Contributors

Malinda Elizabeth Berry is a doctoral student at Union Theological Seminary in New York City. Her work focuses on theological anthropology and the authority of Scripture. In addition to serving on the Reference Committee of the Peace and Justice Support Network of Mennonite Church USA, she is a member of Manhattan Mennonite Fellowship.

Jo-Ann Brant is Professor of Bible, Religion, and Philosophy at Goshen (Ind.) College. Her research interests lie in the philosophy of language and in the gospel of John. She is a member of College Mennonite Church where she serves as the coordinator for the MYF Sunday school program.

Owen Burkholder is Conference Minister for Virginia Mennonite Conference. He is the former pastor of Community Mennonite and Park View Mennonite Churches of Harrisonburg, Virginia, and a former moderator of the Mennonite Church (1995-1997). He is a member of Park View Mennonite Church.

Ron Byler is Associate Executive Director of Mennonite Church USA. He and his wife, Mim Shirk, live in Goshen, Indiana. where they are members of Eighth Street Mennonite Church.

Lin Garber is a retired concert and church singer. A 1957 graduate of Goshen College, he does occasional editing and research work and some freelance writing. He is an active member of the Mennonite Congregation of Boston.

Ray Gingerich is Professor Emeritus of Theology and Church History at Eastern Mennonite University. His doctoral work focused on Anabaptist mission. He refers to the Anabaptists as the sixteenth-century Base Christian Communities. His recent writings include an essay, "Resurrection: The Nonviolent Politics of God." He and his wife are life-time war tax resisters and longtime members of the Fellowship of Reconciliation. He is a member of Community Mennonite Church in Harrisonburg, Virginia.

Roy Hange is Co-Pastor, with his wife Maren, of Charlottesville Mennonite Church in Charlottesville, Virginia. Previous to this assignment he served for ten years with Mennonite Central Committee in the countries of Egypt, Syria and Iran. He also speaks and writes in the area of religious identity and peacemaking.

Nancy Heisey is Associate Professor of Biblical Studies and Church History at Eastern Mennonite University, and currently President of Mennonite World Conference. She is a member of Community Mennonite Church in Harrisonburg, Virginia and also a member of Cross Roads Brethren in Christ Church, Mount Joy, Pennsylvania.

John Kampen is Academic Dean and Professor of New Testament at Methodist Theological School in Ohio. He is the former Academic Dean of Bluffton University and Payne Theological Seminary. He is the author of various books and journal articles including *The Hasideans and the Origin of Pharisaism: A Study of 1 and 2 Macabees*. A good deal of his research has centered on the Dead Sea Scrolls.

Richard A. Kauffman is Senior Editor and Book Review Editor for the *Christian Century* magazine, Senior Editor of *Leader* magazine published by the Mennonite Church USA and Mennonite Church Canada, and a member of Lombard (Ill.) Mennonite Church.

Paul Keim is Professor of Bible, Religion and Biblical Languages at Goshen (Ind.) College. His primary fields of expertise are in Old Testament, and Ancient Near Eastern languages and literatures. He formerly served as Academic Dean at Hesston College and at Goshen College. Among other writings, he has authored chapters on Mennonite higher education, biblical nonviolence, and Ancient Near Eastern maledictions. He and his wife Julie have three children, Anna Beth, Naomi, and Ian.

Marilyn Rayle Kern served as Assistant Pastor of First Mennonite Church in Bluffton, Ohio, and Pastor of the Chicago Community Mennonite Church (formerly Oak Park Mennonite Church) in Chicago. She is retired and lives in Findlay, Ohio.

Phil Kniss is Pastor of Park View Mennonite Church, Harrisonburg, Virginia. He is married to Irene Hershberger Kniss, and they are parents of three daughters, all of whom are currently students in Mennonite colleges.

James R. Krabill is Senior Executive for Global Ministries at Mennonite Mission Network. He and his wife, Jeanette, have three children, Matthew, Elisabeth and Mary Laura, all born in West Africa during their years of mission service there, 1978-1996. They currently live in Elkhart, Indiana, and attend the Prairie Street Mennonite Church.

Elizabeth Landis is a graduate of Associated Mennonite Biblical Seminary, Elkhart, Indiana. She currently lives in Lancaster, Pennsylvania and is employed by the Octorara Area School District as a Violence Prevention Coordinator.

Susan Mark Landis leads and organizes peace and justice advocacy work for Mennonite Church USA. In that role, she ensures a peace and justice presence at Mennonite Church USA Assemblies, serves on the Executive Board anti-racism team, and provides a link to Mennonite World Conference, Christian Peacemaker Teams, and Peace Tax Fund. Her joys are time with family (including husband Dennis and teen-agers Laura and Joel) and friends, working in the perennial bed, baking bread, and thoughtful drama.

Cynthia Lapp, Mt. Rainier, Maryland, is Co-Pastor at Hyattsville (Md.) Mennonite Church just outside Washington, D.C.. She is married to Eric Stoltzfus and mother of three young children, Cecilia, Jamie and Elijah.

Craig Maven is the Senior Pastor at First Mennonite Church, Berne, Indiana. He is currently enrolled at Asbury Theological Seminary in the Doctor of Ministry program. He is married with two daughters.

Keith Graber Miller is Professor of Bible, Religion, and Philosophy at Goshen College, teaching primarily in the areas of ethics and theology. He is the author of *Wise as Serpents, Innocent as Doves: American Mennonites Engage Washington* (University of Tennessee Press, 1996), editor or co-editor of two other books, and contributor of chapters to a dozen other texts. He is a member of Assembly Mennonite Church in Goshen, husband of Ann Graber Miller, and father of Niles, Mia, and Simon.

Lee Snyder was President of Bluffton (Oh.) University until her recent retirement, and before arriving at Bluffton in 1996, she was Vice-President and Academic Dean at Eastern Mennonite University. Lee has served as a resource in various leadership institutes and on community, church, and education boards. She and her husband Del attend First Mennonite Church in Bluffton and are the parents of two daughters.

Dorothy Jean Weaver is Professor of New Testament at Eastern Mennonite Seminary, Harrisonburg, Virgnia. She is the author of *Matthew's Missionary Discourse: A Literary Critical Analysis* and the compiler/editor of *Bread for the Enemy: A Peace and Justice Lectionary.* Dorothy Jean is a member of Community Mennonite Church, Harrisonburg.

J. Denny Weaver was Professor of Religion and The Harry and Jean Yoder Scholar in Bible and Religion at Bluffton (Oh.) University until his recent retirement and is a member of First Mennonite Church of Bluffton. His recent publications include *The Nonviolent Atonement* and *Teaching Peace: Nonviolence and the Liberal Arts,* which he co-edited with Gerald Biesecker-Mast. He continues to serve Bluffton University as editor of the C. Henry Smith Series.

Earl Zimmerman is the Assistant Professor of Bible and Religion at Eastern Mennonite University, Harrisonburg, Virginia, and a Pastor at Shalom Mennonite Congregation. He recently completed his Ph.D. dissertation "A Praxis of Peace: The 'Politics of Jesus' according to John Howard Yoder," soon to be published in the C. Henry Smith series by Cascadia. He and his wife Ruth are the parents of three grown children, Krista, Stephen, and Sara.

Printed in the United States
61735LVS00003B/10

9 781931 038362